Making the White Man's Indian

Making the White Man's Indian

NATIVE AMERICANS AND HOLLYWOOD MOVIES

Angela Aleiss

PRAEGER

Westport, Connecticut
London

Library of Congress Cataloging-in-Publication Data

Aleiss, Angela.
    Making the white man's Indian : native Americans and Hollywood
movies / Angela Aleiss ; foreword by Kevin Brownlow.
       p. cm.
    Includes bibliographical references and index.
    ISBN 0–275–98396–X (alk. paper)
1. Indians in motion pictures. 2. Motion pictures—United States.   I.   Title.
PN1995.9.I48A44 2005
791.43'652997—dc22   2004028188

British Library Cataloguing in Publication Data is available.

Library of Congress Catalog Card Number: 2004028188
ISBN: 978–0–313–36133–3 (pbk.)

First published in 2005

Praeger Publishers, 88 Post Road West, Westport, CT 06881
An imprint of Greenwood Publishing Group, Inc.
www.praeger.com

Printed in the United States of America

∞

The paper used in this book complies with the
Permanent Paper Standard issued by the National
Information Standards Organization (Z39.48–1984).

10 9 8 7 6 5 4 3 2 1

In Memory of Rudy E. Martin (Navajo-Tewa-Apache) (1952–1993)

Composer, Playwright, Entertainer, and Public Relations Director
of the American Indian Community House, New York City.

Contents

Foreword

Redskin Raiders was one of the first films I bought as a schoolboy film collector. The title was irresistible. Indians attack a wagon train, the wagons form a circle, and soldiers and settlers wipe out the Sioux. The film only lasted two minutes, but all my friends wanted to see it, and I ran it to death. It turned out to be an extract from a 1936 picture called *The Glory Trail*. (In those days, studios duplicated short scenes from feature films and sold them to individual collectors.) When I acquired Westerns from a decade earlier, I saw where the makers had got their history from. They took it not so much from the record as from other films. We are now told that only one wagon train ever formed that classic circle under an Indian attack.

History was at the heart of these films, however, and similar events were within living memory. In the 1930s, you could still have met people who had crossed the continent in covered wagons who might have told you terrifying tales of Indian attacks.

And there were Native Americans who had risked their lives to defend their land, just as the Founding Fathers had fought, a century before, for theirs. The advance of the white race must have seemed as threatening to the Indians as that of the Panzers to Russian peasants in World War II. The settlers may have been less heavily armed, but behind them came the cavalry and the unstoppable march of progress, with the McCormick Reaper in the van!

In the early days of cinema, attitudes towards Indians were sharply divided between hostility and admiration. Theodore

Roosevelt, with his pleas for conservation, aroused the nation to the plight of the Indian, and film companies reflected this with "Noble Red Man" scenarios. Sometimes the same filmmaker would express both points of view, as with D. W. Griffith, who must hold the record for sympathetic Indian portrayals and yet who made *America* in 1924, with its scenes of Indian atrocities in the Mohawk Valley during the Revolutionary War.

Incredibly, the legendary Buffalo Bill Cody made *The Indian Wars* (1914), a film about Wounded Knee, with the involvement of former Indian fighters, including veterans of the Seventh Cavalry. They presented the tragedy as a battle rather than as a massacre, but their attitude had clearly undergone a significant change. A reporter on the location kept hearing the phrase, "When did the white men or the government ever keep a treaty with the Indians?"

The period in which these early films were made was undeniably racist. One might even say cheerfully racist. Vaudeville comics made jokes at everyone's expense—Irish, Jew, Pole. In one sense, this was healthy, for with everyone fair game, prejudices were on the surface. The dark side was the rebirth of the Ku Klux Klan, whose members would happily have exterminated anything on two legs that failed to resemble them. (A surprise of this book is that a celebrated Indian actor tried to join the Ku Klux Klan since he regarded himself as 100 percent American.)

I recall that one of the most despised figures on the silent screen was the half-breed (although Aleiss argues otherwise). I found it ironic to think that the full-blooded Indian was regarded as the Noble Savage in those days, but the moment that the Noble Savage procreated with a white woman, the offspring became a vicious character, addicted to redeye and lurking at the back of saloons, ready to commit foul deeds, and usually played by one of the screen's stock villains, Frank Lackteen. When Douglas Fairbanks played the title role in *The Half-Breed* (1916), the movie's director, Allan Dwan, later told me that the actor's wife insisted he'd be shown diving naked into a river in case anyone mistook him for a dirty half-breed.

With such prejudice, why was the Indian so deeply admired that outsiders posed as red men? When I was writing *The War, the West and the Wilderness* (New York: Knopf, 1978), I devoted a section to silent films about Native Americans. And I highlighted those players who claimed Indian origin. Several have since been shown to be impostors: Mona Darkfeather, whom original references listed as a Seminole (real name Josephine Workman!) and Buffalo Child Long Lance. There was even an Indian director, James Young Deer—now there is doubt even about him. In my research, I sought advice from an "authentic Indian," Iron Eyes Cody, who had played in nearly a hundred films and was the iconic American Indian in the antipollution commercials. He received me in his Hollywood home, which was decorated with the brilliantly colored headdresses and robes that marked him out as a true authority.

True authority be damned! Aleiss reveals him to be not a Native American but an Italian American. I thought there was something odd about him. He claimed to have acted in *The Covered Wagon* (1923) and *The Iron Horse* (1924), but he remembered virtually nothing. I knew more of their production history than he did.

And there was the strange case of Grey Owl, who posed as an Apache Indian environmentalist. (In 1999, Richard Attenborough made the Canadian film *Grey Owl* starring Pierce Brosnan.) Years ago, I bought a biography of Grey Owl, and as soon as I saw his photograph, I recognized the face as typical of the area I come from: not the southwestern United States, but the backwaters of Sussex, England.

I would love to know how these people were able to sustain their pretenses. Did the Indians believe that these imposters could speak on their behalf more eloquently than their own people?

This fascinating history is hard on Hollywood. So bear in mind that Westerns were not made for educational purposes, but simply to make money. They had to be as entertaining as possible, and if that meant putting Sioux war bonnets on Navajo Indians, so be it. Worse mistakes were made in other movies, and producers knew that few in the audience cared.

We may still feel romantic about the U.S. Cavalry, thanks to the films of John Ford and the performances of John Wayne. Had we seen evidence of what the Cavalry did in our name—as in *Soldier Blue* (1970), a film I still cannot bring myself to look at—then those beautiful Ford films might now be repellent to our gaze.

Now that the true history of the Old West has been told, and we have learned how appallingly the Indian was treated, some of us may feel guilty at how much we enjoyed these simplistic dramas. Nonetheless, it is fascinating to follow the development of films that had such an effect on us all. Aleiss' book provides a behind-the-scenes view on why these films were made, and while it won't change the images, it adds a new perspective of the Indians' place in Hollywood history.

Kevin Brownlow
London, England

Acknowledgments

This book took an unusual journey to publication. Initially, Cambridge University Press solicited the manuscript for a reader's comments and asked me to revise and resubmit. Alas, by the time I completed the revisions, Cambridge had ceased publishing film books (a fate since affecting several university publishers). Nevertheless, the Cambridge reader provided many valuable comments and much encouragement.

Thanks to Cambridge, the book had significantly improved by the time it found its way to Praeger Publishers. Since then, I've been extremely grateful to my editor, Eric Levy, for his guidance and suggestions. I'm also indebted to Steven Bingen, Kevin Brownlow, Annette Insdorf, Richard Koszarski, and Russell Thornton for their time and attention to this manuscript.

I owe much thanks to the numerous individuals who were especially helpful in guiding me through the maze of archival materials. Many have been supportive in my recent endeavors to expand my previous works on this subject: Sandra Taylor at the Lilly Library, Indiana University; James D'Arc at the Harold B. Lee Library, Brigham Young University; Howard Proutie and Jenny Romero at the Margaret Herrick Library, Academy of Motion Picture Arts and Sciences; Ned Comstock of the Cinema-Television Library, University of Southern California; Charles Bell at the Harry Ransom Humanities Research Center, University of Texas at Austin; Scott Feiner at the Wisconsin Historical Society; and Julie Graham at the University of California, Los Angeles, Arts Library Special

Collections. Marc Wanamaker of Bison Archives provided much expertise on early silent film history.

I am indeed grateful to the Institute of American Cultures/ American Indian Studies Center at the University of California, Los Angeles and the Ball Brothers Foundation, Lilly Library, Indiana University for their financial support. Additionally, the Canada-U.S. Fulbright Program provided me the opportunity to study as a Fulbright Scholar at the University of Toronto.

Finally, this book would not have been possible without the generous assistance of the late William K. Everson, who opened his vast collection of rare Westerns and answered my numerous telephone queries for more than a decade. The unwavering support of both Bill and his wife, Karen, extended well beyond any scholar's expectations.

Introduction

While studying for my doctorate in film history at Columbia University, I once listened to a friend of mine lament how Hollywood Westerns always showed white cowboy heroes clearing the land of its marauding Native Americans. My friend grew up on the Navajo reservation, and for reasons of which I was never clear, he was forced to stay after school and watch old Westerns. Naturally, he quickly tired of the Indian-as-obstacle formula and was able to replay the movies' dialogue line by line. I inquired whether he thought Hollywood had ever created any sympathetic images of Native Americans. But my friend responded that his school never showed any movies with "good" Indians.

This brief encounter motivated me to look more closely at the American Indian's image in Hollywood. Why, I wondered, have movies that perpetuate the image of Indians as civilization's obstacles—*The Plainsman* (1937) and *Stagecoach* (1939)—grown immensely popular, while those depicting the tradition and lifestyle of America's Natives—*The Silent Enemy* (1930) and *Eskimo* (1933)—faded quickly from the public's memory? From the earliest silent era to the present, motion pictures have created diverse Indian characters that have spanned the range from bloodthirsty savages or nymph-like children to a few notable portrayals of a people with their own distinct cultures and identities. Arguably, these Indian-themed films tell whites more about their own attitudes toward Indians than about Indians themselves. Regardless of Hollywood's motives (and profit was surely one of them), the studios developed Indian characters that embodied the ideals and failures of its producers, directors, and writers. This book will show how the motion-picture industry created the Native American's screen image and why it transformed over time. Ultimately, these Indian portrayals were more ambiguous than what my initial studies led me to believe.

Previous works on Hollywood's Indian portrayals have been especially critical of the industry's seemingly endless patterns of negative stereotypes. No doubt some of Hollywood's filmmakers were blatantly racist. But "Hollywood bashing" has become, in some circles, an acceptable trend at the expense of a more serious inquiry into the industry's history. Authors Ralph and Natasha Friar, for example, castigate the movie industry for its cultural distortions and historical inaccuracies. In *The Only Good Indian ... The Hollywood Gospel* (1972), the Friars' attacks against Hollywood are matched by glaring omissions and noticeable errors regarding motion-picture history. The Friars understandably have their own political agenda, labeling Hollywood as a racist institution; their distortion of important facts, however, only weakens their main point.[1] Furthermore, the authors' generalizations overlook key films that are major exceptions to the screen's "traditional negative images" of Indians.

Many scholars have traced the American Indian's evolving screen image while offering an interesting perspective of how cultural perceptions can shape the movies' representations. Gretchen Bataille and Charles Silet's *The Pretend Indians: Images of Native Americans in the Movies* (1980) is a compilation of previously published articles from trade papers, magazines, and journals; Michael Hilger's *From Savage to Nobleman: Images of Native Americans in Films* (1995) traces these images chronologically through the 1990s. More recently, *Hollywood's Indian: The Portrayal of the Native American in Film* (1998; rpt. 1999; Peter C. Rollins and John E. O'Connor, eds.) offers a compilation of scholars' essays that reinterprets individual movies. Similarly, Jacquelyn Kilpatrick's *Celluloid Indians: Native Americans and Film* (1999) discusses a history of Hollywood's Indians based upon excerpts from previously published materials and the movies themselves. Armando José Prats' *Invisible Natives: Myth and Identity in the American Western* (2002), is an interesting poststructural analysis that examines how Western movies with Indians reflect society's cultural transformations.

John E. O'Connor's *The Hollywood Indian: Stereotypes of Native Americans in Film* (1980) is the only work on this subject that examines studio production data and its relationship to the screen's

Indian portrayals. True to his profession as a historian, O'Connor delved into behind-the-scenes studio archival material and studied scripts, memoranda, financial records, and executives' correspondence relating to ten key Indian-themed films. O'Connor's "booklet," however, was written as a supplement to a 1980 exhibit at the New Jersey State Museum and contains only eighty pages. His brief work signaled that a more extensive examination of primary source materials is needed in this field. Ultimately, the studios and individual filmmakers created the Indian's screen representations, and few scholars have explored Hollywood's input into these images. One of the main goals of this book, then, is to fill that gap.

But we must remember that film is an art as well as an illusion. While the method of comparing the movies' misrepresentations and distortions to historical and cultural documentation is popular, it adds little insight into Hollywood's formation of its Indian images. A close examination of how and why Hollywood filmmakers chose to represent Indians reveals several recurring themes: (1) the movies' Indian characters have evolved in cycles over the past one hundred years instead of a consistent linear pattern; (2) stories about contemporary Indian society—from *Laughing Boy* (1934) to *Thunderheart* (1992)—continually draw low turnouts at movie theaters; (3) many non-Indian actors easily pass themselves off as Native Americans both in front of and behind the camera (conversely, Indians can pass easily in roles that demand conventional portrayals without regard to race, as in the significant *non-Indian* roles of Native American actors Wes Studi and the late Will Rogers); and (4) Hollywood has continually vacillated on the subject of Indian/white miscegenation (intermarriage). When examined at this level, these films become powerful indications of the industry's struggle to define the American Indian's identity.

Production materials can help shed light on how Hollywood studios created its Indian characters. A study of the filmmakers' correspondence, writers' evolving scripts, and studio publicity materials provides clues to how the movie industry responded to the changing political climate that would ultimately shape the screen's Indian images. Reactions from industry trade papers, film critics, and Native American groups expose existing misconceptions of both American Indian images and Hollywood history. An examination of the files of the movies' self-censorship organization (formerly, the "Hays Office") shows that Indian characters were portrayed differently from their Black American contemporaries. Although these behind-the-scenes materials are at best scanty, taken together, they open up unexplored territory and even challenge the belief that "the only good [Hollywood] Indian was a dead Indian."

Yet such an ambitious endeavor for this book contains built-in obstacles. A major problem for film historians—especially those covering a large time span—is that studio and filmmakers' production files are often inaccessible. Production materials, scripts, correspondence, and so on, are a part of a studio's corporate files, and unless otherwise stipulated, are not in the public domain. As private corporations, studios have the right to exercise discretion over who has access to their files, when, and how much.[2] Scholars of early cinema history have an especially difficult problem: from the 1890s through the late 1920s (the "silent film" era), a vast amount of production materials and the movies themselves are presumably lost.[3] Years later, many studios unfortunately discarded or destroyed their records due to a perceived lack of continuing value to the companies.

Most of this book's discussion, therefore, deals with movie material readily available to scholars. The papers of John Ford (Indiana University), Cecil B. DeMille (Brigham Young University), and David O. Selznick (University of Texas at Austin) are indexed and stored in archives open to scholars. The University of California, Los Angeles contains the Ralph Nelson Papers and many of Darryl Zanuck's script notations while he was head of production at Twentieth Century Fox. The University of Southern California provides researchers access to Warner Bros. corporate files (through 1967) as well as early scripts and correspondence of Metro-Goldwyn-Mayer. The Wisconsin Historical Society contains the Abraham Polonsky Collection. The Margaret Herrick Library at the Academy of Motion Picture Arts and Sciences holds the Production Code Administration files (from the late 1920s to approximately 1966) along with the Paramount Collection (although sparse during some years) and the Elliot Silverstein Collection.

Many of these archives, however, are accessible only to a certain point; studios that maintain their corporate correspondence since the late 1960s have yet to open them to scholars. For the majority of contemporary films, the only materials available are newspaper and magazine clippings as well as a few interviews with major artists. Thus, archival accessibility and the amount of available supporting materials become key factors when choosing to discuss specific movies. Other important factors include whether the film is an "A" movie (a big production budget released through a major studio) or a "B" movie (a cheaply and quickly made movie to fill the bottom half of a double bill when double features were standard); the film's impact in terms of box-office appeal (non-Western movies with Indians typically drew poor turnouts); how well the film exemplifies a pattern of that particular era; and the specific time frame represented during the film's release. Readers should view the evidence in this book as a starting point; hopefully, in the future, studios will open additional materials for scholarly research.

Regarding my Navajo friend, he grew up (along with many of us) watching countless negative Indian images in movies sold to television. Back then, the smaller studios sold only their cheaply produced independent products, or B pictures, to TV. The sympathetic treatment of movie Indians, on the other hand, was mostly confined to the A Western. Unlike the A Westerns, the B Westerns relied upon simple formulaic plots, stock villains, recycled stunt footage, and minimal dialogue (with obvious grammatical errors). Many of their characters (including but not limited to Indians) therefore emerged as unattractive and one-dimensional. Not until the late 1950s would studios begin to sell their better quality and big-name movies—including A Westerns—to television; many, in fact, didn't air until the early 1960s. But today's wide availability of these movies on cable, video, and DVD should encourage future generations to look even more closely at Hollywood's enduring Native American images.

1
Hollywood and the Silent American

LAISSEZ FAIRE IN THE MOVIES

A rowdy group of cowboys enters a general store. They taunt a young Indian woman and kidnap a white boy. The mother pleads in vain; the Indian woman dons trousers and a hat and leaps on a horse in hot pursuit. She follows the culprits to their campsite, shoots a guarding cowboy, and retrieves the shaken lad.

But the white villains persevere. The Indian woman scales a steep cliff and bounds across a canyon crevice, all with the child tied to her back. As her pursuers inch closer, she severs their connecting rope and sends them hurtling far below. The settlers cheer as the Indian heroine returns the boy to his grateful parents.

Back in 1908, the French motion picture company, Pathé Frères, began producing one- and two-reel films (a reel is about 1,000 feet, or ten minutes) at their new American studio facility in New Jersey. Pathé's weekly shorts of comedies, dramas, and Westerns included *The Red Girl and the Child*, released in August of 1910 and produced by James Gordon Young Deer. The filmmaker had worked briefly for several movie companies (then based on the East Coast), serving as a production assistant, writer, and actor. Young Deer boasted of his Indian heritage (although his background has since proven to be most enigmatic), and trade papers identified him as a Winnebago born in Dakota City, Nebraska. While at the Vitagraph Company of America, Young Deer earned praise for what were considered authentic portrayals of Indian people and their customs.[1]

When Pathé Frères opened its West Coast division in Los Angeles, Young Deer became one of its first producers.[2]

The Red Girl and the Child cleverly reversed gender stereotypes by portraying the Indian woman as an unconventional swashbuckling heroine. Young Deer was not alone: filmmakers adhered to a policy of laissez faire during an era in which studio monopolies and censorship organizations had yet to dictate motion picture content. The Indian as a noble hero actually preceded the cowboy star: the screen's first real Western star, G. M. "Broncho Billy" Anderson, appeared in *Broncho Billy and the Baby* in 1908, but studios like the Lubin Manufacturing Company and the Kalem Company had already portrayed sympathetic Indian characters prior to that time. Indian-themed pictures were especially popular from 1910 to 1912, when studios released approximately twelve to fifteen of them per month.[3] Some of these stories proved to be more audacious than what the standards of the time dictated. Tales of ruthless whites would parallel those of hostile warriors, lasting interracial marriages would complement the Indian/white relationships that failed, sympathetic half-breeds would occasionally offset the treacherous ones, and an Indian's heroic sacrifice might be matched by a white man's generosity. And many films delivered a sharp indictment against civilization and its unfair treatment of Native Americans.

During his productive three-year reign as Pathé's West Coast producer, Young Deer created some unusual tales. Many of his films were idyllic Indian love triangles or tragic stories of an Indian's heroic sacrifice, but others proved to be more daring and rather unconventional. When an Indian woman discovers that a Mexican rival has snatched her lover in *The Yaqui Girl* (1910), she has the man shot so that no one can ever claim him again. The white man in *For the Squaw* (1911) marries an Indian woman, has a child, but returns to his eastern sweetheart. His white fiancée instead scolds the unfaithful man and sends him back to his Indian family.[4] In *The Squaw's Mistaken Love* (1911), an Indian maiden actually makes love to a white man, but soon discovers that he is really a woman in disguise. "Surely, this is a new incident in Western pictures," remarked one dumbfounded reviewer.[5]

The early endeavors of Young Deer and his contemporaries only rarely promoted Indian assimilation into white society. Recent federal policies (post 1880s) advocating divestment of Indian land, compulsory boarding schools, and the eradication of Indian tradition and lifestyle were attempts to erase cultural differences

James Young Deer (*front, right*) with his wife Lillian St. Cyr (*left*) and the Bison Company in New Jersey, 1909–1910.

Courtesy of Bison Archives.

between Indians and whites and absorb Native Americans into mainstream American society. For the most part, Indian people resented the forced intrusion and mandatory efforts by educational, religious, and government institutions to "civilize" them. By the 1890s, Indians had been herded onto reservations; they were supposed to be "tame" and their so-called savage attacks belonged to the past. Filmmakers (and other artists) could now concoct romantic fables of a presumably lost culture within their own comfortable worlds of nostalgia.

What often fascinated these artists and their audiences was the "exoticism" of American Indians—their adorned clothing and Native rituals—which belonged to a race and culture distinctly different from white America. As early as 1894, the company of Thomas A. Edison Inc. staged *The Sioux Ghost Dance* in its primitive West Orange, New Jersey movie studio.[6] The single scene of three warriors stomping around in head feathers and breechcloth lasts only a few minutes, and by today's standards seems theatrically crude. Longer narrative films continued to highlight perceived differences between Indians and whites: Biograph's *Kit Carson* (1903) shows savage warriors attacking the soldiers' campsite and waving a bloody scalp. The "civilized" white hero, with the aid of an "attractive" Indian maiden, escapes from the "bloodthirsty" Indians and returns to white society.

EARLY COMEDIES AND DRAMAS

In early Western comedies, the red man's apparent difference from the white man became a source of mockery. Biograph's *A Midnight Phantasy* (1903) employs the images of savage Indians to satirize Victorian morality: a jealous warrior presents a ballerina with the bloody scalp of her pompous suitor. An even more absurd tale is *Oh, That Indian!* a 1910 short by the New York–based Powers Company. The Indian represents nature's child gone wild: He ingests a little too much alcohol and scalps the bartender, a Chinaman, and his (white) companion's wife. He then forces gasoline down his poor friend, whose lighted cigar sets off a messy explosion.[7]

The more serious Indian-themed pictures, however, were simplistic and loosely based adaptations of literary tales. The classic story of John Rolfe's marriage to the young Powhatan maiden, Pocahontas, was filmed by the Edison studios in 1908 and by the Thanhouser Film Corporation in 1910. The Independent Motion

Picture Company produced Henry Longfellow's immortal poem *Hiawatha* in 1909, followed by its sequel *The Death of Minnehaha* in 1910. Biograph brought Helen Hunt Jackson's poignant tale of *Ramona* (1910) to the screen, and the Selig Polyscope Company followed with *Ramona's Father* (1911), a rather morose story in which both the white hero and the Indian heroine are stabbed and killed. There was even *An Indian Romeo and Juliet* (1912), Vitagraph's version of Shakespeare's tragedy in which a young Huron lad falls in love with an enemy Mohawk maiden.[8]

GRIFFITH AND RACIAL SEPARATION

Whether the movies' Indian characters were sympathetic, evil, or totally ludicrous, their traditional lifestyle and customs were incompatible with their non-Indian counterparts. This concept of a separate Indian/white culture, or a "racial pluralism," was central to the films of American movie pioneer, David Wark (D. W.) Griffith. Born 1875 in Kentucky and surrounded with colorful Civil War stories of his Confederate officer father, Griffith sprang from an era ripe with racial segregation. By the time he had arrived at New York's American Mutoscope and Biograph studios in 1908, Jim Crow laws had separated Black Americans from their white counterparts, Indians had been herded onto reservations, and European immigrants became targets of eugenic theorists. To Griffith, the rapidly emerging multiethnic, multiracial American society was more of a dissolution than an amalgamation: "It never appeared like a *melting* pot to me. It seemed more like a *boiling* pot," he observed of the city streets and its newly arrived immigrants.[9]

In Griffith's Westerns, whites were often evil and lecherous, and at times, responsible for the Indians' viciousness. His Indian characters were often by nature loyal and kind; Griffith's thirty Indian-themed films included only eight with Native Americans as villains (most noticeably in *The Battle at Elderbush Gulch* in 1914). Indians might be harmful, as those who besiege a family's cabin in *Fighting Blood* (1911) or attack a covered wagon in *The Last Drop of Water* (1911), but villainous whites often provoked their behavior. "If he [the Indian] has been guilty of any lawlessness, it has been induced by his misanthropic attitude towards the white man, and can we blame him?" warns the advertisement to Griffith's *Comata, the Sioux* (1909).[10] The white physician in *A Mohawk's Way* (1910) whips his Black servant, drinks too much liquor, and "refuses to waste his time on an Indian." His compassionate wife instead aids a sick Indian baby; the husband is killed and she is safely carried off to the British. The white woman's parting kiss to the Indian mother shows that mutual respect can cross racial lines.

Unlike his portrayals of Black Americans, Griffith's Indians occupied a somewhat different social strata. Blacks were diabolical beasts who threatened social order and preyed upon white women (Gus the rapist in the 1915 *Birth of a Nation*) or they were loyal, self-sacrificing servants (George the faithful guardian in *His Trust* and *His Trust Fulfilled*, both 1911). Indians instead might be worthy of assimilation, but white bigotry would prevent it.[11] "Civilization and education cannot bleach his tawdry epidermis," noted Biograph's advertisement of Griffith's *The Call of the Wild* (1908), "and that will always prove an insurmountable barrier to social distinction."[12] The Indian in this film has attended college and wears starched suits: He has become civilized and temporarily joins the ranks of society's upper class. But his skin color reveals his Indianness and sends him back to the reservation. Similarly, in *A Romance of the Western Hills* (1910), an Indian girl is adopted by white tourists but is later mistreated by their philandering nephew. She soon discovers that "civilization [is] a gift not yet perfect" and returns to her own people.

Whether villains or heroes, Griffith's Indian characters remained separate and apart from white society. Their encounters may have been peaceful and friendly, but neither race would become culturally or socially assimilated into the other. Griffith's first Western, *The Red Man and the Child* (1908), emphasizes apparent differences between the races in order to spotlight the Indian hero as a noble savage: The Sioux warrior is "as kind-hearted as a woman and as brave as a lion"; the outlaws are "a couple of low-down human coyotes." A Sioux warrior forms an enduring friendship with a young white boy when he avenges the murder of the boy's grandfather and wrestles the outlaws to their death. In the final scene, the Indian paddles the canoe back to the campsite, with the child safely asleep by his side.

Like many of his contemporaries, Griffith popularized the noble savage as if to revere a lost culture. Many of his all-Indian tales were simply idyllic love triangles in which the absence of whites hinted at the isolated and yet virtuous existence of his Native American characters. The titles themselves suggest a Romantic nostalgia: *The Squaw's Love* (1911), or "An Indian Poem of Love in Pictures," is framed among scenic lakes, dense forests, and steep cliffs. *The Mended Lute* (1909), or "A Stirring Romance in the Dakotas," features an Indian and his attractive maiden embracing against a picturesque waterfall. Young Deer served as a technical advisor on this film, and his efforts were duly noted: "Much thought and time given to many details . . . having been supervised by an expert in the matter."[13]

But true to Griffith's belief of a racial separation, Indian/white romances were futile endeavors. In *The Chief's Daughter* (1911), a white man's seduction of an Indian woman causes his angry fiancée to break off the engagement, and the rejected Indian maiden returns to her people. *Heredity* (1912) pairs off a white renegade with his purchased bride, an Indian woman. When the couple's half-breed son is born, the "racial difference between father and son is felt."[14] The man becomes ashamed of his Indian wife and child, and his crimes against the Native people bring about his own destruction. Mother and boy return to the tribe, where the call of blood proves stronger than marital ties.

AMBIVALENT ROMANCES

Although Griffith's Indian/white romances precluded a happy cohabitation, other filmmakers occasionally binded an interracial liaison. These short, idyllic romances could never really grapple with the problems of assimilating one partner into the culture of another, since their brief lengths concluded with little more than the couple's happy marriage. Lubin's *The White Chief* (1908), for example, is the story of an American trapper and his love for and subsequent marriage to an Indian maiden. A year later, Edison's *A Cry from the Wilderness* (1909) was the unusual tale of a white trader who renounces civilization in order to marry his Inuit wife.[15]

For the most part, the filmmakers' portrayals of interracial romances were ambivalent. A favorite theme was from *The Squaw Man* (a popular 1905 play by Edwin Milton Royle that would resurface in three movie versions), in which a white man marries an Indian woman, produces a child, and abandons her. Stranded and heartbroken, the woman kills herself. Biograph had shown it in *The Kentuckian* (1908), as did the New York Motion Picture Company (NYMPC) with *A Squaw's Sacrifice* (1909) and the American Film Manufacturing Company in *The Squaw and the Man* (1911).

Conversely, the distraught warrior in Vitagraph's *The Indian Flute* (1911) plunges into the rapids when his Indian lover marries a white trapper.[16] Young Deer created his own twist on this weepy theme: *White Fawn's Devotion* (1910) was the tale of an abandoned Indian wife who feigns death, then suddenly reappears to save her white husband from the tribe's vengeance. It was a lesson fit for any wandering spouse.

Movie reviewers of the period found these depictions of Indian/white marriages most distasteful. Apparently, the films' interracial unions were more liberal than what the Victorian-minded critics could tolerate. Particularly unsettling to the *Moving Picture World* was the Champion Film Company's production of *The Indian Land Grab* (1910), the somewhat implausible story of a white woman who deceives a young chief, but later trails him to become his wife. "There is an inseparable racial gulf which is repugnant to see crossed," the writer remarked. The happy union between a white woman and an Indian warrior in Pathé's *Red Deer's Devotion* (1911) raised another objection. "Still, there is a feeling of disgust which cannot be overcome when this sort of thing is depicted as plainly as it is here," was the paper's reaction to this James Young Deer film.[17]

THE PROBLEMATIC HALF-BREED

Reviewers clung to similar conventions regarding Indian/white mixed bloods, or half-breeds. Often, the movies' half-breeds were either loyal or treacherous: evil half-breeds might steal Indian women from their lovers or plot an ambush against innocent settlers, while honest ones might aid whites in danger or willingly sacrifice themselves. Selig's portrayal of a half-breed as insidious and deceitful in *An Indian Wife's Devotion* (1909) drew much praise: "The picture clearly depicts the despicable characteristics of the average half-breed and undoubtedly represents him as he is—a dangerous and treacherous foe." But two years later, Champion released *The Half-Breed's Courage* (1911), the story of a half-breed who sacrifices himself to save a white man. "Possibly, this is a trait of half-breeds which hitherto has not been sufficiently understood or appreciated," was the paper's somewhat contrite response.[18]

Meanwhile, Kalem took a close look at the half-breed's plight within a racially intolerant society. With studios dispersed throughout New York, New Jersey, Florida, and southern California, Kalem enjoyed ample scenery and a natural environment for its Indian-themed pictures. The persistent tension between Indians and whites dominated Kalem's films; its stories of civilization's corruption of Indian lifestyle underlined the notion that white society would not accommodate Indian people.

Kalem's *Lo, the Poor Indian* (1910) was a classic example: *Moving Picture World* noted how the film revealed that "the two [races] will always conflict no matter how earnest the effort to reconcile them."[19] Similarly, education cannot erase Indian hereditary in Kalem's *The White Man Takes a Red Wife* (1910): A white man marries an Indian woman, has a child, and then abandons them. Years later, the man sends his half-breed daughter to college, but "the call" ultimately beckons her Indian half back to her mother's people. Conversely, in *The Blackfoot Halfbreed* (1911), the educated half-breed daughter renounces her mother's tribe and joins her father's upper-class white community. The heroine "becomes white," but in doing so she must abandon her Native heritage.

INDIANS SPEAK OUT

As Kalem lamented the plight of the poor Indian, critics lauded the studio for its departure from "the dime novel class of Indian pictures." *Moving Picture World* was quick to point out its use of Indian actors in *Chief Blackfoot's Vindication* (1910): "The public is no longer satisfied with white men who attempt to represent Indian life. The actors must be real Indians." The company's painstaking efforts to reproduce Indian lifestyle were noted by one Native American viewer, who spotted occasional mistakes but nevertheless described Kalem's Indian portrayals as "very accurate."[20]

Not all Indians agreed. In the spring of 1911, a delegation of Chippewa voiced strong opposition against what they perceived to be alleged libels in moving pictures. Arriving in Washington DC, the Indians demanded that President William H. Taft impose congressional regulation to halt the movies' distortions. Further west, a chorus of Shoshone, Cheyenne, and Arapaho voiced similar objections to the Bureau of Indian Affairs in Washington. Robert G. Valentine, commissioner of the Office of Indian Affairs (1909–1912) and a proponent of federal assimilation policies, promised his assistance in eliminating the films' objectionable features.[21] Valentine had been busy developing programs in industry and agriculture to help civilize America's Natives, so stories of idyllic romances, wagon-train attacks, and worst of all, educated Indian heroes who abandon civilization were simply sending the wrong message.

Selig's production of *The Curse of the Red Man* (1911) was a glaring example. The angry Chippewa labeled the film "a false representation of Indian life" and objected to the depiction of an educated Indian as drunk and destitute. The film's story of a Sherman Institute graduate and a celebrated college football player showed how educated Indians could become social pariahs within their own culture. The Indian character returns home in a suit and tie and discovers his own tribe refuses to accept his modern teachings. His people subsequently order him out; three years later, he "meets the curse" (whiskey) and wanders among society's fringes. When he kills a brutal bartender, he flees to the desert and the sheriff's posse hunts him down.

The Selig company quickly rose to the defense. "The Indian reviewer who criticized the film as a false portrayal of Indian life is mistaken," politely explained the story's writer and assistant director, Hobart Bosworth (who also portrayed the movie's lead character). "The film is a dramatization from real life of an event that occurred in the Eastern California and Western Nevada deserts some four years ago."[22] The film's tragic hero was supposed to be "Willie Boy," the young Paiute and Chemehuevi Indian who allegedly murdered a man, then led his pursuers on a wild chase across the desert. Dozens of contradictory accounts have since told the story—the most popular being the 1969 movie, *Tell Them Willie Boy Is Here*.[23] Selig's production was especially controversial because it implied that federal assimilation policies were futile against traditional Indian practices. "We are trying to teach the Indian that he should be a good farmer and forget about being a warrior," groaned a southern California Indian reservation superintendent in 1911, "and when he visits the city and sees nothing but the [movie] Indian depicted with gun or arrow in his hands, instead of a hoe or rake, he becomes sadly confused."[24]

LIFE IN INCEVILLE

The Native American outcry did little to immediately effect Western films. Studios continued to seek natural locations and real Indian actors, and many ventured into remote Indian communities for on-site filming. In 1910, Griffith and his Biograph players had traveled to Piru and the Camulos Ranch in southern California to film the first screen version of Helen Hunt Jackson's tale of *Ramona*.[25] By 1911, the Essanay Film Manufacturing Company (whose logo was an Indian's head) staged a series of Native American plays using members from the local Indian community near their Redlands studio (just east of Los Angeles).[26] But the NYMPC and Bison Life Motion Pictures would lift Westerns to a new height and redefine the Indian's screen character.

The Bison company arrived in Los Angeles in 1909. One of Bison's regular stars of its Indian and Western dramas was Princess Mona Darkfeather. Under the tutelage of her husband/director Frank E. Montgomery, Darkfeather played Indian and several Spanish leads in many Bison productions before moving on to Kalem and Universal. She was given the title "Princess" by a Chief Big Thunder when the Blackfoot tribe made her a blood member. Darkfeather was actually a descendent of the Workman family pioneers who emigrated from Northern England to southern California in the nineteenth century. She was born in Los Angeles and also claimed Spanish ancestry. Her real name was Josephine Workman.[27]

Besides Darkfeather, Bison included its cadre of cowboys, Indians, and trick riders for its weekly staple of one-reel Westerns. Many were stories of Native American life in the wilderness long before white civilization appeared; they exalted Romanticism and the noble savage and condemned the hostile warrior. Others were a ménage à trois of two warriors pursuing the same attractive maiden, or an Indian's steadfast loyalty to a white. Occasionally, a Bison short might reveal the ruthless invasion of greedy frontiersmen upon Indian land: "It is a tale which will bear constant repeating," noted *Moving Picture World* of *The Red Man's Persecution* (1910). "The people of this country cannot know it any too well." Bison's Indian romances were rather amusing oddities: *An Indian Love Story* (1911) was the tale of two dissatisfied Indian couples who actually swap partners.[28]

By late 1911, the quality of Bison's Westerns was waning. Their stories may have been numerous and varied, but their Indian characters were at best flat and one-dimensional. The popular Indian tales that had dominated the screen since the turn of the century were now cliché: reviewers in particular tired of the stereotypical noble versus savage portrayals and faulted filmmakers for exaggerating the public's demand. "Too much of a good thing is bad," moaned a weary writer. "Give the public just a little rest."[29] *Moving Picture World* even cited Bison's products for being downright shoddy: "No Bison picture in a long time has been so poor in photo-play as [*An Indian Hero*, 1911]."[30]

A surprise came in December of 1911, when the NYMPC announced that it was abandoning its simplistic cowboy-and-Indian pictures in favor of more spectacular Westerns. In their place came stories that were supposedly "real and true to life." The move was a bold attempt to rescue Westerns from their primitive dime-novel status. To ensure realism, the Bison company had leased the Miller Brothers' 101 Ranch Real Wild West Show and its company of daring riders, horses, and stuntmen. The partnership, which came to be known as Bison-101, promised elaborate historical recreations and an expansion from one- to two-reel subjects.[31]

The successful merger with the Miller Brothers' Ranch was the brainwork of Thomas Harper Ince. Born in Rhode Island, Ince had grown up in the theater then later moved on to acting and directing in motion pictures.[32] When the NYMPC hired Ince to revive their ailing Bison Westerns, the producer quickly went to work. He set up Hollywood's first assembly-line production unit, employing men and women to take charge of various departments and overseeing ten or more directors simultaneously. He created his own scenarios, or movie scripts (often in collaboration with other writers), and supervised the filming and editing of every story. Although many Ince films were actually directed by others, he took credit and placed his name on all as supervising director.[33] His elaborate stock company of technicians, artists, and cowboys—nestled in the Santa Monica Mountains overlooking the Pacific Ocean—came to be known appropriately as "Inceville."

This scenic mountainside community was dotted with tipis belonging to the Oglala Sioux Indians from South Dakota's Pine Ridge Reservation. Ince had signed an agreement with the federal government to secure a large group of Indians, all of whom were under his daily care. Entire Oglala families of men, women, and children camped out along the mountain range for six months, when a new group would replace the previous one. By 1913, Ince's Indian performers were receiving $7 to $10 per week, plus expenses.[34]

Life in Inceville had its occasional headaches. Ince complained that the Oglala might simply refuse to work: "They were stolid and non-communicative and had a strong dislike for doing anything that did not happen to appeal to them at the moment," he wrote. Pieces of the set would disappear into the Indian camp, and Ince soon discovered that his Native American actors had an unexplainable attraction to bright-colored props. But bigger problems occurred when a few Indians regularly visited the local saloons and became intoxicated. Ince, worried that these incidents could prompt the government to cancel his contract, threatened the saloon keepers with prosecution if they continued to sell alcohol to his Indian performers.[35]

Despite these obstacles, Ince and the Oglala made more than eighty Westerns together. From 1912 to 1917, Ince boasted, these Indians "appeared in many of my two-reel pictures and did some truly remarkably [sic] work."[36] In 1916, Ince's team drew upon plans to build a two-story schoolhouse and offer classes in "the rudiments of the elementary subjects" to his Indian community. The Sioux tribe already boasted several Carlisle graduates who became candidates for assistant instructor positions at the school. "There is no reason in the world why these Indians should not be given an education," Ince mused.[37]

The success of Inceville's movies attracted its imitators. Colonel William F. "Buffalo Bill" Cody's Historical Picture Company of Colorado hired the Oglala for *The Indian Wars* (1914), an eight-reel picture re-creating Custer's Last Stand and the Wounded Knee Massacre. The Black Hills Feature Film Company in Nebraska also employed the Oglala for *In the Days of '75 and '76* (1915), a seven-reel picture about James "Wild Bill" Hickok and Martha "Calamity Jane" Cannary.[38] The Universal Film Manufacturing Company transported 300 Arizona and New Mexico Indians to its 20,000-acre Oak Crest Ranch in San Fernando Valley (just north of Los Angeles) for its Westerns.[39] Occasionally, Universal's Indians donned Confederate soldier uniforms in Civil War epics; at other times, they metamorphosed into supernatural creatures. Universal's *The Werewolf* (1913) appeared to be an early forerunner of the studio's horror film cycle: a mixed-blooded daughter avenges her Indian mother's murder by turning into a wolf.[40]

Ince's Westerns left an indelible mark on the movies' Indian portrayals. His stories were epic in scope and took a close look at interracial relations. Unlike Griffith, Ince rarely bothered with idyllic Indian tales or moral themes; rather, his concern was for individuals and their relationship to class, culture, or race as a whole. Griffith's Indian stories were timeless, often with social messages and references to class conflicts. Ince's Westerns, on the other hand, adopted a James Fenimore Cooper outlook: His

Tom Ince (*seated center, left*) with Sioux actors at Inceville, 1914.
Courtesy of Bison Archives.

explanations were historical and his tone elegiac. Often, his films looked at the individual's futile struggle against social and political forces.

In *The Indian Massacre* (1912), civilization's corrupt influence adversely affects the quiet, traditional life of an Indian village.[41] Ince shows how greedy frontiersmen deplete the Indians' food supply by killing buffalo, and how they shoot at Indians for mere sport. Understandably, the warriors agree to drive the whites from their hunting grounds: they attack the settlers' homes and kidnap a white child as a replacement for their own lost one. The final shot of the Indian mother grieving her child's death powerfully illustrates the maternal bond.

Ince's Westerns did not pretend to favor Indians. The producer's more sympathetic portrayals were matched by negative ones; even *Moving Picture World* noted that overall, Ince's Indian-themed films adopted "a middle course that is nicely balanced."[42] The well-known *Custer's Last Fight* (1912; reissued in 1925) takes a decidedly patriotic view of the army officer's involvement in the Battle of Little Bighorn.[43] The Sioux and Cheyenne are impediments to civilization who eventually "overwhelm Custer with a red mass of destruction." In *Blazing the Trail* (1912), a family of naive settlers welcomes the Indians into their camp and feeds them. But the warriors kill the mother and father, wound the son, and capture the young daughter. The final shot of the parents' two grave markers becomes a grim warning to Western immigrants.

Whether Ince's Indians were hostile or sympathetic, they were never assimilated into white society. Like Griffith's Native American portrayals, Ince's fell short of a permanent Indian/white cohabitation: an Indian girl's marriage to a white man ends in her tragic death in *His Squaw* (1912), and a colonel unknowingly shoots his adopted Indian daughter in *The Colonel's Adopted Daughter* (1914). Griffith's *The Battle at Elderbush Gulch* (1914) and Ince's *The Hour of Reckoning* (1914) both include a climactic Indian attack and a noticeable commentary against miscegenation. In Ince's version, the white woman's husband slips out of the besieged cabin and is immediately killed by the attacking warriors. Death becomes preferable to the threat of forced interracial relations: "Seeing that they are outnumbered and will undoubtedly fall into the hands of Indians, the woman makes her cowboy friend kill her and then himself."[44] The same theme previously appeared in the 1893 play, *The Girl I Left Behind Me*, by David Belasco and Franklin Fyles.

Directors Cecil B. DeMille (*Union Pacific*) and John Ford (*Stagecoach*) would repeat it twenty-five years later.

PATHÉ AND YOUNG DEER

While Inceville and Universal studios boasted of all-Indian stock companies, Pathé's West Coast division claimed an American Indian producer. Around December of 1910, Pathé Frères opened a studio in Edendale, California (northeastern Los Angeles) and placed James Young Deer in charge of production. The filmmaker wasted no time in expanding Pathé's complex, hiring a troupe of actors and even inventing an ingenious photographic process for scenes lit by fires or the moon. Not to be outdone by his competitors, Young Deer traveled on location to Orange County in California, Santa Catalina Island, and southwestern Arizona to film his Indian- and Spanish-themed pictures. The producer hired one of the Nestor Film Company's acclaimed performers, George Gebhardt Jr., and announced that the non-Indian actor would play all of Pathé's Indian leads.[45] Pathé's female lead was Lillian St. Cyr, a Winnebago Indian commonly known in Hollywood as Princess Redwing. She was also Young Deer's wife.[46]

Young Deer apparently led a rather fast and elusive lifestyle. He spent much of his early years performing in circuses and Wild West Shows, and as a filmmaker he made frequent trips across country and later to Great Britain. Young Deer's taste for adventure sometimes competed with his own movie stories. At a Los Angeles country club, he startled guests when he cracked a whiskey glass with his teeth and pretended to swallow it. He then cut his hand on the glass and fainted; the hospital's diagnosis was "alcoholic hysteria."[47] Once during filming, Young Deer hogtied a horse and pushed it over a cliff in an attempt to create a "realistic" effect. Local residents were horrified at the animal's screams and *Moving Picture World* was outraged. The court subsequently fined Pathé $60.[48]

In late 1913, Young Deer's prolific life in motion pictures came to a halt. The trouble began when local maidens named the producer as a coconspirator in a white slave ring. The Los Angeles County Sheriff's office personally delivered a subpoena to him on location in Orange County, and Young Deer was subsequently forced to answer some embarrassing questions concerning his affiliation with the ring's millionaire leaders. Months of public scandal followed before the case was settled and Young Deer was free,[49] but not for long.

Two months later, another woman stepped forward and accused Young Deer of taking money "under a false promise to give her work." Shortly thereafter, a fifteen-year-old girl accused Young Deer of a statutory offense against a juvenile. Again the law went after the producer, who jumped his $1,500 bail and headed for New York. Scared and penniless, Young Deer blamed "the vengeance the white men meted out to Indians," and called himself "the black sheep of the whole [white slave] happening." He then fled to England but a year later, returned to face charges in Los Angeles. Fortunately for him, his female accusers had left town.[50] The case against Young Deer was dropped, but so was his lucrative movie career.

Young Deer's misfortunes coincided with a major transition in early motion picture history. By 1912, feature films of five reels or more began to replace the short one- and two-reelers. Furthermore, Westerns declined as historical dramas and popular novels superceded cowboy-and-Indian pictures. "The cowboy is waning by the side of a declining Indian maid," observed the New York Times in a piece on Hollywood's "passing fashions." A year later, Moving Picture World's verdict was in: Indian dramas had finally played themselves out. "So give your attentions to something else," was its advice to aspiring writers.[51]

Production companies thus turned their efforts to other subjects. As audiences demanded longer and more complex narratives, the all-Indian idyllic tales slowly faded from the American screen. Short Indian-themed pictures continued to appear, but their simplistic formats could no longer compete with feature films. A few notable Indian actors and even a director later surfaced in Hollywood. But many years would pass before Native Americans could again achieve the stature they once enjoyed in the early motion picture industry.

2

A Cultural Division*

THE SQUAW MAN

The publicity for Jesse Lasky's *The Squaw Man* (1914) clearly spelled out the risks of an Indian/white marriage: "When you fall in love with an Indian girl, she does not stand aside when you fight. No siree, she comes of a terrible ancestry." The ad's message that Indian women will "kill the other fellow before you can" made light of the belief that whites ought not to marry Indians.[1] But for all its movie hype, *The Squaw Man* exposed the layers of contradictions that afflicted these interracial unions and examined the obvious problem of social prejudice. The miscegenation theme was particularly troublesome, for silent filmmakers continued to wrestle with it in later feature films including *The Vanishing American* (1925). In many of these stories, Native American existence remained futile within a white-dominated world.

Hollywood's short, idyllic Indian tales also faced a dismal future. Brief stories of charming maidens pursued by amorous warriors or noble Indians doomed to extinction could hardly compete with the longer, more serious feature Westerns like *The Squaw Man*. Movie director James Young Deer, whose career flourished during the early silent years, bemoaned the decline of Indian stories

*Excerpts from Angela Aleiss, "The Vanishing American: Hollywood's Compromise to Indian Reform," *Journal of American Studies* 25(1991): 467–472, were reprinted with the permission of Cambridge University Press.

(as well as his reputation) and temporarily sought refuge in the British film industry.[2] The financial success of *The Squaw Man* and other feature films eventually drove the shorter Indian tales of Young Deer and his contemporaries out of the movie business.

The release of Jesse Lasky's *The Squaw Man* in 1914 marked the first time a feature film was made in what is now Hollywood. *The Squaw Man*'s length of six reels—approximately 90 minutes—explored the Indians' plight in more detail than its one- and two-reel predecessors. Silent feature films still offered the same variety of Indian-themed stories, however. Noble warriors were matched by Indian villains, and interracial romances brought various outcomes. Silent epic Westerns revived the Indian-as-obstacle formula, while the rare docudramas offered a glimpse of Native American lifestyle untouched by civilization. As these longer films allowed a more in-depth exploration of underlying racial tensions, they nonetheless reinforced the belief that Indians remained separate and apart from white civilization.

But the movie industry itself was rapidly changing. The early teens signaled a pattern of growth for the motion picture industry, and many studios were well on their way to becoming modern factories. By late 1914, feature films had triumphed almost completely over the one- and two-reel shorts, sending some companies to success and others (like Kalem and the Méliès Manufacturing Company) to oblivion. Paramount Pictures Corporation was founded in 1914 (initially as a distribution organization), First National was created in 1917 (and later acquired by Warner Bros.), and in 1915, Universal Pictures officially opened a studio in the San Fernando Valley. These companies produced their longer feature films more slowly and with larger budgets than the one- and two-reelers. Their sophisticated narratives were more structured and less creative; at the same time, their visual artistry set higher standards throughout the industry.

As longer feature films became more of a financial gamble, studios needed solid evidence that their movies would indeed sell to audiences. Consequently, they sought established plays, novels, and even reputable stage actors to build their productions. Paramount Pictures, through its initial production origins of the Famous Players Film Company and the Jesse L. Lasky Feature Play Company, signed major Broadway stars and playwrights to its studios. Paramount regularly developed features based upon popular literary sources, from Broadway plays to classic novels, including the mass-produced works of Zane Grey. Another author, Edwin Milton Royle (also a lyricist and director) wrote the well-known and successful play *The Squaw Man*, which would become the basis for the 1914 movie version.

The Squaw Man first opened in New York City in 1905. Reviewers praised the story as sincere with a "deep and lasting pathos" and noted that the play showed Indians in a more genuine light than the sentimental and Romantic depictions of the past.[3] The play's tragic story of a marriage between an Englishman and a Ute Indian woman had similar literary roots in the first dime novel, *Malaeska: the Indian Wife of the White Hunter* (1860). In *Malaeska*, the woman promises her dying husband to raise their son in white society, but she and her son both die as he is about to marry a white woman. In *The Squaw Man*, the marriage is also doomed: the Indian woman kills a white villain in order to save the Englishman's life. She marries and has a son by him, but the town's sheriff is after her for the murder. Meanwhile, her husband must send their son to England for a proper education. Her life in danger and her only child removed, the Indian woman kills herself.

As Hollywood's first feature Western, *The Squaw Man* underscores the belief that white civilization has no room for American Indians. Its message is bold: society rejects Native Americans and simultaneously destroys their kinship. (Cecil B. DeMille shared the movie's direction with Oscar C. Apfel.) For the leading roles, DeMille cast the well-known stage idol Dustin Farnum as the Englishman (Farnum had appeared in the play's 1911 revival) and Redwing as the ill-fated Indian woman. Redwing was actually Lillian St. Cyr of the Winnebago tribe, and DeMille chose her because he wanted a real Indian to play her part.[4]

The Squaw Man earned a hefty net profit of $244,700, enough to establish that feature-length movies were here to stay.[5] Its financial success prompted DeMille to remake the movie in 1918 and 1931 (the latter is a talkie version starring Warner Baxter and Lupe Velez). Producer Lasky again teamed up with Royle to make *The Squaw Man's Son* (1917), a rather quirky sequel to its 1914 predecessor. The movie was based upon Royle's novel, *The Silent Call* (1910) and simply picked up where *The Squaw Man* left off: the mixed-blooded son ultimately abandons his drug-addicted (Caucasian) wife for a pretty, educated Indian woman. Here again, the movie's conclusion suggested that Indians should remain with Indians.[6]

In *The Squaw Man* (1914), James Wynnegate (Dustin Farnum) cautions Nat-U-Rich (Lillian St. Cyr) against talking after she's killed the white villain.

Courtesy of Bison Archives.

RECYCLED ROMANCES

For the most part, however, feature filmmakers wrestled with contradictory resolutions to Indian/white romances. The subject of racial miscegenation was tricky: unlike the movies' Black Americans, Native Americans could marry whites without fear of censorship reprisals. Anti-miscegenation laws in California were also a mixed bag: the state forbade Black/white unions until 1948, but Indian/white marriages were acceptable.[7] Producers thus groped to clarify the Indian's relationship with white America while their stories suggested the industry's ambivalence toward the subject.

DeMille repeated *The Squaw Man*'s theme of an interracial marriage—this time with a happier outcome—for *The Woman God Forgot* (1917). The director had already explored the cultural and class tensions underlying the relationship between a Turkish nobleman and a Montenegrin woman in *The Captive* (1915). In *The Woman God Forgot*, the captain of Cortez' army (Wallace Reid) falls in love with Montezuma's attractive Aztec daughter (Geraldine Farrar, a Metropolitan Opera star). The couple's final union, however, carefully eschews any cultural compromise: following Montezuma's defeat, the two flee the arid desert and retreat to the secluded forest. The movie concludes with an uneasy alliance between its two protagonists: they each remain in their own traditional attire, a symbol of their separate cultural identities (a similar resolution had occurred in *The Captive*). Even *Variety* was quick to note that Farrar's skin was distinctly lighter than all other members of her tribe, a fact that simultaneously seemed to mask her Indian heritage.[8]

Other features successfully paired Indians with whites, but the relationship seemed strained by underlying conflicts. In *The Red Woman* (1917), a chief's daughter (Broadway actress Gail Kane) earns high honors at an eastern college but is scorned by her non-Indian peers. She returns to her own people, falls in love with a white man, watches him depart for the East, then gives birth to their child. He later joins her and they are married, far removed from civilization's bigotry. (*Variety* had no qualms with the interracial romance but frowned upon the child's birth prior to the marriage ceremony.) Similarly, in *The Son of The Wolf* (1922), based on a Jack London short story, an Alaskan gold miner falls in love with the chief's daughter and even kills his Indian competitor for her affections. The happy couple then departs for civilization, an affirmation of white heritage over Native American tradition.[9]

A common element among Indian/white movie romances was the discovery that the Indian hero (or heroine) is actually white. The topic was rare in short silents, but features provided a more expansive forum to explore the ambiguities that underlie these tensions. The typical storyline dictates that the Indian and white fall in love but encounter obstacles because of their mixed racial status. The Indian's discovery that he or she is really white was one way for skittish filmmakers to resolve all social dilemmas and avoid taboos against Indian/white miscegenation. Thus, the outcome is neat and predictable: boy meets girl, boy loses girl, and boy returns to girl of the same race. In *The Test of Donald Norton* (1926), the hero flees his abusive Indian stepmother and vows to kill himself if he's sent back to the Indians. He falls in love with a Caucasian woman and discovers that he, too, is really white.

Many Indian/white romances did survive, but safely outside society's boundaries. Typically, the pair is destined to live among society's fringes or retreat from white civilization. *Laughing Bill Hyde* (1918) was based upon the short story by Rex Ellingwood Beach, who joined the gold rush to Alaska in 1898 and subsequently set many of his novels in that territory (including *The Spoilers*, filmed five times). *Laughing Bill Hyde* successfully pairs a white ex-con to a decent mixed-blooded Indian woman. In a sense, both white and Indian are social outcasts, confined to the sparse settlements of the far North. The movie was the feature film debut of William Penn Adair Rogers ("Will Rogers"), the notable Cherokee actor/comedian who established himself as a movie star playing non-Indian characters.[10]

James Fenimore Cooper's *The Last of the Mohicans* prompted many movie variations of the 1826 classic novel. Griffith started the trend with *Leather Stocking* in 1909, and both the Thanhouser and Power companies each made their own versions in 1911. Not to be left out, Vitagraph released *The Deerslayer* the same year, with Wallace Reid as the wise Chingachgook. In 1924, Pathé created its own ten-part serial, *Leatherstocking*. Cooper's Indians were essentially types: Chingachgook and his son Uncas represent the last of the noble Mohicans while Magua embodies all that is savage and evil. While Cooper spoke of ideal times before whites forced Indians to part with their lands, his mood is ultimately elegiac and his tone melancholic.

The 1920 version of *The Last of the Mohicans*, codirected by Maurice Tourneur and Clarence Brown, paints a similarly somber portrayal of America's Native inhabitants. The film seems to idolize its Indian subjects among the rising sun, flickering torch lights, and graceful shadows that glide from one end of the screen to another. Tourneur and Brown place their Indian characters against a multi-layered perspective: a cave entrance in the foreground frames a highlighted middle ground containing human silhouettes, which recedes into a darkened background of forests and mountains.[11] But these shots suggest that Native American heritage, like the receding background, will eventually fade with the progress of civilization. The brief romantic attraction between Cora (the daughter of an English colonel) and Uncas ends tragically when a lecherous Magua pries her loose from the rocky precipice and she falls to her death.[12] Magua (played by a young Boris Karloff) also kills Uncas, and as the wounded Mohican lies near Cora, he grasps her hand. In line with Cooper's story, the movie offers a bleak view of how historical forces (the French and Indian War) determine human relationships.

The tragic story of *Ramona*, however, became the most popular of Indian/white romances. Based upon Helen Hunt Jackson's weepy novel of 1884, the story shows how an interracial marriage is doomed within a bigoted American society. Griffith had filmed the tale in 1910, but the movie's ten-minute length allowed little time for plot or character development. Set in the late nineteenth century, *Ramona* reveals the Indians' struggle to survive among apathetic agents and bigoted whites in southern California. The heroine is a mixture of Scottish and Cahuilla Indian ancestry, and her misfortunes include her Indian husband's death at the hands of greedy whites. Ultimately, she marries a wealthy Mexican but must flee America to find peace and happiness. Two silent feature versions of *Ramona* (1916 and 1928) followed, with the former boasting a length of three hours and "a plea for justice for the red man."[13] The 1928 version, starring Dolores Del Rio and Warner Baxter, was the creation of Chickasaw filmmaker Edwin Carewe (born Jay Fox), a director of more than sixty features during his career.[14]

CULTURAL MARGINALITY

Braveheart

The plight of the Indian caught between two cultures and at home in neither world often resulted in the Indian's rejection by

Chickasaw filmmaker Edwin Carewe (*center*) with production crew on the set of *My Son* (1925).
Courtesy of Bison Archives.

both societies. The theme of the marginal man was frequently a by-product of Indian/white romances and grappled with the same social dilemmas. Earlier silents had already explored the disturbing effects of marginality, often citing civilization's intolerance as the culprit (as in *The Curse of the Red Man*). In some cases, the resolution was death: white bigotry may prevent the Indian's successful assimilation, but disease would also take its toll. In *A Sacrifice to Civilization* (1911), death by disease became another reinforcement of Indian/white barriers.[15]

With feature films, the most popular of these marginal man themes reinforces Indian/white cultural separation by the Indian's return to a traditional lifestyle. *Braveheart* (1925), a silent feature directed by Alan Hale and produced by DeMille, illustrates the painful dilemma of cultural marginality: burdened by his own tribal conflicts and the persecution of white society, the film's protagonist is caught between two hostile worlds. *Braveheart* shows that the Indian as noble savage seldom adapted to white culture. The story is based upon the 1905 Broadway play, *Strongheart*, written by Cecil's older brother, William de Mille. (The producers had changed the play's original title to avoid confusion with Strongheart the Dog, a popular canine movie star at the time.) A New York theater reviewer noted that William de Mille had "braved public opinion" by placing "a full-blooded Indian on an equal footing with his white brother." "Never before," the reviewer wrote, "has the attempt to set aside the social differences between the white and the red man been so pronounced."[16] The movie version of the play, *Strongheart* (1914), sends a young Indian to Columbia University. But Strongheart is framed by his non-Indian classmates for cheating in a football game, a situation that prompts his retort, "You have taught me I am not one of you." The Indian returns to his village and becomes the tribe's chief.

Braveheart draws a clear boundary between Indians and whites. The differences are not so much based upon moral character or educational status but upon lifestyle. Like *Strongheart*, *Braveheart* also attempts to place Indian characters on an equal footing with whites. The studio even emphasized that the story takes place in 1925 "and deals with the modern Indian and not the savages of '49."[17] In the movie, Braveheart (Rod La Rocque) leaves his northwest tribal village and journeys to college. His education includes some blatant anti-Indian prejudice; when a football coach wrongly accuses Braveheart of cheating, the school expels the Indian. His

Rod La Rocque as the marginal man caught between two hostile worlds in *Braveheart*.

Courtesy of Bison Archives.

own tribe casts him out and women turn their backs on him, but Braveheart defends his tribe's claim to ancient fishing grounds. Eventually, a judge rules in the Indians' favor, and the college apologizes for the false accusation. But Braveheart's love for a white woman is thwarted by his skin color; ultimately, she must return to her own people and he becomes the tribe's chief.

Redskin (1929) restates the marginal man theme (the Indian protagonist is rejected by both races) by highlighting aspects of Native American life through its Technicolor photography. The movie skillfully uses black and white to represent the dull scenes of civilization but reserves two-color Technicolor (red and green) to depict Pueblo Indian life. *Redskin*'s color process was an accurate rendition of the desert shades of reds and greens, for without blue (a color not perfected in feature film until 1935) the elaborate jewelry instead radiates a deep cyan that is unique to the turquoise stones of the southwest.

The Half-Breed

The dilemma of the Indian mixed blood or half-breed also demanded a closer examination. Feature films often depicted the leading character as a marginal man, romancing a white woman while caught between two hostile worlds and struggling with conflicting loyalties. *The Half-Breed* (1916), directed by Allan Dwan and produced by D. W. Griffith, is a strikingly picturesque example. The movie was based on Bret Harte's short story, "In the Carquinez Woods" and was remade in 1918 as *Tongues of Flame*.[18] Harte's sharply etched characters and sentimental tone attracted many filmmakers, and Hollywood made several movie versions of his most popular stories, "The Luck of Roaring Camp" and "The Outcasts of Poker Flat."

The Half-Breed tells the story of Leaping Brook (Douglas Fairbanks), abandoned by his Indian mother when she commits suicide because her white lover deserts her. The young boy is raised by a kindly white man but later flees to the forest when told, "No harm will come to you if you always remember your place as an Indian." He meets Theresa (Alma Rubens), a Mexican woman hiding from authorities for stabbing her unfaithful lover.

In *The Half-Breed*, both Mexican and Indian become social outcasts, sandwiched between two unfriendly worlds. The camera reinforces Leaping Brooks' dilemma by framing him between rocky crevices and giant redwood trees. The hero hides Theresa in his tree trunk home, a symbolic reminder that she is also trapped. A forest fire erupts and Leaping Brook is framed among the engulfing flames: he chooses to save Theresa instead of the sheriff (his real father). The conclusion shows the couple alone in the woods, a natural refuge from society's persecution.

ROMANTIC IMAGES AND VILLAINS

The Indian Docudrama

As Hollywood continued to set Native Americans within a bigoted civilization, a few independent filmmakers looked closely at the Indians' fading culture and lifestyle. These "docudramas," as they are now called, combined dramatic stories with documentary-type footage as if to romanticize a lost tradition. Some studios even pledged to produce movies "historically correct in every detail."[19] Back in the earlier days of the short silent films, a few companies had also attempted to reconstruct Indian lifestyle. Longfellow's epic poem *Hiawatha* enjoyed an even longer remake in 1913 by France's American-based Gaumont Company. *Hiawatha* was shot in upstate New York with a cast of 150 American and Canadian Indians and supposedly re-created the Iroquois False Face Curing Society, in which masked demons are believed to possess spiritual powers.[20]

Later, other movies promised a glimpse of Native American lifestyle when rapid assimilation was eroding Indian culture. Times had changed: in 1898, Thomas Edison studios had released a string of short documentaries, each praising the success of Indian boarding schools. Twenty years later, the same studio mourned the loss of Indian culture. Edison's *The Vanishing Race* (1917) sets an ominous tone: the Blackfeet Indians were once the possessors of a great empire, but now, the film explains, only a few survive on reservations. In the tradition of America's nineteenth-century Romantic artists, *The Vanishing Race* revives the noble but doomed Indian among majestic canyons and lakes, while tiny figures of Indian riders recede into the shadowy background. *Before the White Man Came* (1920) employed the local Crow and Cheyenne as actors and was photographed on the Wyoming and Montana reservations. The movie's story of Indian mysticism and romance includes traditional dancing and sweat lodges. Tinted footage (like red for fire) highlights dramatic black-and-white scenes.

A few docudramas successfully combined a traditional story line with a glimpse of indigenous culture to the far north. Robert J. Flaherty re-created life among an Inuit (Eskimo) family for *Nanook of the North* (1922; distributed by Pathé). Originally an explorer who had spent long periods in the Arctic, Flaherty set out to combine realistic, stark footage of Inuit life with a loose story line and a central character. *Nanook* gave viewers a feeling of intimacy that set it apart from the bland, impersonal travelogues of that era. "[*Nanook*'s] people, as they appear to the spectator, are not acting but living," noted the *New York Times*. The *Los Angeles Times* admitted that one look at *Nanook* was not enough. "[It's] a picture that can live forever," the newspaper crooned.[21]

Flaherty's film about life in the Arctic became a kind of watershed. Hollywood studios soon capitalized on *Nanook*'s popularity, producing feature movies with an Inuit theme: *Justice of the Far North* (1926), *Frozen Justice* (1929), *Igloo* (1932), and *Eskimo* (1933). (See Chapter 3.) "Nanookmania," in fact, became a marketing craze that produced dozens of trademarks including Eskimo Pie ice cream.[22] "Never before in its history has Alaska been so much in the public eye," said the president of the Alaska Moving Pictures Corporation of *Nanook*'s influence.[23]

Eight years before Flaherty's *Nanook of the North*, photographer Edward S. Curtis had also merged elements of documentary and fiction into *In the Land of the Head-Hunters* (1914). The movie is actually a saga of love, jealousy, and war among the Kwakiutl Indians on Vancouver Island and features an all-Indian cast. The dramatic story holds together a series of scenes illustrating traditional Kwakiutl lifestyle. (Curtis had spent five seasons on location working with the Native Canadians.) Its painstaking recreation of the hunting, war, feasts, customs, and religion of the Kwakiutl notwithstanding, *In the Land of the Head-Hunters* enjoyed only a short burst of glory, then faded from sight for many years.[24]

The Indian as Obstacle

By the mid-1920s, the rise of cowboy stars William S. Hart, Tom Mix, Tim McCoy, and Harry Carey offered competition to Hollywood's Romantic and tragic Indian heroes. But the release of Paramount's *The Covered Wagon* in 1923 paved the way for epic Westerns and Indian villains. *Variety* announced that the movie was "the biggest thing the screen has done since Griffith made *The Birth of a Nation*" and predicted a wave of successors. The movie was based upon Emerson Hough's 1922 novel, which established the standard story of wagon trains rolling along the Oregon Trail. Hough glamorized cowboy life and offered stirring action combined with a romantic love interest. The film's budget of $850,000 was quickly recouped: after eleven months at New York's Criterion Theatre, *The Covered Wagon* broke all previous records.[25] Its huge cast included Indian extras: producer Jesse Lasky refused to "hire Filipinos, slap wigs on top of their heads, and call them Indians," so he assembled a tribe of Arapaho and paid them each $5/day (plus $1 extra for a horse and tipi). Future cowboy star Tim McCoy, formerly an Indian agent, served as the movie's technical advisor.[26]

The Covered Wagon's story was simple. Its plot of a wagon train bound for Oregon included bloody fights between hero and villain, a sweeping buffalo hunt, and a large-scale Indian attack. The Indians emerge as a menace to white civilization: Hungry settlers kill the buffalo, and the Indians retaliate. So begins the pioneers' struggle against the recalcitrant Natives who steal horses, burn wagons, and even plug an arrow into the shoulder of a bride-to-be. Clearly, whites and Indians could not live together peacefully.

But the ballyhoo that surrounded *The Covered Wagon* suggested that hostile warriors were of long ago. Famed impresario Sid Grauman, known for his lavish stage prologues that appeared before the feature film, imported the movie's Arapaho extras for its premiere at his prestigious Egyptian Theatre on Hollywood Boulevard. By now, real Indians were a novelty. The evening's prologue featured twenty-five peaceful Indian chiefs "just off the reservation, the real Americans with their squaws and papooses," according to the Egyptian's program.[27] The Arapaho had traveled from Wyoming's Wind River Reservation to Hollywood and pitched camp on the sage and scrub-covered hills of Cahuenga Pass. Behind the Indians' encampment of tipis, water wagons, frolicking children, and wandering dogs was a large sign of white electric light bulbs that spelled out "Grauman's *Covered Wagon* Indian Village." Locals were simply dazzled.[28]

The Covered Wagon's success temporarily revived the formula of evil Indians who blocked westward expansion. In Paramount's *North of 36* (1924; another Emerson Hough story), "each night brings the fear of an Indian attack," and in Sunset Productions' *General Custer at Little Big Horn* (1926), the U.S. Cavalry scouts for concealed "naked savages." In *America* (1924), Griffith's revolutionary

Technical advisor and translator Tim McCoy poses with Native American actors on the set of *The Covered Wagon.*

Courtesy of Bison Archives.

war saga, Mohawk Indians aid British enemies, attacking colonial forts and gorging themselves on food and alcohol. *With Sitting Bull at the "Spirit Lake Massacre"* (1927), featuring Yakima Indian Daniel Simmons in the title role, introduces the Indian leader who "more than any other, struck terror into the hearts of whites."[29]

The anti-Indian theme is most graphically displayed in *The Devil Horse* (1924) written and produced by Hal Roach (known for "Our Gang" and "Laurel and Hardy" comedy series). The Devil Horse is a wild, black stallion and the cherished pet of a young white boy. When the Indians kill the boy's family, the horse develops a life-long hatred toward the tribes. His fury "kindled by an Indian smell," the horse terrorizes Indians by hunting them down and trampling them to death. The crafty "Chief Prowling Wolf" earns his name by spying on whites; the movie plays up the anti-miscegenation theme by showing him trying to kidnap the reluctant white heroine as his bride. Clashes between Indians and whites were inevitable, *The Devil Horse* suggests, and mounting atrocities fuel hatred on both sides.

THE VANISHING AMERICAN

As images of hostile warriors and noble savages dominated silent feature Westerns, a few movies took a serious look at the Indians' struggle within contemporary society. *The Vanishing American* (1925) revealed the deterioration and mismanagement on America's Indian reservations and actually faulted white agents for the Indians' plight. The movie's underlying message is that white civilization—in the form of education, technology, government, and disease—will eventually eradicate Indian heritage. The film underscores the cultural loss within Indian society, and its hero's death and appeal to Christianity reinforces the belief that Indians must aspire to and accept white civilization.

The Vanishing American was released at a time when Indian supporters and social reformers were attacking inadequate government programs and futile missionary efforts. Artists, writers, and painters rallied to the Indians' cause, and one of them, Zane Grey, devoted several novels to Indians as victims of white greed and abuse. Grey wrote approximately seventy-eight books, many dealing with the historical West. Although critics faulted his novels for lacking sophistication and character depth, Hollywood recycled his stories into dozens of silent and sound Westerns, and television later aired the Western anthology series *Dick Powell's Zane Grey Theatre*. Grey was one of the few writers whose name actually appeared above the film's title as a selling point, and he successfully established his own Zane Grey Productions at Paramount studios.

The idea for *The Vanishing American* was conceived in 1922, when Grey invited Jesse Lasky (then vice president of production at Paramount) and Lucien Hubbard (editorial supervisor for Zane Grey Productions) to spend a few months in the scenic desert region of northern Arizona. Lasky suggested the area as a background for a motion picture, so Grey began writing *The Vanishing American*.[30] The story first appeared in 1922 as a serial in *Ladies Home Journal*, and Harper & Brothers planned for the book's publication to coincide with the film's release. Grey faulted whites for the destruction of Indian culture and failure to obtain workable solutions; he accused agents and missionaries of robbing Indians of their possessions and stripping them of their heritage. But combined pressure from both religious and social groups convinced Harper editors to alter the story before publication. Harper responded by suggesting changes in *The Vanishing American*, a move that caused Grey to consider withdrawing his manuscript. The recent debates in religious circles and disclosures about the Indian Bureau, Grey explained, made 1924 the ideal time to publish his book.[31]

The Vanishing American initially dramatizes the Indians' struggle for survival. The movie opens with a half-hour (Darwinian) prologue illustrating human evolutionary history, tracing the loss of Native American power and strength against invading Europeans. The story continues on the fictitious Nopah reservation (Nopah refers to the Navajo tribe) just prior to World War I, where corrupt agents cheat Indians out of their horses and relocate them to poor lands. One of them, Booker, even kicks elderly Indians aside when they block the door, and he sexually attacks Marion (the reservation's white schoolteacher). Nophaie (Richard Dix), the story's Indian hero, returns from the war in France and discovers his tribe dying of starvation.

In contrast to Grey's novel, no missionary appears in the film. Booker instead embodies all that is evil. The movie also removes the book's references to Nophaie's eastern education and stresses his cultural lag; Marion, for example, must teach him to read the Bible. Nophaie's lack of a white education eliminates deeply rooted cultural conflicts, as he does not truly encounter white culture until he enlists in the army.

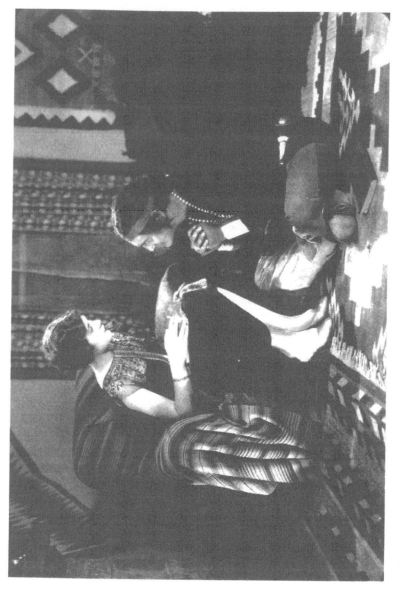

Marion (Lois Wilson) reads the Bible to Nophaie (Richard Dix) in *The Vanishing American.* Courtesy of Bison Archives.

The film's conclusion examines the Indians' fate against white civilization. Assimilation, disguised as Christianity, becomes the solution to Nopah survival. The Indians gather en masse to put an end to agent exploitation, and the whites respond with machine-gun fire. The Nopahs retaliate, and Nophaie is accidentally shot by a shell-shocked Indian soldier who unknowingly fires into the crowd. As Nophaie lies dying, Marion reads from the Bible that he who loses life will receive it, and he nods in agreement. The fighting ceases, and the hero's death symbolically saves the Nopahs from mass extermination.

The movie's conclusion was a significant departure from Grey's story. In *Ladies Home Journal*, Nophaie dies of influenza—as a white man: "His eyes were those of an Indian, but his face seemed that of a white man." Although many Nopahs who died of the plague turned black, the hero's death appears as a final gesture to relinquish his own Indian identity. His parting words to Marion reveal that whites and Indians should not intermarry: "White woman ... go back to your people." Nophaie thus becomes a martyr for white injustice yet dies an Indian as he admits his racial incompatibility with Marion. In another unpublished version, the romance between Nophaie and Marion actually leads to an interracial marriage.[32] Paramount instead dispensed with the magazine's conclusion of Nophaie dying from influenza and offered assimilation in the guise of Christianity as a solution to the Nopahs' fate. Hollywood, it seems, was a long way from accepting Native Americans as cultural equals.

Although Paramount planned another one of their massive publicity campaigns for *The Vanishing American*, the film was far from a box-office winner. The Indians' predicament was hardly entertainment for audiences hooked on action-packed cowboy epics. The movie peaked at $10,735 in October 1925 but fell to only $6,000 by December 12 (*Stella Dallas*, for example, brought in almost $15,000 the week ending November 28).[33] Viewers who expected another Western spectacle were disappointed: Following its long prologue, *The Vanishing American* lapsed into a dramatic tale of individual relations that was tedious. Not until 1934 would Hollywood again deal with modern-day reservations and corrupt white agents in *Massacre*.

By 1927, silent feature movies had brought the noble versus savage warrior full cycle and thus laid the foundation for a non-Western, American Indian genre. That same year talking pictures arrived (via Warner Bros. *The Jazz Singer*), and the limitations of early sound equipment drove Westerns into a hiatus. Thus, the savage Indian attacks briefly faded along with the dwindling cowboys.[34] Ironically, a whole new non-Western genre would soon emerge—one that would celebrate Native American autonomy and lifestyle and would dominate Hollywood's Indian-themed movies.

3

Indian Adventures and Interracial Romances

The decline of the epic Western was a blessing to the Hollywood Indian. The absence of cowboy heroes initially brought a wave of pro-Indian movies and for a while, Native Americans enjoyed the cinematic spotlight. The trend coincided with an era of adventure: The explorer couple Martin and Osa Johnson had recently returned from the African continent with thousands of feet of wildlife footage, and the American Museum of Natural History in New York City sponsored a number of photographing expeditions to Asia and the Arctic. From the South Pacific Islands of *White Shadows in the South Seas* (1928), *The Pagan* (1929), and *Tabu* (1931), to the African deserts and savannahs of *The Four Feathers* (1929) and *Trader Horn* (1930), to the rugged mountains of Persia in *Grass* (1925) and the Siamese jungle of *Chang* (1927), filmmakers attempted to capture the "exotic" lifestyle of indigenous people in remote parts of the world. American Indians were no exception.

THE COWBOY'S BRIEF RETURN

Hollywood's Indian adventures took off to a slow start, however. Cowboy-and-Indian pictures temporarily bounced back in 1929— this time with a talking soundtrack—when *Variety* announced a "big demand for Westerns in all sections." Indian characters reemerged in big-budget frontier epics, or A Westerns, produced by major studios and filmed on location to capture all the rugged terrain and scenic splendors that the wilderness could offer.[1] Film companies transported cast and crew to re-create American legends in *The Virginian* (1929), *In Old Arizona* (1929), and *Billy the Kid* (1930). The Academy Award–winning *Cimarron* (1930) told the story of the Oklahoma land rush and included noticeable compassion toward its Black American characters, a heroic portrayal of its female protagonist, and the successful marriage of the hero's white son to the Indian servant. Fox's *The Big Trail* (1930) featured the young actor, John Wayne, in his first leading role. Wayne escorts a wagon train across the American frontier and explains that the Indians are his friends. "Feed 'em right and treat 'em well, and we'll have no trouble," he tells the wary settlers. The Indian attack in *The Big Trail* is clearly provoked by white encroachment: Cheyenne and Shoshone warriors descend upon the wagon train because they are fed up with trespassers.

The Big Trail brought a big financial disappointment. Fox's $2 million Western was supposed to reap huge profits as well as introduce the seventy millimeter wide-screen format to movie theaters. The picture was critically well received, but the box-office returns barely covered the studio's hefty investment. Furthermore, *Variety* had observed that loyal Western fans were now lured by the rough-and-tough action of gangster films.[2] The epic cowboy-and-Indian picture thus retreated to a hiatus, wide screen was off the movie screen (at least for the next twenty-three years), and newcomer John Wayne was temporarily relegated to B Westerns.

The most simplistic plots of good versus bad Indian characters appeared in B Westerns. These independent, low-budget cowboy pictures were usually made for the second half of the theater's double bill, and their limited finances severely restricted their production resources. Costly scenes of Indian attacks or buffalo stampedes would be reused in subsequent pictures, and whites in Indian make-up would serve as inexpensive substitutes for Indian extras. Some Bs portrayed Indians as friendly: *The Fighting Cowboy* (1933), with Buffalo Bill Jr. (Jay Wilsey), includes an Indian woman who aids the hero against villains, and in *'Neath the Arizona Skies* (1934), John Wayne protects an Osage Indian girl (an heiress to oil lands) from a gang of greedy outlaws. Other B Westerns cast Indians as an evil menace: in *Mystery Ranch* (1932), the Apache Indian "Muto" (whose tongue was cut out) emerges from dark shadows to strangle his unsuspecting victims.

NATIVE AMERICAN ADVENTURES

The Silent Enemy

The decline of epic cowboy-and-Indian pictures ushered in a cycle of non-Western, American Indian adventures. Even though the movies' Indians still remained an exotic people, separate and apart from the white race, their key presence signaled a brief attempt at creating an American Indian genre within early talking pictures. These adventures also made use of actual locations and in some cases, Native American actors and dialogue in the authentic language. But the films' weak box-office returns demonstrated that the Hollywood Indian's screen image was inextricably tied to the Western. After a brief appearance, these Indian adventures—sandwiched between two cycles of cowboy epics—disappeared. The Indian as a primary subject, it seemed, was simply not exciting enough for American audiences.

Nevertheless, a few studios gambled with the topic, at least for the time being. *The Silent Enemy* (1930; produced by Screenart and distributed by Paramount Pictures), an account of Ojibwa life before European arrival, was the decade's first film to depict Indian survival within a rapidly changing world. The story was filmed in northern Ontario, and members of the Ojibwa tribe actually served as the film's actors. Although much of the movie is silent, it opens with an emotional talking sequence by Chauncy Yellow Robe (Sioux), who portrays Chief Chetoga in the picture.[3] Yellow Robe explains that *The Silent Enemy* shows how his people lived, hunted, celebrated, and worshipped before civilization trampled upon the forests and destroyed the Indians' food supply. The film's coproducer, Douglas Burden, had based the story upon the voluminous seventeenth-century Jesuit *Relations*, the French missionaries' painstaking research of northeastern Indian tribal culture, and had borrowed clothing and objects from the American Museum of Natural History.

Burden's choice of Buffalo Child Long Lance to play the story's robust hunter raised a sticky issue. Long Lance claimed genuine Canadian Blackfoot ancestry, complete with a childhood in the Montana and Alberta plains, hunting buffalo and fighting Indian wars. In 1928, he published *Long Lance: The Autobiography of a Blackfoot Indian Chief*. But the Blackfoot chief from Canada was really the son of mixed white/Black/Indian parents from Winston-Salem, North Carolina. Yellow Robe spotted many contradictions in

Long Lance's background and contacted the Bureau of Indian Affairs in Washington. Long Lance was from North Carolina, he discovered, and informed the movie's legal counsel that they had an imposter on their hands. The studio feared charges of false publicity and instantly sent an envoy to Winston-Salem to check out Long Lance's murky past. The report came back: Long Lance was certainly not from the Western plains, but his parents claimed mixed Indian and white heritage. The studio was satisfied and subsequently promoted Long Lance as an "authentic Indian" in all the movie's publicity.[4]

Long Lance's authenticity—or lack of it—did little to bolster *The Silent Enemy*'s short life at the box office. A cinematographer from the American Museum of Natural History had forewarned coproducer Burden early in production that the American Indian had become "too commonplace" to contemporary audiences. The public wanted exotic people from far away places, he explained, and not Romantic images of America's past. "It is the strange and unknown that thrill and hold the blasé public today," he added.[5] *Variety* praised the movie's spectacular wildlife footage (especially the caribou stampede), but agreed that the movie "has not the commercial draw exhibitors look for."[6]

Eskimo

The fate of Metro-Goldwyn-Mayer's *Eskimo* (1933) was not much better. The film's adventurous scenes were certainly impressive, but few Americans would be stirred by Inuit survival in the far north.[7] Furthermore, the Inuit spoke in their own language, which although novel for its time (and decades before Canada's release of *The Fast Runner*), demanded that audiences sit through nearly two hours of English intertitles. Based upon a series of books by the German explorer, Peter Freuchen, *Eskimo* told the story of civilization's corrupt influence upon an isolated Alaska Native community. The picture's director was W. S. Van Dyke, whose past successes with *The Pagan*, *White Shadows in the South Seas*, and *Tarzan the Ape Man* (the 1932 talkie version starring Johnny Weissmuller) promised yet another adventurous epic of exotic people from a far away place. For *Eskimo*, Van Dyke would drive home the theme of white contamination upon Native lifestyle, as he had done in *White Shadows in the South Seas*.[8]

The film's producer, Hunt Stromberg, was a stickler for authenticity. "See that we don't overlook any opportunity nor miss any details," he would write director Van Dyke on location in the chilly northern Alaska Territory. Stromberg's insistence on authenticity extended to the film's actors and dialogue as well. Most of the minor and supporting roles were filled by Alaska Natives, but the casting for the male lead (Mala) worried Stromberg "to death," as he put it. "The audience must love him from the very start of the picture," explained Stromberg.[9] The studio tested several Inuit actors for the part and eventually hired one of them. But the demands of movie making were too much for the inexperienced actor, and he simply walked off the picture.[10]

The young unknown actor Ray Theodore Wise was an ideal second choice. Born in the Alaska Territory, Wise's Jewish father had emigrated from Russia to San Francisco and his Inuit mother came from Alaska. Wise had previously appeared in Universal's *Igloo* (1932) as the tribe's robust young hunter (he was also an assistant cameraman in Hollywood); his tall, chiseled physique, dark hair and complexion, and a natural athletic ability to perform his own stunts were a perfect combination for *Eskimo*'s leading Inuit man. "He looks and acts very real—you honestly believe he's a native Eskimo," observed Stromberg.[11]

The film's incorporation of Inuit dialogue caused some concerns. Both Stromberg and Van Dyke initially wanted the Alaska Natives speaking their own language, but executives at Metro-Goldywn-Mayer (MGM) believed that English intertitles were simply too old-fashioned and disconcerting. "An audience reading titles might squirm in their seats," Stromberg concurred, but later realized that replacing scenes already shot in Inuit dialogue with an English soundtrack would be too costly and time consuming.[12] The final decision: keep the Inuit dialogue and add English intertitles.

Eskimo's fatalistic tone notwithstanding, the film delivered an upbeat conclusion. MGM departed from the foreboding theme of *White Shadows in the South Seas* (in which civilization eventually eradicates Native Polynesian lifestyle) and instead suggested that Inuit people would perhaps fare a bit better. Mala avenges the rape of his wife by harpooning the European trader but is later captured by the Royal Canadian Mounted Police (one of whom is played by director Van Dyke). He escapes, and was initially supposed to meet his death beneath the cold Arctic waters. MGM instead chose a happier ending, with Mala and his second wife drifting safely across the narrow Arctic inlet.[13]

The trend toward romanticizing America's northern neighbors apparently caught on. A year later, RKO Radio Pictures (RKO) would

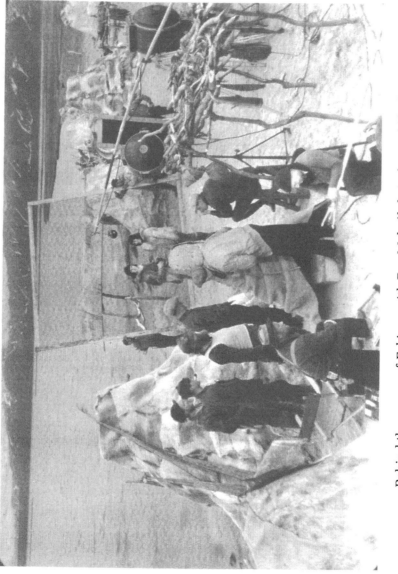

Behind the scenes of *Eskimo*, with Ray Mala (*left, in front of filter*).
Courtesy of Bison Archives.

also abandon its tragic conclusion in *Man of Two Worlds* (1934). Initially, the story of an Inuit man (Francis Lederer) whose contact with civilization brings him disillusionment and despair was supposed to end with his suicidal death in the frigid Greenland snow. But the studio devised a new ending in which the hero's people find him and bring him home to his wife and son. "Their chief, their mighty hunter, has come back to them," the studio outlined in its script revisions.[14]

As for *Eskimo*, reviewers were apparently more impressed than moviegoers. "It's a remarkable film," observed the *New York Times*, and compared its scenes of Alaska Native customs and lifestyle to Flaherty's *Nanook of the North* (Flaherty had collaborated with Van Dyke on *White Shadows in the South Seas*).[15] The movie's editor, Conrad Nervig, even picked up an Academy Award. But *Variety* kept a wary eye on the box office and predicted that a story about life in the Arctic was as icy as the film's title. (Indeed, after a sluggish opening in New York City, MGM quickly decided to change the title to the more sexy *Eskimo Wife-Traders*.[16]) *Eskimo*'s eventual loss of $236,000 at the box office was an embarrassment compared to the hefty profits from previous MGM adventures.

Laughing Boy

A year later, MGM's *Laughing Boy* (1934) was another well-intentioned Indian film that brought a box-office disaster. The film

Table 3.1 Cost and Profit (Loss) of MGM Adventure Films, 1928–1934

Film Title[1]	Year Released	Production Cost $	Profit (Loss) $
White Shadows in the South Seas	1928	365,000	450,000
The Pagan	1929	293,000	562,000
Trader Horn	1930	1,322,000	937,000
The Squaw Man	1931	731,000	(340,000)
Tarzan the Ape Man	1932	660,000	919,000
Eskimo	1933	935,000	(236,000)
Laughing Boy	1934	518,000	(383,000)

[1]Indian-themed films are in boldface.
Source: The E. J. Mannix Ledger, "Loew's Inc. MGM Studios Operating Results by Pictures," Margaret Herrick Library, Academy of Motion Picture Arts and Sciences.

was based upon Oliver La Farge's Pulitzer Prize–winning novel of the same title, and its theme of civilization's corruption of Indian culture was suitable for liberals and reformers who had been lamenting the Indian's plight. But MGM ran up against government agents, Christian missionaries, schoolteachers, and other "friends of the Indians" who were disturbed with *Laughing Boy*'s unmistakable message: "The inescapable failure of any attempts to make Indians over into whites."[17]

The story of Laughing Boy, a Navajo warrior, and his love for Slim Girl, a woman from the same clan, grappled with the cultural dilemma between white and Indian worlds. Laughing Boy is raised a traditional Navajo with little exposure to white civilization: he is a sharp contrast to the educated Slim Girl, whose sexual favors for a greedy white man bring material comforts to her own marriage. In the film, Laughing Boy discovers his Navajo wife in the arms of her white lover, and he accidentally shoots and kills her with an arrow meant for the other man. The saddened Indian hero returns to his tribe, vowing to never again relinquish his traditional ways.

Universal Pictures initially attempted to bring La Farge's tragic story to the screen, with John Huston as screenwriter and William Wyler as director. La Farge thoroughly combed Huston's script and reminded the writer that southwestern tourists were well acquainted with Navajo ceremonials. "So you'd better get it right," La Farge warned.[18] But anxious letters from Indian agencies, civic groups, and religious educators soon plagued the studio. B. D. Weeks, president of Bacone (Baptist) College in Oklahoma, lambasted the movie industry for complete ignorance on the subject. "[These films about white corruption of Indian people] reflect badly upon the red man, and cheapen him in the eyes of the world," he thundered. Weeks subsequently demanded that Will Hays (head of the Hays Office, the industry's self-regulatory censorship agency) intercede on behalf of the Indians. But one Hays official pointed out that these "defenders" of Indian welfare were "more interested in keeping such facts off the screen than they are in protecting the poor Indian."[19] Universal subsequently dropped the project.

Laughing Boy was to endure a controversial revival at MGM. Writer John Lee Mahin, who had recently completed the script for *Eskimo*, apparently convinced MGM to buy the rights to La Farge's novel.[20] Producer Hunt Stromberg decided to replay "the feeling of contamination imposed by the white man," and again demanded

Laughing Boy (Ramon Novarro) shares an intimate moment with Slim Girl (Lupe Velez) in *Laughing Boy*.

Courtesy of Bison Archives.

fidelity to detail. This time, however, the movie's Indians must speak English.[21] Furthermore, the producers believed that the casting of matinee idol Ramon Novarro (a Mexican) as Laughing Boy opposite the fiery Lupe Velez (also of Mexican descent) as Slim Girl might attract a larger audience.

The film's illicit Indian/white love affair was another matter. The Production Code (the Hays Office criteria of "decency" for motion pictures) stipulated that miscegenation between black and white races was strictly forbidden, but was silent on the Indian/white issue.[22] Nevertheless, the steamy adulterous relationship between the married Slim Girl and her white lover infuriated the Production Code's staunch Catholic enforcer, Joseph Breen. No sooner than Breen had read the script, he declared it "a sordid, vile and dirty story that is definitely not suited for screen entertainment."[23] The New York State Board of Censors banned the film, but a month later approved it with two pages of deletions.[24] But MGM defended its project: the story's indictment of white corruption upon Indian culture was in accord with public opinion, the studio claimed, and quickly submitted the script to the Department of the Interior for its approval.[25]

Despite its star performers and prize-winning story, *Laughing Boy* was another box-office flop. *Variety* labeled the film as "below average entertainment" and sneered that Ramon Novarro's contrived Indian accent sounded like Maurice Chevalier speaking bad French.[26] MGM had invested $518,000 in the picture, but its loss of $383,000 was even worse than *Eskimo*'s. Furthermore, the studio's release of Cecil B. DeMille's third version of *The Squaw Man* in 1931 also suffered a financial loss.

Massacre

At Warner Bros., Indian-themed pictures would experience a similar fate. This time, however, the studio would look at the Native American's plight on modern-day reservations. Warner Bros.' release of *Massacre* in 1934 foreshadowed the country's pending "Indian New Deal" legislation by targeting widespread corruption and mismanagement upon Indian reservations. As a part of Warner's social consciousness series (*I Am a Fugitive from a Chain Gang*, 1932, *Wild Boys of the Road*, 1933, and *Bordertown*, 1935), *Massacre* presented a plea for reform within a troubled American society. But the film's message that the federal government would eventually resolve the Indians' problems was a low priority for Depression America.

Massacre's release came just prior to the Indian Reorganization Act (IRA) of 1934, a sweeping attempt to reverse decades of government neglect and grabbing of Indian lands. The IRA's policy of economic growth, self-determination, cultural plurality, and a revival of tribalism among Native American societies were designed to give Indians control over their own livelihoods. *Massacre* openly indicted federal agents and their exploitation of America's Indians but simultaneously promoted the government's long-range goals in Indian affairs. Columbia studios had already advocated the same theme in *The End of the Trail* (1932), a story that criticizes the U.S. Army for its mismanagement of Indian affairs. The leading character (played by Tim McCoy) is an Army officer, but he defends the Indians' rights and refers to them as his "red brothers." Determined to fight military corruption and incompetence, McCoy pleads for justice from the Great White Father in Washington, a plan that the Army adamantly opposes. But the government resolves all conflicts: McCoy averts further warfare and becomes the first Indian agent to serve on the Fort's new reservation.

In *Massacre*, a newly enlightened government descends upon the mistreated Indians and promises to right past wrongs. The film's leading character, Joe Thunderhorse (Richard Barthelmess), is a Sioux Indian who routinely performs at fairs and rodeos and enjoys all the expensive commodities of white society. But when Thunderhorse visits his sick father on the reservation, he discovers rampant corruption and exploitation of his own people. One of the story's white villains rapes Thunderhorse's own sister, and he retaliates by hitching a rope to his car and dragging the culprit along the road. The police arrest the Indian for attempted murder, and he is sentenced to ninety days of hard labor.

Massacre's remaining story endorses federal Indian policies. Thunderhorse escapes prison, and travels to Washington to visit the commissioner of Indian Affairs. (Along the way, he alights on a freight car that bears the familiar National Recovery Administration's Blue Eagle logo representing Warner Bros. support for Roosevelt's New Deal programs.) Thunderhorse's accusations against the widespread corruption prompt an immediate Senate investigation, but angry Indians declare the justice system a sham and burn the courthouse. Thunderhorse instead believes in the government's ability to rectify social wrongs: the court finds

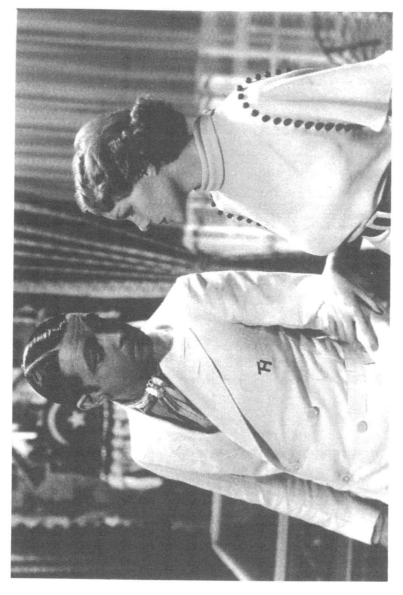

Joe Thunderhorse (Richard Barthelmess) listens as Claire Dodd expresses her concerns in *Massacre*. Courtesy of Bison Archives.

in his favor, and Washington invites him to serve as Indian commissioner.

Realizing its timeliness, Warner seized upon *Massacre*'s urgent plea for Indian reform. "The Indians are already beginning to kick over," associate producer Robert Presnell glibly announced early in production, "and the government in Washington will undoubtedly do something about it in the very near future."[27] *Massacre*'s Indians were to be on the brink of pathos and despair: crooked agents, shyster lawyers, and drug-addicted physicians would haunt the reservations. But key Roosevelt aides were not pleased: a film exposing the corruption and squalor upon America's reservations implied that Washington was ignoring the Indians' plight. Weeks later, executive producer Hal B. Wallis informed Presnell of the bad news: the Interior Department was worried because of the pending "deal" [IRA] with American Indians. Warner Bros.' version of *Massacre*, it seemed, would only undermine the government's New Deal efforts. Wallis felt the pressure and groped for a more politically safe theme. "Don't you think this would be just as good a story if we change the Indians to Jews and laid it in the Ghetto instead of an Indian reservation?" he asked, and suggested that actor Joe E. Brown replace Barthelmess in the title role.[28]

As supporters of FDR, the Warners decided that the government's image clearly could not be tarnished for the Indian's sake. The real hero of *Massacre*, then, would have to be the New Deal and not the American Indian. The studio's newfound loyalty toward the Democratic Party (Jack Warner had recently switched his political allegiance toward Franklin Roosevelt) prompted the appearance of the administration's Blue Eagle logo in *The Gold Diggers* of 1933 and *Wild Boys of the Road* (also 1933). *Massacre* would be no exception. "Substitute the word 'agent' for 'government' to keep the latter in the clear," the Hays Office advised the Warners. Otherwise, *Massacre* "may be interpreted as reflecting unfavorably upon the government's conduct of Indian affairs."[29]

Massacre's plea for the desperately exploited Indian passed largely unnoticed. While New York reviewers generally praised the film for its sincerity, *Variety* complained that "the story is very complicated and rambles off on too many tacks."[30] The film played to a tepid reception and brought a profit of only $129,000, a far cry from the $1.6 million of Warner Bros.' *I Am a Fugitive from a Chain Gang*.[31] Thus, *Massacre*, along with Hollywood's cycle of other Indian adventures, would soon recede into the dusty vaults of the motion picture archivists.

AMBIVALENT ROMANCES

The box-office failures of the Indian adventures reinforced the country's tradition that its Native American images were deeply rooted in the Western. Audiences may have yearned for the exotic or the unknown, but Americans seemed unable to extract Indians from the dime novel or Romantic settings of the Old West. A noticeable exception were the films of Will Rogers, whose lead roles as a non-Indian in several John Ford movies (*Doctor Bull*, 1933, *Judge Priest*, 1934, and *Steamboat 'Round the Bend*, 1935) helped to establish him as the "successful" Indian actor in contemporary society. But for the most part, Hollywood Indians somehow remained different from mainstream white America. Whether the movies portrayed Indians as good or evil, comical or straight, they played up perceived differences between Indian and white cultures as if to expose the audiences' own hidden prejudices.

RKO's romantic comedy, *Annie Oakley* (1935), points out that Indians are indeed aliens—although benevolent ones—among white civilization. The story about the legendary sharpshooter and her travels with Buffalo Bill's Wild West Show features Sitting Bull (Chief Thunderbird, a Cheyenne Indian) whose skills as a medicine man ultimately unite Oakley with her male rival.[32] Sitting Bull's introduction to modern civilization (he abandons his soft bed for the hard floor and shoots out the room's lights) reveals that Indian and non-Indian attitudes are essentially incompatible within American society.

Meanwhile, a few studios continued to experiment with interracial romances between Indians and whites. The subject was often left to producers' ambiguous interpretations, however, and a successful Indian/white union rarely delved beyond its fairy-tale ending. Paramount's *Behold My Wife!* (1935) pairs a wealthy white man with an Indian woman, an arrangement designed to spite his snobbish parents. The story, based upon Sir Gilbert Parker's novel, *The Translation of a Savage*, had been filmed previously in 1913 (Edison Studios) and 1920 (Paramount), but Paramount's sound version made substantial narrative changes. The studio even tried to change the title to the more vivid "Red Woman," but the Hays Office advised against it.[33] The 1935 remake sets the story in contemporary New York City, and the man travels to a western reservation where he meets an educated Apache woman. The movie's interracial marriage is a satire of upper-class American values. The white man marries the Apache woman as a vendetta against his family for driving his former (Caucasian) fiancée to suicide; ultimately, and perhaps unrealistically, the Apache woman and white man happily unite as if all cultural and class differences magically disappear.

Typically, however, Indians and whites each settled within their own racial boundaries. Fox's *Call Her Savage* (1932) shows how Indian heritage can be a powerful social detriment. The film casts the coquettish Clara Bow in the title role of Naza, a half-Indian and half-white woman. The movie was Bow's first since she experienced a nervous breakdown and took a temporary retirement from the screen. As America's "flapper girl" of the 1920s, the wide-eyed Bow possessed the vitality and energy for her role as a tomboyish and somewhat unruly mixed-blooded woman. *Call Her Savage* was only a moderate success at the box office and was Bow's penultimate film before her retirement from Hollywood.[34]

The story raised a red flag for the Hays Office. *Call Her Savage* was based upon the book of the same title by Tiffany Thayer, which contained elements of promiscuity, sadism, and lesbianism. Hays apparently was not happy with the property, and his office advised Fox studios to clean it up.[35] Fox thus removed much of the movie's theme and offensive sexual material, including a scene in which Naza bathes in the nude then makes love to an Indian boy. Gone also were scenes of Naza's attempted rape as well as her street solicitation to strange men.[36]

Still, the studio struggled with how to explain Naza's rather boisterous behavior. The movie's underlying message, they reasoned, would be that Naza is "driven by forces within herself [that] she does not fully understand." But the audience would know from the beginning that these forces "are attributable to the mixed blood in her veins." Naza's outburst and tomboyishness were more than just "savagery in the sense that she is a hellion"; they amount to "the call of blood to blood."[37] Thus, Naza's Indian ancestry would dictate her behavior and somehow explain that she is different from mainstream white America.

In *Call Her Savage*, Naza is born into a wealthy white family, but she is unaware that her mother's affair with an Indian lover had produced her own racially mixed heritage. The film points to Naza's Indianness as the cause for her flamboyant behavior: She frolics on the floor with her Great Danes, playfully lashes her half-breed suitor with a riding whip, instigates fistfights with her fiancé's former lover, and bashes a guitar over the head of a Mexican singer. Indeed,

Naza's unpredictable behavior puzzles even her: "Why can't I be like other girls?" she pouts.

But Naza is a victim of tragic circumstances, a painful reminder that she will never be fully accepted into American society. Her white stepfather disowns her because he cannot "tame" her, and her first marriage to an alcoholic (white) man ends in disaster. She even loses her only child in a fire. A later romance with a wealthy white man is shattered when his conventional father objects to the woman's unruly behavior. Ultimately, Naza discovers her true heritage: "It makes clear many things I never understood before," she confesses. Her Indian identity revealed, she retreats to the wilderness with her half-breed suitor.

THE INDIAN ACTORS ASSOCIATION

As studios pondered the tepid box-office returns of their Native American adventures and interracial romances, the nation's faltering economy gave Indian actors worries of their own. Of particular concern was the casting of non-Indians in Native American roles, although the issue was hardly clear cut. Many non-Indians, with a little dark make-up and long hair, could easily pass as Indians, and some even convinced producers that they were actually of Native American descent. To make matters worse, the country's economic depression and the Westerns' hiatus left many "real" Indian actors unemployed. When a few Westerns did appear, these frustrated Indian actors found themselves competing against "Syrians, Swedes, Arabs, and Latins who were manufactured by sun-oil and braided wigs."[38] Fed up with the lack of work and rival Indian wannabes, the constituency eventually banded together to form the Indian Actors Association (an affiliate of the Screen Actors Guild), which demanded that only real Indians play Indians.

The leader of this outspoken group was Luther Standing Bear, a member of the Lakota [Sioux] tribe and one of America's celebrated Indian authors.[39] (Following Standing Bear's death in 1939, Many Treaties, or Bill Hazlett, chaired the Indian Actors Association.) This Hollywood-based, nonprofit organization began around 1936 and established a closed shop agreement for its Indian-member actors. The Association decried "the practice among some studios of engaging pseudo-Indians for leading roles that not only misrepresent the action of the Indian but fake his dialect." Particularly annoying was that the movies' Indians would "talk and grunt like morons,"

In *Call Her Savage*, Naza (Clara Bow), the tomboy, frolics in the wilderness. Courtesy of Bison Archives.

as one member put it. The Association suggested that studios instead use Indian technical experts, and they sponsored courses in Indian sign language and pictography. A crucial issue was equal pay: while non-Indian extras received $11/day Indians earned only $5.50. The Association's vocal protests eventually won their members identical salaries.[40]

But studios also had their gripes, one of which was the inability to discern real Indians from the phony ones. "All is not Indian that glitters," observed the *New York Times* and voiced producers' headaches in rounding up enough Indian extras in Hollywood. Many non-Indians passed themselves off as authentic, while some Native Americans were actually "too modernized" with their tattooed chests and closely cropped haircuts.[41] Studios easily solved these problems by employing Native Americans from reservations, a practice that infuriated the former Indian Olympic athlete, Jim Thorpe.

Since the early thirties, Thorpe had acted as Indian spokesperson against the industry's practice of hiring non-Indians as Indian extras. With the assistance of the Department of Labor, Thorpe scanned Hollywood in search of illegal Mexicans and Italians who posed as Indians in order to find employment. His discovery that only 40 percent of the Indian extras were "honest" prompted his demand that casting offices hire only from his own group of 250 "real" Indians and that all phonies appear before the bar of justice.[42] (A U.S. attorney, however, pointed out that studio-hiring practices of using non-Indians for Indian roles were exempt from federal law.[43])

Thorpe's anger exploded when producer/director DeMille instead chose to hire Indians from the reservation for *The Plainsman*. Times were lean for Hollywood Indians: the sympathetic cycle of the early 1930s had faded into movie history, and the epic or A Western had still not recovered from its financial scars of *The Big Trail*. At Warner Bros., executive Jack Warner echoed the opinions of other studio moguls when he complained that Western pictures with Indians had become too old fashioned and hokey.[44] Thorpe, who had provided his Indians for *Annie Oakley*, had reason to worry if his troupe would soon see another paycheck. "There are only a few pictures each year that we can work in," he lamented, "and when they use white men it just means we can't make a living."[45]

But DeMille had plans of his own. For *The Plainsman*, he instead chose to employ the Cheyenne Indians residing near Lame Deer in Montana, and spent $200,000 on location sequences to obtain their services. Indignant, Thorpe fired a letter of protest to President Roosevelt, arguing that only "bona-fide" Indians should play Indians on the screen. (Thorpe himself had offered Mexicans and Hawaiians of his own extras that he could make up as Indians.) Why, wondered the former Indian athlete, did DeMille not hire from his own cadre of talented performers, many of who could speak Indian languages and ride bareback? "I wanted Indians that looked like real Indians, not the Hollywood variety," DeMille snapped.[46] But the producer's casting of two non-Indians (Victor Varconi and Paul Harvey) to play Indian chiefs added only more fuel to Thorpe's fire.

What Thorpe did not realize was that *The Plainsman* would sweep American movie theaters and revive the traditional cowboy-and-Indian epic. The days of Indian adventures and interracial romances were over. By the mid-1930s, big-budget cowboy-and-Indian Westerns were back on the American screen. But for a while, these stories of the country's conquest, taming, and expansion forced Native Americans into a subsidiary role: a separate race and culture hostile to the advance of white civilization. Not until World War II would America begin to reexamine its racial relations and would the Indian's role in society—and in Hollywood—reemerge in a different light.

4

War and Its Indian Allies*

World War II laid the foundation for a reevaluation of the American
Indian's screen image. Even before "tolerance," "brotherhood," and
"unity" became catchwords within a society engaged in another
world conflict, the movie industry had responded to the growing
fascism in Europe with more ambiguity in its Indian portrayals. Like
Black Americans who would find a place in the racially integrated
units of Hollywood's war films (years before actual military desegre-
gation), movie Indians would form a political alliance with their
white counterparts.[1] Images of menacing warriors who blocked
westward expansion gradually began to fade into one in which
Indians stood as allies—rather than as enemies—alongside America's
frontier heroes.

But during the mid-1930s, the nineteenth-century belief in a
Manifest Destiny would dominate Hollywood Westerns. Studios
emphasized the concept of a unified nation while demonstrating the
government's potency to eliminate evil threats. The cowboy represented law and order: he was the benevolent hero who drove Indians
from the plains and made the frontier safe for families. Cecil B.
DeMille's *The Plainsman* (1937) successfully revived the cowboy-
and-Indian formula, which for several years became the staple for
Hollywood Westerns.

*Excerpts from Angela Aleiss, "Prelude to World War II: Racial Unity and the
Hollywood Indian," *Journal of American Culture* 18 (Summer 1995): 25–34, were reprinted with the permission of Blackwell Publishing Ltd.

THE EPIC WESTERN RETURNS

The Plainsman, released by Paramount studios in January of 1937, revolves around the theme of America's Manifest Destiny and resurrected the epic Western with its hostile Indians. The film's story, as the titles inform, is an attempt to "do justice" to the plainsmen: the characters of Buffalo Bill Cody (James Ellison) and Wild Bill Hickok (Gary Cooper) appear as American legends that fight to turn a savage frontier into a civilized nation. Paramount's advertising campaign portrayed Cody and Hickok as history's "glamorous personalities," slashing an empire from savage hands and fighting with blood and fire to make America great.[2]

DeMille's film immortalizes the plainsmen's heroic deeds and casts American Indians as unwelcome guests. *The Plainsman* presents Indians as an obstruction to Lincoln's plans of expanding America's boundaries: their very presence poses a threat to white civilization. The image of aggressive warriors had to be established early, prior to the capture of Bill Hickok and Calamity Jane. Production personnel advised DeMille that the audience must initially recognize the Indians as "really a menace—burning settlements and massacring whites."[3] (The film includes early scenes of an Indian attack, followed later by the torture of Hickok.) DeMille insisted that the film's Indians physically represent aggressive, hostile warriors. Apparently, the gentile features of actor Bruce Cabot were all wrong for Painted Horse (a Cheyenne warrior); the crew had to search for another "heavier" type, perhaps a Mexican or an Italian "with a strong, brutal face."[4] The racial boundaries were clear: white heroism against a red menace, the latter bordering on barbarism and savagery.

The popular theme of Western expansion against recalcitrant Indians dominated John Ford's *Stagecoach* (1939): the film flatly—and unambiguously—declared that white civilization had no room for American Indians. The opening titles warn of the Indians' "savage struggle" to oust innocent settlers, and the final attack upon the stage suggests that America will be safe only when its hostile Natives vanish forever. King Vidor's *Texas Rangers* (1936), for example, shows that while "savages" rule the plains Texas is hardly a safe place. Only when the Rangers "put them on the reservation for good" can Texas look forward to real progress. *The Last of the Mohicans*, the 1936 remake of the classic James Fenimore Cooper tale, is a far cry from Tourneur's silent version. Gone are the Romantic, idealized

Indian images of 1920; instead, bloodthirsty, scalp-hungry Hurons literally scream into the camera and massacre the inhabitants at Fort William Henry. The villainous Magua is "as evil a Huron as ever" and his actions "are even more ghastly than those of the text itself," declared the *New York Times*.[5]

Audiences flocked to see DeMille's epic Western that glorified American conquest and wiped out its Indian obstacles. The Box Office Blue Ribbon Award named *The Plainsman* the "Best Picture of the Month for the Whole Family," and *Variety* reported that the film was an "outstanding smash" during its first week at New York's Paramount Theater.[6] Two years later, *Stagecoach* boasted earnings of $85,000 in its first week at New York's Radio City Music Hall, $26,000 more than DeMille's *The Plainsman*.[7] Contemporary stories of Native American life disappeared as Americans apparently preferred epic scenes of heroic cowboys and hostile Indian attacks.

AMBIGUOUS HEROES AND INDIANS

In 1939, the United States was immersed in a rapidly changing world, and Hollywood began to rethink its evil Indian images. Although many Americans believed that their country could retain the policy of nonintervention and isolation that had characterized society since the First World War, government officials responded by concentrating upon foreign affairs rather than domestic issues. By 1940, the Office of Indian Affairs focused its attention upon war preparedness and gradually directed its goals toward global efforts. Commissioner John Collier's ideal of a pluralistic nation began to fade as growing international strife forced him to change perspective. The American Indians' ability to contribute to national defense became more important than who they were, and the government lost no opportunity in targeting them as a resource. As the desire for a strong defense in the face of an encroaching world war seeped into Bureau policies, it brought about a move toward racial unity—an assimilation of Indian culture into white society.

The trend to a postwar assimilation of Indians and whites appeared gradually in Hollywood Westerns. The industry continued to portray American Indians as obstacles to Western settlement during the late 1930s, but the increasing conflict in Europe began to arouse filmmakers' sympathies and consequently to reshape Indian images as early as 1939. Previous Westerns could boast of conquest, but a national campaign to purge the land of its Indian inhabitants smacked of fascist genocide. Furthermore, selective service was enforced by 1940, and scenes of the U.S. Cavalry killing Indians en masse could easily equate American militarism with Gestapo leadership. At the very least, Manifest Destiny was beginning to paint a racially intolerant picture of America's frontier heroes.

Beginning in 1936, the Hollywood Anti-Nazi League had openly condemned German fascism and the Japanese invasion of China; so vocal was their opposition that isolationist groups criticized the industry's prointerventionist (and leftist) politics. Many studio executives proclaimed national unity a powerful weapon against fascism, a political ideal that would help to reshape the Indians' image at least two years before America's entry into the war.

Geronimo

Paramount glorified America's ability to rid the West of its marauding Natives in *Geronimo* (1939). Director Paul Sloane introduces *Geronimo* as "the story of a great enemy," then informs viewers that the Indian leader remains unconquered. The movie's portrayal of "that most feared Apache that ever ravaged the West" was a fitting parallel to the fascist enemy in Europe: Geronimo emerges as cunning and deceitful, and Paramount's publicity describes him as "the red terror of the American screen."[8] Joseph Breen was apparently concerned about the movie's treatment of its Indians, for he advised Paramount to submit it to the commissioner of Indian Affairs for an opinion. Paramount shrugged off the suggestion: much of *Geronimo*'s action was stock footage from *The Plainsman, Texas Rangers*, and *The Texans*, which had recently been shown on the screen.[9]

But while *Geronimo* bolstered military conquest and the country's strength in national defense, it simultaneously promoted diplomacy in dealing with America's enemies. As agents for a national state, the army displays considerable restraint in the "humane" capture of Geronimo, thus exemplifying that democracy—and not fascism—dictates a prisoner's treatment during war. The Apache surround the cavalry, and the general tells his men to "die like soldiers"; Geronimo, meanwhile, disguises himself as an army officer (he recently killed the captain) and sneaks into the encampment. Like a Nazi spy, he clandestinely infiltrates enemy territory and attempts to murder its leader. But troop reinforcements arrive, and as Geronimo tries to stab the general, his son seizes the Indian leader with a dignified, "Your prisoner, sir."

Geronimo's final scene required cooperation with the U.S. Army. Paramount believed that the movie should "cash in on the current national interest in patriotic American subjects" and hoped to promote "a flag-waving ending" by having the general present a posthumous medal.[10] The army's assistance was contingent upon an agreement to give the War Department final approval of *Geronimo*'s scenes, dialogue, and titles before Paramount released it to the public. The agreement also spelled out that the War Department reserved the right "to eliminate the whole film or any part thereof deemed objectionable."[11] The fact that Geronimo actually surrendered apparently seemed unattractive during an era in which the government wished to glorify military strength and American diplomacy. Instead, the military would capture the Apache leader and show restraint and tact when dealing with America's "hostile" Indians.

Critics balked at *Geronimo*. The movie's weak script and mechanical acting overshadowed any political theme. The *New York Daily News* admitted that while the film was a good thriller, the story was ludicrously off the mark at its trumped-up conclusion. One reviewer described Geronimo as "a remarkably genuine redskin with a vocabulary of one grunt and a histrionic repertoire of two expressions: grim, and very grim."[12] Another expressed surprise that "Chief Thundercloud," the actor who portrayed the Chiricahua Apache leader, could actually act. "This quality is unusual," the writer explained, because "Indians ordinarily are not adept in the finer nuances of portrayal."[13]

Chief Thundercloud (Victor Daniels) could indeed act, and his impressive list of screen credits proved it. Prior to *Geronimo*, he achieved recognition as the screen's first Tonto in Republic's serials of *The Lone Ranger* (1938) and *The Lone Ranger Rides Again* (1939). Paramount's menacing and treacherous Geronimo, however, was a far cry from the loyal Tonto.[14] Thundercloud himself was uneasy playing a villain, so he was much relieved when director Sloane deleted a scalping scene from the picture. "If I did a scene like that," moaned the actor, "every child in America would hate me."[15]

Northwest Passage

Despite *Geronimo*'s evil Apache leader, Hollywood was gradually beginning to redefine its Indian villains. King Vidor's *Northwest*

Chief Thundercloud (Victor Daniels) in a menacing publicity pose for *Geronimo*.
Courtesy of Bison Archives.

Passage, for example, shows early signs of ambiguity toward its Indian characters. Released in early 1940 by MGM, *Northwest Passage* is the story of Rogers' Rangers and their 1759 expedition to destroy the French and Indian military forces in their war against England. Major Robert Rangers (Spencer Tracy) refers to the enemy Abenaki Indians as "red hellions" who hack and murder whites, steal women, and brain babies. "If it were over quick," he explains, "they were lucky." Rogers and his men descend upon the French/ Abenaki stronghold—spotted with human scalps—and burn every visible tipi.

But *Northwest Passage* includes its Indian allies as well. The movie's analysis chart, completed for each production by the Hays Office, indicated that its Indian characters were unsympathetic as well as sympathetic.[16] Rogers enlists a Mohawk as his scout, and he orders a young Indian boy to help one of his wounded men. During the village ambush, Rogers instructs his men to kill only "every fighting Indian," and later tells his troop to release the Indian prisoners. The random slaughter of Indians is punished: One deranged Ranger tries to attack two Indian women and a child and murders a warrior out of sheer delight. (His infuriated comrade retorts: "Haven't you had enough?") The disturbed man pilfers an Indian head and his own madness sends him hurling off a cliff. (The Production Code Administration insisted upon a moral compensation within motion pictures. Loosely interpreted, this meant that a wrongful death was to be compensated by punishment—preferably death—of the perpetrator. In *Northwest Passage*, the deranged Ranger who plunges to his death became the film's retribution toward an unfit soldier.[17])

Critics raved about *Northwest Passage*. *Variety* called it one of the "foremost adventure narratives, and a great man's picture."[18] Vidor's film certainly promoted the patriotic themes and American chivalry that bolstered the interventionist effort during the war: audiences packed into New York's Capitol Theater and paid $45,000 the first week to watch a "great picturization of American history."[19]

North West Mounted Police

The Canadian wilderness also provided a setting for a strong American/British alliance with its Indian neighbors in DeMille's *North West Mounted Police* (1940). DeMille's most recent Westerns had championed the theme of Manifest Destiny with Indians as the frontier's obstacles. In *Union Pacific* (1939), the story's timely message of "preserving the unity of this nation" embraced Irish laborers and Chinese coolies, but not the recalcitrant Indians.[20] Released in April of 1939, the film portrayed the construction of the transcontinental railroad plagued by white villains and Indian attacks. "The railroad builders are continually harassed by Indians, who stole supplies, burned houses and killed workmen," the picture's titles warn. The film's final Indian attack and its last-minute cavalry rescue include a man raising his gun to the heroine's head to save her from Indian contact. Like Griffith in *The Battle at Elderbush Gulch* and Ford in *Stagecoach*, DeMille was structuring separate societies in which Indians were civilization's worst enemies.

A year later, however, DeMille's *North West Mounted Police* would reevaluate the white relationship to America's Natives. The 1885 Métis uprising in Saskatchewan of the French and Indian mixed bloods and their Cree support against the Canadian government (the "Riel Rebellion") was the basis for DeMille's first Technicolor film. DeMille portrayed the French as enemies to Canadian progress and extolled the growth of the British Empire. The producer/ director "never had any doubt, from the outbreak of World War II, where America must and eventually would take her stand."[21]

The film's story of the friendship and mutual respect between Canada and the United States now included its Indian allies. The Cree Indians, led by Chief Big Bear (Walter Hampden), initially defy British allegiance and become caught in a power struggle between the Métis and the Canadian government; the Mounties, however, succeed in retaining the chief's loyalty to the British. The American interest is represented by a Texas Ranger (Gary Cooper), who pursues a criminal across the Canadian border where the Mounted Police claim he is also wanted for murder. Americans and Mounties unite to capture the man (Louis Riel, leader of the Métis uprising) and succeed in preventing "a war that might have torn Canada to fragments."[22]

DeMille's respect for historical accuracy extended as far as his Anglo-American sympathies would allow. Numerous notations on Indian sign language and dialect accompanied careful research on Cree costumes and equipment; citations included a glossary of Blackfoot words gathered by Henry Schoolcraft and descriptions of Cree camps by Edward Curtis.[23] "History should be honestly and diligently respected," DeMille said in a 1939 interview, but he noted that dramatic license sometimes took precedent over historical truth. "For the sake of dramatic construction, I am justified in making some contradictions or compressions of historical details, so long as I stick to the main facts," he added.[24]

DeMille did take liberties in the portrayal of Big Bear by combining his character with Crowfoot, leader of the Blackfoot, who prevented his people from joining the Riel Rebellion.[25] (Big Bear actually had joined the Métis and was later imprisoned for his part in the rebellion.) In *North West Mounted Police*, Big Bear's composite character supports the British and emerges as a timely metaphor for wartime propaganda: Indians would clearly remain on the side of Canadian and American—rather than French—political interests. When a New York newspaper questioned Big Bear's ability to speak fluent English, DeMille replied with three pages of quoted passages from Crowfoot's eloquent oratory. (The director had explained that both leaders were impressive speakers.) His detailed response carefully positioned Indian chiefs among the ranks of other legendary American heroes:

> The Indians of the American continent have produced some great men, and I fear we are all a little apt to confuse these fine philosophers and statesmen with the Indians of the comic strip, whose accepted rhetorical attainment is "ugh!"[26]

The film's villains, then, are the French and Indian Métis. Their leader's daughter is Louvette (Paulette Goddard), whose unsavory habits are intended as a reflection of her French and Indian ancestry. Louvette's treachery against Canadian/American forces represents Anglo-American suspicion toward French cooperation with Nazi Germany during World War II. Louvette eats on the dirt floor with her hands, prowls barefoot around the campsite, and entices a naive Mountie away from his post when she learns of an attack. Originally named "Loupette" (a parody on the word lupine), she "has the instincts of a wolf, lives by robbing traps, and gets into every possible difficulty."[27] Louvette's connivery is akin to treason: when she seduces the Mountie, she fails to warn Canadian forces of an ambush.

INDIANS AS ALLIES

The Sympathies of Darryl Zanuck

At Twentieth Century Fox, Darryl Zanuck's sympathy toward the North American cause developed years before U.S. entry into the

The treacherous Louvette (Paulette Goddard) casts a furtive glance at Madeleine Carroll in *North West Mounted Police.*

Courtesy of Bison Archives.

war. (As vice president of production, Zanuck closely supervised each film script and insisted upon numerous modifications.) His stance against religious/racial persecution frequently surfaced during America's prewar years. In 1934, Zanuck revealed the evils of anti-Semitism in *The House of Rothschild*, and he preached religious tolerance in *Brigham Young—Frontiersman* (1940). Among his Westerns, a similar theme prevailed: *Hudson's Bay* (1941) favored a British/Canadian alliance against its French enemies, a part of history obscured by France because of the hero's alliance with the Anglo cause.[28] Zanuck advised that a Canadian/Indian alliance dominate the film and that both Indians and whites should show allegiance to the British flag.[29]

Zanuck's 1939 film, *Susannah of the Mounties*, was an earlier World War II Western whose political tone was noticeably one of racial tolerance. Directed by William A. Seiter and starring a preadolescent Shirley Temple, *Susannah* promotes a pacifist theme that leads to interracial harmony. Susannah is the only survivor of a wagon train massacre; despite the fact that the Indians have killed her grandfather, she befriends a Blackfoot boy and brings peace between both races.[30] The chief agrees to help locate the Indians who raided the wagon and offers his son "Little Chief" (portrayed by Martin Goodrider, a Blackfeet Indian) as a token of promise to the whites.[31] Susannah and Little Chief, after a few cultural clashes (he orders her to walk behind him "like a squaw") develop a mutual friendship. Later, they join their fingers in a "blood brother" ceremony—a symbolic gesture that breaks the barriers of Manifest Destiny separating Indian and white societies and points toward racial unity.

The underlying message is that Canada, England, and the Blackfoot are all united in the national welfare. Canadian expansion occurs through a peaceful resolution—rather than a hostile clash—between both races. Zanuck's ally sympathies helped to shape the film's Indian portrayals. "Don't give [the] impression that the Queen Mother will send soldiers to annihilate the Indians," he warned, "as this may get us in trouble with England."[32] The conclusion shows the Mountie, Susannah, and two Indians sitting underneath the British flag and sharing the peace pipe—the film's gesture of solidarity during the present European conflict.

Newspapers approvingly took note of *Susannah*'s theme. The *New York Evening Journal* announced that Temple "showed the red man and white man how to live together like brothers." The *Star*

Telegram argued that the Indians were the movie's real heroes: Little Chief had taught "hostile Susannah how to ride, how to do Indian war dances ... and at last the meaning of blood brotherhood." Other reviewers were less than enthusiastic with the film's newfound interracial harmony: "The Indian raids and fights are rather unimpressive," *Variety* alerted exhibitors.[33] Perhaps American audiences were not quite ready to accept Hollywood's plea for an Indian/white alliance.

But the pro-ally sympathies of Zanuck, DeMille and other studio moguls were gradually becoming the rule—rather than the exception—in Hollywood. "The film industry will not shirk from its chance to aid immeasurably in the strengthening of national morale," a *Variety* editorial announced in 1940. Hollywood supported military readiness by providing studio facilities for the making of Army training films and reshaping the movies' content in response to a world fascist threat. Westerns followed with a step toward racial unity: a year before Pearl Harbor, one veteran producer observed that scheming businessmen and crooked bankers began to replace Indians as the frontier's villains. By 1942, the trend had become noticeable: when MGM resorted to the cowboy versus Indian formula in *Apache Trail*, the results were hackneyed. "The uprising of the Apaches against the whites is something that's long since seen its best picture days," *Variety* complained.[34]

The Politics of Jack Warner

At Warner Bros., the concept of racial brotherhood began to influence its Indian/white portrayals at least two years before America's entry into the war. Vice President of Production, Jack Warner, also saw to it that his ally sympathies shaped the movies' political themes. In 1940, Warner had sent money to Britain for the purchase of two fighter planes and produced *London Can Take It*, a documentary that raised thousands toward British aid. His feature films of the late 1930s conveyed strong anti-Nazi sentiments: *Confessions of a Nazi Spy* (1939) and *Underground* (1940) both elicited sharp criticisms from pro-German sympathizers (namely, the German-American Bund) as well as the nation's isolationist groups.[35]

National unity was a powerful weapon against fascism, and Warner Bros. promoted this political theme even in its Westerns. *Dodge City* (1939) celebrated the building of the West and the settlement of a Kansas town: when a citizen drives a golden spike through the town's railroad terminal, an Indian holds it steady. The community is plagued by villainous cowboys (who were initially reprimanded for killing buffalo on Indian Territory); the new threat to law and order is civilization's corruption and greed. Warner's *Santa Fe Trail* (1940) was another variation on the Western theme without the usual cowboy-and-Indian skirmishes and wagon-train attacks. Its pro-Southern sympathy notwithstanding, the movie's friendly Indian character is a barometer of America's changing sentiments during World War II.

A year later, the shift at Warner Bros. toward Indian/white solidarity grew even more pronounced in *They Died with Their Boots On*, another biography of George Armstrong Custer. "Most Westerns had depicted the Indian as a painted, vicious savage," director Raoul Walsh explained of his 1941 film, in which the real villains are the unscrupulous railroad companies. "In *They Died with Their Boots On*, I tried to show him as an individual who only turned vindictive when his rights as defined by treaty were violated by white men."[36]

Noting its timely release, Warner Bros. seized the opportunity to exemplify American militarism. "In preparing this scenario," screenwriter Aeneas MacKenzie explained in 1941, "all possible consideration was given to the construction of a story which would have the best effect upon public morale in these present days of a national crisis."[37] Hence, the studio built an image of an efficient—albeit pompous and bureaucratic—American military. "I need not mention," MacKenzie continued, "that this picture will be released at a moment when thousands of youths are being trained for commissions, and when hundreds of new and traditionless units are being formed."[38] Warner Bros. research noted that during President Grant's era, army officers were appointed as acting superintendents for the Indian Service, making "an impressive show of efficiency by enforcing programs for Indian welfare with prompt military action."[39] Such gestures failed to impress the War Department, which criticized the script's depiction of officers and enlisted men as corrupt or drunk. Executive producer Hal B. Wallis believed that although the military would not assist in the movie's production, Warner Bros. should incorporate the army's suggestions so as not to "build up antagonism against possible future cooperation."[40] In *They Died with Their Boots On*, the U.S. Army would protect the Indians' best interests.

White paternalism replaced Manifest Destiny as hostile interracial relations became politically unwise for a nation in the throes of fighting genocide in Europe. Warner Bros. thus whitewashed

Custer's career to create a more racially "sympathetic" hero: the Lieutenant Colonel's massacre of the Cheyenne village in the Battle of Washita was completely ignored, and the events at the Little Bighorn were rearranged so that the loss would not "result from Custer's greed for glory." (The studio's liberal interpretation of history prompted MacKenzie to comment that Warner had "an eye more to generosity than to fact."[41]) Further, the hero's feats result from luck rather than foresight: Custer is promoted to (brevet) Major General by an administrative error, and he claims a victory medal during the Civil War by flouting orders and saving an entire regiment from extermination.

But the movie's Indian characters were to have a human dimension. "The Indians need not be presented as lay figures whose sole function in life is to 'mas[s]acre' and be wiped out," advised studio executive Melvin Levy, "but as real people having desires, hopes, loves, and hates." Levy thus attempted to convince associate producer Robert Fellows to create a relationship of respect and friendship between Custer and Crazy Horse, as it was "a basis of actuality."[42] Fellows solicited the opinion of his close friend (and history buff) Lee Ryan, who recommended a scene in which Sitting Bull speaks to the chiefs, and Chief Joseph (White Bull) of the Minneconjou Sioux outlines battle strategy. It was "a bit gushy," Ryan explained, to have Custer as the last survivor in a battle not borne out by a conversation with Sioux braves.[43]

The movie's Custer hero (Errol Flynn) thus emerges as the guardian of Indian welfare. He defends the Sioux's treaty rights and even admires the tactical abilities of the Oglala leader, Crazy Horse (Anthony Quinn). Custer temporarily imprisons Crazy Horse for attacking his wagon train, but he reminds the regiment to treat the Indian leader well. When Crazy Horse escapes, Custer actually praises him as "the only cavalryman I've seen around this fort so far." Crazy Horse demands a peace powwow with Custer: Framed equally in low-angle shots, the two face each other mounted on horseback. The Indian leader says that his people will give up everything but the Black Hills, and Custer promises to defend the sacred land against whites. "I listen to my brother," the officer assures him in another wartime gesture toward interracial cooperation.

The Western Railroad Land & Trading Company, however, has other ideas. The railroad's only route is through the Black Hills, and its corrupt owners (including Custer's former West Point classmate) devise a plan to wipe out the Sioux and snatch their territory.

Newspapers announce a "Second California Gold Rush" in the Black Hills, and Custer warns officials that the Indians will unite in retaliation. "If I were an Indian, I'd fight beside Crazy Horse to the last drop of my blood!" the officer thunders during his court-martial.

Meanwhile, Crazy Horse invites Sitting Bull to a war council, and Indians from several nations convene to plan an attack. The night before, Custer requests that an English soldier escape with a message because he does not want to endanger a foreigner's life. The Briton refuses to leave, and in the spirit of Anglo-American wartime solidarity and racial tolerance, he adds that Indians are the only real Americans. Custer ultimately "sacrifices" his regiment at the Battle of Little Bighorn to protect General Alfred Terry and his men; his dying declaration stipulates that the Indians be protected in their right to the existence in their own country—a request that General Philip Sheridan pledges to enforce. (The movie's depiction of Custer's heroic sacrifice prompted studio head Jack Warner to remark: "If Custer died like that, we should applaud him!"[44])

The November 20, 1941 premiere of *They Died with Their Boots On* was just seventeen days prior to America's entrance into World War II. The movie's theme of an Indian/white alliance was not far from wartime rhetoric: as Indians fought in the battlefields, they stood alongside white Americans and gradually melted into society. The Office of Indian Affairs announced that, despite years of discrimination, Native Americans "responded earnestly and enthusiastically" to the challenge of war, and tribes even dropped claims against the United States for "patriotic reasons." The Iroquois Confederacy had issued a declaration of war upon the Axis Powers in 1942, and 18,000 Indians had joined the armed services by 1943. Indians stood beside whites and captured military honors: seventy-five received the Purple Heart and sixteen the Distinguished Flying Cross, while a Second Lieutenant Childers (a Creek) picked up the Congressional Medal of Honor.[45] Perhaps the most memorable event occurred on Mount Suribachi in Iwo Jima, where the Pima Indian Ira Hayes was one of six men who helped raise the American flag.

THE OFFICE OF WAR INFORMATION

For a nation on the brink of another world conflict, Hollywood's Indian/white portrayals offered a powerful message about America's emerging solidarity with its Indians. Even before the formation of the Office of War Information (OWI) in early 1942 (a federal agency

Wartime brotherhood: Errol Flynn in "blood brother" ceremony with Indians in New York's Central Park as a promotion for *They Died with Their Boots On*.

Courtesy of Bison Archives.

that advised the film industry on its promotion of war-related themes at home and abroad), major Hollywood studios had taken a step toward an Indian/white alliance. "Any form of racial discrimination or religious intolerance, special privileges of any citizen are manifestations of Fascism, and should be exposed as such," the OWI lectured Hollywood studios.[46] In order to address these issues, the OWI devised a handy guidebook for the film industry. Hollywood proceeded to lump Blacks, Mexicans, and Indians in a "melting pot" of racial minorities united with white America against the fascist enemy. Hence, Indians, like Blacks, would be fighting for the same democratic principles without regard to race or color.

The OWI routinely recommended script modifications, advising producers to treat "dark-skinned peoples" as allies to American heroes. "Our sincerity," the agency explained, "is judged by the attitude and treatment we accord those dark-skinned peoples within our own borders."[47] Previous movies like *Susannah of the Mounties* and *They Died with Their Boots On* had already anticipated these wartime sentiments of unity and tolerance, but now both Hollywood and the government openly cooperated and acknowledged the film industry's duty to actively assist in the war effort. The OWI scolded Republic Pictures for their "disparaging treatment of Eskimos" in *Road to God's Country* (1943). "Is it fair," they cried, "to show the Eskimos fleeing inland rather than facing an enemy when in fact they have been giving assistance to our Alaskan troops?"[48] (In 1942, the largest single purchase of war bonds in Alaskan Territory had come from Indians and Alaska Natives.[49])

The OWI admonished studios for any representation of minorities that might be harmful to the national image of a "racial brotherhood." Republic's story of a Pawnee Indian who earns a medical degree and returns to his tribe followed the familiar "marginal man" theme, but a corrupt Indian commissioner, a jealous Indian leader ("Claw Tooth"), and an Indian-hating sheriff all collaborate to remove Fleetwing from his newly appointed position as tribal chief in order to confiscate Indian land. Tensions erupt when Fleetwing, framed for the murder of a rancher, is sentenced to hang and the Pawnees storm the town. Eventually, order is restored and Indian Territory is returned to the Pawnees. But such a mélange of crime, hatred, and treachery was hardly the essence of wartime propaganda. "The entire story adds up to a most unpleasant picture of warfare between whites and dark-skinned peoples," the OWI's Bureau of Motion Pictures objected.[50]

[The conflict] is not conducive to amicable relations between our country and the dark-skinned peoples abroad whom we are seeking to enlist in the cause of the United Nations or who are already fighting with us.[51]

Thus, the movie's image of ruthless Americans trampling over the rights of "dark-skinned peoples" was the wrong message to send abroad.

At the height of wartime activities, scheming businessmen, crooked agents, and even Nazi spies emerged as the frontier's foes, but Indians would clearly remain on the side of Western heroes. The popular, low-budget B Westerns soon followed suit: Columbia's *Frontier Fury* (1943) was the story of an honest Indian agent who loses his job when thieves steal the tribe's income, but he continues to "fight to death for his cold and hungry Indian friends."[52] Monogram Productions's *The Law Rides Again*, also 1943, showed Ken Maynard and Hoot Gibson befriending Indians while pursuing a villainous white agent.[53] Chief Thundercloud joined "Trail Blazers" Bob Steele and Hoot Gibson tracking down villains in *Outlaw Trail* and *Sonora Stagecoach* (both 1944), and "Little Beaver" (a very young Robert "Bobby" Blake) rode alongside Wild Bill Elliott and Rocky Lane through twenty-three "Red Ryder" adventure films (1944–1948).

As the war dragged on, the public demanded even more escapist action. Epic Westerns, with their Technicolor photography, top box-office names, and sweeping panoramic landscapes, emerged as appealing antidotes to gloomy battlefield dramas. Warner Bros. planned to honor a town of the past in *San Antonio* (1945), Gary Cooper would star and produce in *Along Came Jones* (1945), and Paramount would remake Owen Wister's classic, *The Virginian* (1946), with Joel McCrea in the lead. But Twentieth Century Fox's *Buffalo Bill* signaled the return for more Western epics that would take a closer look at Indian/white relations. Following the themes of United Artists' *Kit Carson* (1940), Republic's *Young Bill Hickok* (1940), MGM's *Billy the Kid* (1941), and its own *Jesse James* (1939), Fox created another romanticized version of a Western hero—and one who would demonstrate noticeable tolerance toward his Indian counterparts.

BUFFALO BILL

The story of William Frederick Cody has always provided choice material for Western pictures. *Buffalo Bill*, released in April 1944, lauds the former pony express rider, Indian scout, and international showman as a symbol of freedom and fairness to the Indians of the American West. Cody (Joel McCrea)—like Warner Bros. Custer—is the Indians' friend and protector. "Indians are good people if you leave them alone," he tells Ned Buntline, who eventually capitalizes on Cody's exploits for his popular dime novel series. Cody's skill as a rifleman is quickly noticed. "We need more men like you to exterminate these savages," suggests one Indian-hater. "They must be wiped out." Cody responds that some white men also need wiping out, especially those who have made the Indians drunk with whiskey.

The film's villains are the railroad owners. The company demands that the Cheyenne step aside for Western expansion, but Yellow Hand (Anthony Quinn) refuses. When a craze for buffalo hides sweeps the East, the Cheyenne and the Sioux declare war. In a dual at War Bonnet Gorge, Cody kills Yellow Hand. An Indian schoolteacher (and friend of Cody's) also dies in the battle, and he carries her limp body across the field. Studio executive Darryl Zanuck had no desire to reveal America's mistreatment of its Indians—especially during a racially motivated war in Europe. The film's original dedication alluded to the Indians' removal from the West, a fact that troubled him. "In this we are reminded of a situation which we would rather not have brought up: our ignoble treatment of the American Indian. Perhaps the writer can devise something else for this."[54]

Adhering to his concept of racial tolerance, Zanuck portrayed Cody as more than just a "protector" of Indian welfare. His suggestion that Cody recognize the chiefs as heads of any other nation and bring them to Washington respects Indians as allies to white America.[55] The hero's relationship with Indians is more personalized than Warners' Custer: Cody actually holds the dead Indian teacher in his arms and says, "They are *all* friends of mine."[56]

Buffalo Bill was a box-office success. *Variety* reported that the film gained $92,000 the first week at New York's Roxy Theater, a rarity for wartime Westerns in large Broadway houses.[57] Yet disappointingly, some critics seemed to prefer hostile Indian/white clashes to peace parleys. The *Brooklyn Daily Eagle* complained that the Indians' fancy regalia just didn't look blood-curdling enough: "We aren't scared, and in Indian fights we expect to be."[58] As critics overlooked the film's plea for Indian/white tolerance, they clung to traditional stereotypes.

Cody (Joel McCrea) is captured by Indians in *Buffalo Bill*. Yellow Hand (Anthony Quinn) stands at his right.

Courtesy of Bison Archives.

Nevertheless, the return of the Western to a more spectacular form lured viewers to theaters, where they would be reeducated in the Indian's newfound image. World War II had brought the hostile, conniving Indians of *The Plainsman* and *Stagecoach* to a point where they would stand in friendship alongside the frontier's heroes of *Buffalo Bill*. Even though films like *Valley of the Sun* (1942) showed a disregard for cultural accuracy (the film's Apaches of Arizona erroneously live in tipis and pull a travois), they nonetheless included a white protagonist who protected his Indian friends against corrupt agents and greedy cattlemen. This sympathetic trend served as a transition from a racially segregated society to one in which assimilation would dominate the Westerns' themes. Whether the industry openly acknowledged these political implications or not, the Hollywood Indian was gradually being transformed into an image of white America.

5

Red Becomes White

In the popular *Broken Arrow*, Thomas Jeffords asks the Apache leader Cochise if they might live together as brothers. "Walk with me so my people will see us together," Cochise replies. Although the movie's gesture symbolizing Indian/white brotherhood was hardly new, it signaled that tolerance was now Hollywood's weapon against frontier discrimination as well as the solution to hostile race relations. But beneath *Broken Arrow*'s appeal for reform was a plea for Indian assimilation into white society. Hollywood Indians could now stand alongside the movie's white heroes, provided they compromised their heritage.

Several years before Indian assimilation appeared as a desirable subject for Westerns, Hollywood began exploring the insidious effects of racial bigotry. While the movies' portrayals of Blacks, Indians, and Mexicans had already been scrutinized by the watchful eyes of the Office of War Information, other special-interest groups found the industry lagging in more positive racial depictions. In 1945, the Writers' War Board pointed an accusing finger at Hollywood for perpetuating a "false and mischievous notion that ours is a white, Protestant, Anglo-Saxon country in which all other racial stocks and religious faiths are of lesser dignity."[1] Hollywood Indians soon joined the chorus when they formed the American Indian Citizens League (with Will Rogers Jr. as its head) to fight discrimination against performers of Native American descent.[2]

The industry's response was an indictment against social prejudice and its disturbing revelations about traditional American values. Political "messages" thus began cropping up in movies condemning anti-Semitism—*Crossfire* (1947) and *Gentleman's Agreement* (1947)—as well as those advocating Black racial tolerance—*Lost Boundaries* (1949), *Intruder in the Dust* (1949), and *The Well* (1951). "The American cinema is apparently preparing to face questions of racial and religious prejudice with more forthright courage than audiences have been accustomed to expect," the *New York Times* noted as early as 1947.[3] Included in this postwar trend were Westerns, which began to examine Indian/white relations in a more serious light.

EARLY POSTWAR WESTERNS

Duel in the Sun

The highly controversial *Duel in the Sun* (1946) was one of Hollywood's first postwar Westerns to challenge racial and parochial boundaries. Niven Busch's 1944 story of the passionate and violent love affair between a half-breed woman and a white man flouted traditional mores by unleashing the carnal instincts that had been previously held in check by the Hays Office's stringent Production Code. Furthermore, the movie's portrayal of Indian-hating white bigots was unusual for an industry emerging from a recent world war. Produced by David O. Selznick, whose profitable credits included *A Star is Born* (1937) and *Gone with the Wind* (1939), *Duel in the Sun* was a colossal epic that cost more than $5 million (surpassing *Gone with the Wind* by $1 million) and drew such a national clamor against its sexy scenes that the industry feared even more censorship.

Duel in the Sun exposes an ugly prejudice on America's frontiers. The setting is the stark desert country of the Texas Panhandle during the nineteenth century, when wealthy cattle owners fought railroad development through their lands. Scott Chavez, sentenced to die for killing his Indian wife and her lover, sends his half-breed daughter Pearl (Jennifer Jones) to his former fiancée Laura Belle McCanles (Lillian Gish) and her husband, Senator Jackson T. McCanles (Lionel Barrymore). The senator is scornful of Pearl and mocks her Indian heritage: his two sons—the Harvard-educated Jesse (Joseph Cotten) and the younger, wanton Lewt (Gregory Peck in an uncharacteristic villainous role)—both have an eye for Pearl, but their father forbids his home to be "turned into an Injun reservation."

Jennifer Jones (*right*), as the sexy Pearl Chavez, attracts the attention of Walter Huston and Lillian Gish in *Duel in the Sun.*

Courtesy of Bison Archives.

Tensions mount within the family when the senator rallies his ranch hands to drive the railroad off his land. Jesse's support of the railroad's expansion infuriates his father, who orders his son to leave the ranch. Meanwhile, Pearl is attacked and raped by Lewt; with Jesse gone, Lewt ardently pursues and wins her over. But when Lewt fails to publicly announce their engagement, Pearl leaves him and agrees to wed a ranch boss. Outraged, Lewt kills Pearl's unarmed fiancé, causing the senator to blame all the family's problems on "that Indian girl." Jesse returns to befriend Pearl, and a trigger-happy Lewt shoots him, although Jesse is only wounded. Burning with rage, Pearl rides to Lewt's mountain hideout to kill him: they shoot each other and die in a bloody embrace beneath the scorching Texas sun, neither "tamed" by civilization.[4]

Duel's fiery conclusion was a point of controversy. Busch's novel actually ended with Pearl marrying the kindly Jesse, even though she had killed his brother in self-defense. Busch initially sold *Duel* to RKO; when Selznick later acquired the movie's rights, he immediately sensed trouble with the conclusion's absence of "compensating moral values." "I don't see how," Selznick pointed out, "the girl's action in killing the killer can be regarded as anything but murder, for which there is no punishment."[5] He was right: the Production Code's rigid watchdog, Joseph Breen, objected to the story's illicit sex and Pearl's murder of Lewt without proper retribution. Furthermore, the idea that Pearl would marry the brother of the man she just killed—especially since she loved the man till his death—appeared unconvincing. "What kind of companions and bed mates [are] Jesse and Pearl going to be with the ghost of the man she has killed between them?" Selznick asked. He preferred to have Pearl irresistibly drawn to Lewt—from start to finish—and Jesse ultimately would discover the pair dead.[6]

But *Duel in the Sun* (dubbed "Lust in the Dust") would release the sexy Indian woman to the screen long before it was fashionable to do so. The image of the risqué Western heroine had already been tested with Howard Hughes' *The Outlaw* (1943), loosely based upon Billy the Kid and featuring Jane Russell's bust line.[7] *Duel*'s half-breed Pearl rattled the rigid guidelines of religious and local censorship organizations and reminded audiences that Indian women could also possess an appetite for sexuality. Actress Jennifer Jones apparently exposed another side to her talent: fresh from her Oscar-winning performance as the pious novice in *The Song of Bernadette* (1944), she had enchanted moviegoers with "her large, sad eyes and soft face."[8] *Duel*'s femme fatale was a far cry from the saintly Bernadette. Besides, the filmmakers reasoned, Pearl's sexy Indian half was safe to exploit because it "does not generally connote the same as a Latin temperament."[9] If the image of the wanton Mexican woman seemed cliché, casting Pearl as an Indian "reduces any emphasis upon over-sex rather than accentuates it," director King Vidor explained. Selznick agreed: Pearl's Indian identity presented no violation of the code's anti-miscegenation clause. "I believe that Mr. Hays has been gracious enough to accept the original Americans as people worthy of sex relationships," he added.[10]

But such audacity outraged the puritanical. The movie's suggestive scenes prompted Archbishop John J. Cantwell of the Los Angeles Catholic Archdiocese to denounce *Duel in the Sun*, and he forbade his Church members to view it. Particularly troublesome were scenes of the minister (Walter Huston) eyeing a half-clad Jennifer Jones, who was "unduly, if not indecently, exposed."[11] The Catholic Church was especially annoyed because Selznick failed to submit the film to its censorial Legion of Decency for approval before theatrical release.[12] The Production Code Administration, on the other hand, placed its seal of approval upon *Duel*, a fact that embarrassed Breen. In a letter to the Legion of Decency, Breen apologized that his organization had "made a serious error," and he only wished he could correct the mistake.[13]

Selznick responded to his Catholic critics by snipping approximately two minutes from his film, thus earning a "B" rating (objectionable only in part) by the Legion.[14] But *Duel*'s fanfare only lured curious audiences, who lined up in droves to see Selznick's blockbuster epic. The picture accumulated a stunning $83,500 during its first week in New York and topped the box-office list for May 1947. Following a two-week exhibition in Los Angeles, *Duel* brought $46,500 to three of the city's theaters, where the *Hollywood Reporter* labeled the film a "truly magnificent smash."[15] While movie censors had watered down much of Naza's sexual escapades in *Call Her Savage*, Selznick's Pearl came to represent the screen's passionate Indian woman.

The Postwar B Western

Duel's message that assimilation was but a dream among the politically liberal was unusual for its time. Stories of bigoted, Indian-hating whites did not really dominate Westerns until John Ford's

The Searchers in 1956. But for a society readjusting to a changing postwar era, tolerance, brotherhood, and equality were convenient themes for an industry targeted with growing criticism. Westerns thus responded with conspicuous tolerance and sympathy toward their Indian characters. True postwar brotherhood could play no racial favorites, so Indian characters gradually assumed nontraditional roles in more sympathetic Westerns. In Howard Hawks' *Red River* (1948), Walter Brennan refers to Chief Yowlatchie, the loyal Indian aide to the chuck wagon, as a "dumb heathen." But when Brennan complains of excessive dust on the trail, the Indian tells him off: "Keep mouth shut. Dust not get in." In *Across the Wide Missouri* (1951), Clark Gable's half-breed son narrates: "My father told me that for the first time he saw these Indians as he had never seen them before—as people with homes and traditions and ways of their own."

The postwar B Westerns followed suit, as many encouraged sympathy toward Indians while softening negative stereotypes. These low-budget Westerns had already begun to modify their Native American images during the war when unscrupulous agents and Nazi spies (as in Monogram's *Cowboy Commandos*, 1943) had replaced the frontier's evil Indians. Some B Westerns tackled the issue of Native American identity: *Daughter of the West* (Martin Mooney Productions, 1949) is the story of a convent-educated Indian, Lolita (Martha Vickers), who is unsure of her heritage and ventures to the Navajo reservation to teach school. She falls in love with an Indian Carlisle graduate and later works with him to prevent a white agent from stealing the tribe's valuable mineral rights. Lolita's journey eventually leads her to discover that she is the daughter of the legendary Ramona.[16]

Many white heroes of these B Westerns fought on the side of Indians and occasionally challenged previous stereotypes. In Columbia's *The Last Round-Up* (1947), singing cowboy Gene Autry protects the Indians' interest when the water department tries to divert water away from their reservation. "What about the Indians? They have rights, too," he informs the official, who immediately suspects Autry of being part Indian. Outside, a group of young boys engage in a game of cowboys-and-Indians, and predictably, one of them feigns a scalping. One lad objects because "Indians don't scalp people anymore"—a reminder that traditional beliefs of Indians as bloodthirsty savages should be passé in a more tolerant postwar society.

Other B Westerns attempted to reinforce the theme of an interracial brotherhood. Monogram's *Black Gold* (1947) appeared to promote this issue on several fronts: Indian, white, and Chinese. "Use tolerance, Americanism to win heavy publicity," the studio advised. "The picture carries a message that will have a wholesome effect upon the community."[17] The story of Black Gold—the thoroughbred winner of the 1924 Kentucky Derby—includes his Indian owner (Anthony Quinn), his educated Indian wife (Katherine DeMille, the adopted daughter of Cecil B. DeMille), and their adopted Chinese son (Ducky Louie). The owner trains the horse for the derby, but when oil is discovered on Indian land, the man is severely injured in an accident and eventually dies. The Chinese boy rides Black Gold at Churchill Downs, winning the Derby.

Cloaked in early postwar "liberalism," *Black Gold*'s signs of tolerance precluded racial assimilation. Traditional stereotypes prevailed, but with a progressive twist: Indians may be different, but they're okay. "*Black Gold* is a fine drama of primitive emotions," a promotional review boasted. Anthony Quinn makes "an irresponsible Indian a good and friendly man, simply unable to overcome the urge of his ancestry," and his Indian wife is "understanding, repressed, and stoical." Reviewers complained that while Quinn "ughed" a bit too much, his character did not harm the movie's theme of racial tolerance.[18] Sketches of the Indian owner and his wife, the Chinese boy, the white schoolteacher, and the "black" horse highlighted the film's posters and promoted its theme of an interracial brotherhood.[19]

HOLLYWOOD INDIANS AND COLD WAR POLITICS

Beneath the Westerns' theme of an interracial brotherhood, however, was a suspicion toward Indian/white differences. Conformity became crucial as a strong feeling of national unity and the prevailing political mood guaranteed that only Anglo-American values were safe. Deviating from white society was suspect, and the activities of Representative John Rankin in Congress—a prelude to those of Senator Joseph McCarthy—made the label "un-American" dangerous to groups or individuals who differed. One by one, Hollywood studios cranked out movies designed to quell accusations by espousing an anti-Red ideology, which, by the films' conclusions, would either reform or doom their communist protagonists. Fox's *The Iron Curtain* (1948), Warner Bros.' *To the Victor* (1948), RKO's *The Red*

Menace (1949) and many others served as a kind of "loyalty test" for an industry suffering from political persecution. Indian characters might even become suspect: A seemingly innocuous film based upon Henry Longfellow's *Hiawatha* was temporarily shelved by Monogram in 1950. The character's message for peace, the studio rationalized, could be regarded as helpful to present communist designs.[20]

A few Westerns thus emerged as allegories of the Cold War mentality. Paramount's *Unconquered*, the story of Pontiac's rebellion, became a fitting analogy to the then-current communist purge. The movie's release in September 1947 was just one month prior to the testimony of Hollywood's nineteen "unfriendly" witnesses before the House Un-American Activities Committee in Washington, in which ten (seven writers, two directors, and one producer) were eventually cited for contempt and sent to prison for refusing to admit whether they were communists.

Unconquered was produced and directed by the redoubtable Cecil B. DeMille, whose political views grew increasingly more conservative during an era of labor strife and anti-communist propaganda. DeMille's dislike for unions and his suspicion toward un-American activities served him well as president of the Motion Picture Industry Council—formed to expose the "communist problem" in Hollywood. He even tried to oust members of the Screen Directors Guild for opposing the anti-communist loyalty oath.[21] By 1956, DeMille provided a prologue to his movie *The Ten Commandments* in which he asks, "Are men the property of the state? Or are they free souls under God?" He then drew a parallel between ancient Egypt and the Cold War by concluding, "This same battle continues throughout the world today."

Beneath its anti-communist rhetoric, *Unconquered* hinted that a person's "Indianness" was politically risky during a Cold War era. Set in the eighteenth-century American wilderness, *Unconquered* refers to those "who push ever forward the frontiers of man's freedom." The obstacles to this freedom are the Ottawa chief Pontiac and his Indian allies, determined to abort British encroachment and restore French ascendancy in the West. DeMille himself believed that American western expansion "might have been halted and people in Ohio today might have been speaking French if the Indian uprising under Pontiac had succeeded in destroying the English outposts on the frontier."[22]

Unconquered begins when Abigail (Paulette Goddard) is transported to the North American colonies as an indentured slave, and aboard ship she meets Garth (Howard Da Silva), an unsavory character married to an Indian woman (Katherine DeMille). Captain Chris Holden (Gary Cooper) claims Abby with the highest bid, and he later discovers that Garth is supplying Pontiac with ammunition in order to attack the British at Fort Pitt.

Like subversive communists, Pontiac and his warriors remain elusive as they conspire against the British Empire. "There are no savages between earth and Mars," quips one colonist, "but there are 10,000 red hot ones between here and the Ohio." The Indians do indeed seem to infest the wilderness, jumping out of trees and popping arrows from everywhere. Garth's Indian wife represents the enemy turned informer. Through her efforts and sacrifice, the Indian woman protects the military and saves the American frontier from the hands of "murderin' devils and redskins." But Garth later abandons his Indian wife for trying to burn Abby at the stake. Spurned by her husband, the angry woman silently warns Chris of the hidden soldiers: a traitor to her people, an enemy of the British, she deliberately walks into the soldiers' gunfire.

The film's conclusion points up the difference between "pagan" Indians and "Christian" Americans as an ideal example of anti-communist propaganda. Chris escapes and again tricks the attacking Indians by filling a wagon with dead soldiers to give the appearance of a large militia. In typical Cold War convention, the scheme prevents a bloody clash and drives the Indians from Fort Pitt. As Garth tries to kidnap Abby, Chris shoots him; he and Abby marry and settle in the West. "Settlers are the new world," Chris tells Abby. "They are strong and free because they have faith in God."

Paramount's promotion for *Unconquered* was a fitting analogy to the postwar communist purge. *Unconquered* "should inspire America to fight red political ideas today as America once fought Red Indians," announced one advertisement. Another asserted more confidence toward the country's ability to ward off communism: "America today resists red ideas as it once resisted Red Indians in the pioneer days of *Unconquered*."[23] The American Legion's endorsement reminded that democracy's enemies—like the Indians who once hid in the forests—now lurk within the nation's corridors: "The lessons of courage and patriotism which it teaches are vitally necessary in these times." An advertising slogan reinforced the desire to snuff out communists, with an eagle's outstretched wings and the words, "Keep America Unconquered" printed across its silhouette.[24]

While *Unconquered* suggested that being Indian was suspect, Hollywood's immediate solution to the frontier's "Indian threat" would be Native American assimilation into white society. The movies' days of Manifest Destiny were over: knocking Indians off one by one was supposed to be unacceptable within a more tolerant postwar society. Westerns must advocate tolerance, and wartime brotherhood would eventually give way to postwar assimilation. The champion filmmaker of Manifest Destiny later admitted that assimilation was the preferable solution to Indian/white tensions. "You educate what primitive peoples you can and bring them to your side if you can," said DeMille, "and not just take the alternative, which destroys them and rules over them."[25]

A LOSS OF INDIAN IDENTITY

Broken Arrow

By 1950, then, peaceful coexistence between Indians and whites was achieved only through the loss of Indian identity. "Good" Indians would conform to white society, "bad" Indians would not. The affirmation of white-Anglo values within Indians themselves became the basis of *Broken Arrow* (1950), the story of the peace agreement between the U.S. Army and the Chiricahua Apache Indians. Directed by Delmer Daves, *Broken Arrow* suggested that while Indian culture and heritage were significant, Indian conformity to civilization was inevitable. ("We wanted to tell the story of the American Indian as a human being," Daves explained in an attempt to "equalize" the two races.[26]) The movie was certainly not the first to portray American Indians sympathetically, but it did propose assimilation as a solution to the "Indian problem."

Daves was ideal for *Broken Arrow*. The Irish American director had briefly lived among the Navajo and Hopi Indians, and his own familial ties to the West (his pioneer grandparents had crossed the country in a covered wagon) sparked his interest at an early age. Daves labored in the movie industry as a screenwriter until his directorial debut with *Destination Tokyo* (1943); *Broken Arrow* was his first of nine Westerns. While John Ford claimed Monument Valley as his turf, Daves staked out the scenic red rock canyons of Sedona, Arizona. Politically, his movies differed from Ford's: Daves favored interracial unions (an Indian/white marriage in *White Feather*, 1955, and a Mulatto/white romance in *Kings Go Forth*,

1958) and he celebrated Anglo values over ethnic heritage. Ford's Indian characters, on the other hand, held firmly to a distinct identity and culture (although not necessarily an accurate one) and never fully embraced white society. When Ford's Cochise in *Fort Apache* (1948) wipes out an entire Army troop and victoriously plunges the cavalry flag into the ground, he simultaneously defeats white invasion of Apache land and refuses to sacrifice Indian heritage.

Broken Arrow was based upon Elliott Arnold's epic novel *Blood Brother*, published in 1947. The film's central theme, according to its producer Julian Blaustein, was the friendship between Thomas Jeffords (James Stewart) and the Apache Indian leader Cochise (Jeff Chandler), which would serve as a basic structure for the story's Indian/white relations. (Screenwriter Michael Blankfort, whose credit initially appeared on the film, was actually a "front" for Albert Maltz, one of Hollywood's blacklisted forbidden to work in the industry.)[27] *Blood Brother* covers nineteen years of southwest history, from 1855—when the whites acquired the land south of the Gila River in what is now Arizona—to 1874, the year Cochise died. The film *Broken Arrow*, however, de-emphasizes the novel's historical setting, eliminating many references to past events that led to current conflicts, and focuses instead upon the relationship between Jeffords and Cochise.

On one level, *Broken Arrow* attempts to distinguish cultural differences between Indians and whites. Twentieth Century Fox delved into anthropological sources and noted everything from Apache games to the Indians' jewelry and clothing.[28] The movie even depicted portions of the girls' traditional puberty rite. The studio's faithful depiction of the wedding scene in *Blood Brother*, however, became a point of critical controversy. *Broken Arrow* duplicates Arnold's passages regarding the wedding: Thomas Jeffords officially "marries" the Apache Indian woman, Sonseeahray (Debra Paget) when the medicine man makes a small incision on their hands and ties both together. As their blood mingles, he recites, "There are two bodies but now there is but one blood in both of them."[29] The movie's wedding ceremony emerges as a metaphorical theme: it is the postwar blood brother ritual displaced into marriage.

But beneath *Broken Arrow*'s message of tolerance was an attempt to erase Indian identity. The movie's avoidance of language differences—while an improvement over the grunts and howls of earlier Hollywood Indians—seemed to blur cultural distinctions. Director Daves believed that *Broken Arrow* could break the racial barrier by indicating at the outset (in Jeffords' opening narration) that the Indians would speak in customary English so the audience could understand them. The goal of understanding, he reasoned, could be achieved by eliminating broken English and replacing it with a more conventional style.[30] (In *Fort Apache*, Cochise speaks in Spanish, a language the Apaches had learned from the Mexicans.) Both races thus speak the same language and sound alike; indeed, Cochise sounds even more eloquent than the stuttering James Stewart.

The film professes an eternal brotherhood between Indians and whites, but Apaches must make the concessions. Cochise and his warriors agree to temporarily permit mail riders to pass safely through Apache territory; those who disagree are banished and appoint Geronimo (Jay Silverheels) as their leader. When a group of Indian-hating miners ambush Jeffords and Cochise, they kill Sonseeahray in the struggle. As Jeffords hold his dead wife, he vows revenge upon the whites, but Cochise reminds him: "No one on my territory will open war again—not even you."[31]

The permanent peace between Apaches and whites, then, becomes possible only through the sacrifice of Jeffords' Indian wife. His final narration reminds the audience that Sonseeahray's death was necessary for the seal of peace.[32]

Broken Arrow thus came to represent the popular solution to Native American survival. The Association of American Indian Affairs, headed by its anthropologist president and author, Oliver La Farge, hinted that the movie would redefine the Indians' new role in American society. *Broken Arrow* discarded traditional stereotypes, La Farge announced, and proved that American Indians must be considered first-class citizens.[33] Such a declaration was in line with his belief that cultural pluralism was passé: "Our basic overall theory of policy is that Indians must become absorbed into the general population. In being thus absorbed, they may not be able to retain enriching elements of their own culture."[34]

Even television picked up the movie's theme of an Indian/white brotherhood. *Broken Arrow*'s popularity prompted Twentieth Century Fox to launch its own TV series, *Broken Arrow* (ABC, 1956–1958), with Michael Ansara as Cochise. Similarly, *Brave Eagle* (CBS, 1955–1956) with Keith Larsen in the title role, took place in an Indian village and preached peace to intrusive whites and warring tribes. The Indian companion also became popular: *Yancy Derringer* (CBS, 1958–1959) featured the mute Pahoo (Jay X Brands) as the

A peaceful coexistence: on the set of *Broken Arrow*, with Jeff Chandler as Cochise (*left*) and James Stewart as Tom Jeffords.

Courtesy of Bison Archives.

loyal aide to the white hero, and *The Lone Ranger* (ABC, CBS; 1949–1961) resurfaced with Jay Silverheels (Mohawk) as Tonto.

Silverheels, who was born Harold J. Smith on Canada's Six Nations Reserve, dedicated much of his professional life to fighting Indian stereotypes in Hollywood. In addition to his sidekick role as Tonto, he appeared in more than thirty films, played lacrosse, and was an amateur middle-weight boxer and a harness racer. For years, Silverheels was the only Indian on the board of directors for the Screen Actors Guild. In 1968, he founded the Indian Actors Workshop, an all-volunteer organization that encouraged Indians to develop their acting talent and offered training in related crafts. "We're trying to provide for Indians an opportunity for education in theater arts that they would not have otherwise," Silverheels said of his organization.[35]

Indian Compromise on the Frontier

Daves continued to preach the theme of assimilation in his subsequent Indian Westerns. *Drum Beat* (1954), written, directed, and produced by Daves, is based upon the story of Kintpuash, leader of the Modoc Indians and known among whites as "Captain Jack." The story begins in 1872, when Indian fighter Johnny MacKay (Alan Ladd) is summoned by President Grant to bring peace to the Modocs of the northern California/Oregon region. Although MacKay's parents were massacred by Indians, he believes that tolerance, and not guns, will bring the Modocs into line.

But Captain Jack, played by a muscular Charles Bronson, only balks at Grant's peace plan. The restless Indian bolts the reservation and sends his warriors on raids and killing sprees. Jack agrees to a peace council, but instead wounds MacKay and kills Brigadier General Edward Canby (the only U.S. general ever killed in an Indian conflict).[36] Eventually, MacKay captures Jack and the army executes the Indian leader. "We could've saved a lot of lives," MacKay scolds Jack, "if *you* hadn't grabbed country that wasn't yours" (italics added). The bad Indian is eliminated, so peace finally becomes possible between Modocs and whites.

Other fifties Westerns reiterated that good Indians would adopt a white peace plan. *Naked in the Sun* (1957), a low-budget film about the Seminole War, features the rebellious leader Osceola and his angry warriors. But Osceola eventually surrenders Indian land and tells his tribe to live in peace. "Enough blood has been spilt," he wearily admits. *Sitting Bull* (1954), the story of the great Hunkpapa Sioux medicine man, riled critics with its many liberties. "And, at the end of this crazy horse opera," scoffed the *New York Times*, "we are led to believe that Grant and Sitting Bull agree on a policy of co-existence between the white man and the red!"[37] (Historically, Sitting Bull had fled to Canada to escape the army's wrath.)

Walk the Proud Land (1956) offers one of the strongest pleas for assimilation. The film recounts the story of agent John P. Clum (Audie Murphy) and his adventures on an Apache Indian reservation. Clum's goal is to assimilate the Indians into mainstream America: he tells an Apache boy to follow white man's ways because "it's his world and you must learn to live in it." The army must make useful citizens out of Indians, Clum believes, and he advises Geronimo to surrender and put himself "under the mercy of the U.S. government." In a special ceremony echoing the wedding sequence in *Broken Arrow*, agent Clum and an Apache Indian are joined together as brothers.

By the 1950s, even the Indian docudrama could not escape Hollywood's newfound agenda. *The Silent Enemy*, *Eskimo*, and *Laughing Boy* had championed Indian lifestyle over white civilization, but *Navajo* (1952) proposed that traditional Indians might eventually abandon their old ways. *Navajo* was shot in black and white and filmed on location in northern Arizona. The story revolves around a rebellious young Indian lad (portrayed by the unknown performer Francis Kee Teller) who distrusts all whites and vows never to join them. The boy escapes the stifling confines of a local boarding school with his kindly white teacher and a Ute scout trailing him through remote canyons. Instructor and guide become injured, but the boy eventually realizes that not all white folks are evil. The final scene of the lad running for assistance suggests that understanding and compassion will convince even the most reluctant Indian to join white society.

Apache's (1954) original message was garbled by Hollywood's assimilation ideals. Director Robert Aldrich initially planned for the movie's Indian character to lead a life of bloodshed and loneliness, rather than one of peace and compromise. Massai (Burt Lancaster) deplores the thought of living on a reservation: a Cherokee's plea for reconciliation ("We found that we could live with the white man, only if we lived like him") sends the warrior scurrying into the remote desert. Like *Drum Beat*'s Captain Jack, Massai leaves a trail of murder and destruction. Taunted by local citizens, pursued by a mob, and even bitten by an unfriendly dog, the Indian has "nothing in him but hate." Yet, love tames a wild soul, and when Massai settles down with an Indian woman, the cries of his newborn child prompt him to toss his rifle aside and call off the war. "He has planted corn," observes one soldier. "Something no other Apache has done before." (Apaches were primarily hunters.)

Apache thus advocated the loss of Indian identity to achieve peaceful coexistence. This was not the film's original ending: director Aldrich preferred that Massai be shot in the back by Federal troops and die an Indian, rather than succumb to civilization. But United Artists insisted that killing a popular star like Burt Lancaster might disappoint audiences, so Massai instead turns into a decent hard-working Indian farmer. Not until 1972 would the Apache hero of Aldrich's *Ulzana's Raid* be allowed the respectable death that Massai was denied.[38]

Jim Thorpe—All American

Jim Thorpe—All American (1951) was one of Hollywood's first postwar attempts to set the Indian within contemporary society. The film preceded another Warner Bros. biography of an Indian entertainer, *The Story of Will Rogers* (1952), featuring Will Rogers Jr. in the lead role.[39] But Rogers was a "success" story and Thorpe's life was fraught with hardship and tribulation. As a biographic representation of the great Olympic athlete, *Jim Thorpe—All American* struggled to find a peaceful Indian/white coexistence within America, a difficult proposition for an account of a man's tragic life. Warner Bros., which hired Thorpe as the movie's technical advisor, announced that the former athlete "did not want to cover up shadowy phases of his career."[40] Thus, Thorpe's feats on the gridiron, track, and baseball fields would be matched by the loss of his Olympic gold medals, the death of his infant son, and his rapid decline into oblivion. On the other hand, producer Everett Freeman leaned more toward the postwar concepts of tolerance and brotherhood: The movie's message, he believed, should "help promote better understanding between white men and their Indian brothers." Freeman advised to soften the movie's tragic Indian theme and instead stress "a tribute to a great athlete."[41]

Warner Bros. thus attempted to reconcile Thorpe's heroic feats in athletics with his personal tragedies. James Francis "Jim" Thorpe was born in 1887 of an Irish/Sac-Fox father and a part French and

Potawatomi/Kickapoo mother in what was formerly Indian Territory in Oklahoma. He attended the Carlisle Indian School where he plunged himself into sports and met the famed football coach, Glenn S. "Pop" Warner. Years of rigorous athletic training and team sports eventually paid off for the husky athlete. In 1912, Thorpe won two gold medals for the pentathlon and decathlon events at the International Olympics in Stockholm, Sweden. But Thorpe's Olympic medals were revoked in 1913 when the Amateur Athletic Union accused him of having played professional baseball.[42] Nevertheless, he remained active and played professional football and baseball and became the first president of the American Professional Football Association (later renamed the National Football League).

Years later, however, a reporter discovered the great athlete digging ditches for a mere $4 a day. When Thorpe was too poor to afford a ticket to the 1932 Olympic Games in Los Angeles, letters and donations poured in. He later sold the rights of his life story, "The Red Son of Carlisle," but the picture was never made. "His existence has been a series of ups and downs with the latter distinctly predominant," the *Los Angeles Times* observed.[43] For the remainder of his life, Thorpe eked a meager living as a minor player in Hollywood movies while campaigning against studios hiring non-Indian actors for Indian roles.

By the time Warner Bros. began filming the athlete's biography, Thorpe had hit rock bottom. "His life had gone to pot," said Burt Lancaster, who portrayed the Indian athlete in *Jim Thorpe—All American.* "But there is no question about it, he never received much encouragement."[44] Aware of Thorpe's various misfortunes and mishaps, Warner executives vacillated over whether to portray him as a victim or a hero. "The theme which occurs to me relies on the fact that Jim Thorpe is an Indian," Warner Bros. producer Milton Sperling wrote early in production. Perhaps Thorpe's ancestry could explain his plight, Sperling reasoned; his stoic character could crack with the death of his son. "Tragedy comes when he is reached emotionally by another human being," Sperling added.[45] But the idea of a world-famous athlete—Indian or not—confined to life's dumps proved unattractive, so the studio opted for a more uplifting conclusion.

Jim Thorpe—All American thus resolves the modern Indian's dilemma by making him an American hero. Jim "just wants a chance" to prove himself but discovers that the road to racial equality is

Carlisle Indian teammates congratulate Thorpe (Burt Lancaster, *center*) after scoring the winning touchdown in *Jim Thorpe—All American.*

Courtesy of Bison Archives.

long and arduous. He's passed over as football coach because he's Indian, and the Olympic committee demands return of his two gold medals. Jim believes that people want him back on the reservation; following his son's death and his marital break-up, he entertains in a carnival sideshow. But the movie returns Thorpe to Oklahoma and appoints him an honored coach of a boys' football team. His dignity restored, Thorpe emerges as the Indian hero who has survived the battle scars of social bigotry and thus successfully adjusted to white American society.[46]

Thus, from the country's Western frontiers to its urban centers, postwar movies had ventured into new territory by suggesting a commonality between Indians and whites. But mutual coexistence demanded a sacrifice of Indian identity, and prospects for Native American cultural survival became bleak indeed. As more Westerns depicted a lasting romantic union between Indians and whites, they simultaneously suggested that civilization would absorb Native American autonomy. *White Feather* (1955) merely reiterates *Broken Arrow*: The white protagonist serves as a peacemaker between the Cheyenne and the cavalry, and he weds the chief's daughter. (The movie was cowritten by Delmer Daves and Leo Townsend.) But *White Feather*'s interracial marriage survives, and the couple's mixed-blooded son ultimately enters the U.S. Military Academy at West Point. America's goal of racial unity finally had been achieved—by Hollywood's standards—yet the postwar ideal of an Indian/white coexistence would eventually crumble in the face of social bigotry.

6

A Shattered Illusion*

The release of John Ford's *The Searchers* in 1956 marked a turning point in Hollywood's classic Westerns. No longer would self-righteous, fair-minded cowboys rectify the town's wrongs, leaving a legacy for the next generation. In Ford's movie, the Western hero is lonely and obsessive, explosive and compulsive; he harbors a deep hatred for American Indians and slaughters them with a vengeance. "The underlying text of racism is brought to the surface in *The Searchers*," wrote film historian James Monaco. "Westerns would never be the same afterwards."[1]

With *The Searchers*, peaceful Indian/white frontier relations were shattered. Gone were the postwar ideals of tolerance and brotherhood, and in their place appeared a pre-sixties anxiety and isolation. Indian assimilation was impossible within a society marred by racial bigotry and social discrimination. *The Searchers* was not the first Western to reveal this prevailing pessimism. But the movie's box-office success established a turning point: Indians became society's victims and faced a life of frustration and alienation on both the Western frontier and in America's urban centers.[2]

*Excerpts from Angela Aleiss, "A Race Divided: The Indian Westerns of John Ford," *American Indian Culture and Research Journal*, 18 (3) (November 1994): 167–186, were reprinted by permission of the American Indian Studies Center, UCLA. © Regents of the University of California.

RACISM RETURNS TO THE FRONTIER

The Searchers

The Searchers acknowledges that while differences exist between Indians and whites, savagery is innate to both races. From *Stagecoach* (1939) to *Wagon Master* (1950), Ford's Indians grew more complex; his white heroes, however, reveal their racism and brutality. Production notations indicate that while Ford planned to "portray the Comanches with as much barbarism as possible," associate producer Patrick Ford (John Ford's son) added similar thoughts about the movie's white protagonists: "They [Ethan and Martin] are only a shade less barbaric than the savages they follow."[3]

The year is 1868, and the place is the stark, primitive Texas countryside. Ford's vision of a stable community with strong familial ties typically remains hopeful in this Western, but his focus is upon the fanatic racism of his protagonist, Ethan Edwards (John Wayne). Ethan, an otherwise noble individual, possesses a blind hatred toward the Comanche for killing his family and abducting his niece. His racism is initially apparent when he sneers that his nephew, Martin Pauly (who is, in fact, part Cherokee), can easily be mistaken for a half-breed. The brutal murder of Ethan's family unleashes his fury: He shoots out the eyes of a dead Comanche, he slaughters the buffalo to deplete the Indians' winter food supply, and he scalps the Comanche chief Scar (Henry Brandon) who murdered his family. Worst of all, Ethan is determined to kill his niece Debbie (Natalie Wood) for becoming the chief's wife.

But Ethan is an eerie mirror image of Chief Scar, a reflection of the Indian's savagery. Both men had witnessed their families' brutal slayings by the other race, and each is determined to avenge their deaths. Chief Scar is "tall, savage, with a hatred for white people because they have killed his sons"; Ethan is "rentless in his hatred of Indians, and of all things pertaining to them."[4] Ethan whistles like a bird before attacking Scar's camp, just like the Indians had done before descending upon the Edwards' ranch. This peculiar reflection of both characters is also evident in Ethan and Scar's initial meeting:

ETHAN: You speak pretty good American ... for a Comanch'. Someone teach you?

SCAR (later): You speak good Comanch'. Someone teach you?

Monument Valley, Arizona, provides a scenic backdrop for *The Searchers*, with Ethan (John Wayne, *center*), his Cherokee nephew, Jeffrey Hunter (*left*), and Harry Carey Jr. (*right*).

Courtesy of Bison Archives.

Driven by a fierce determination, Ethan's search for his niece is obsessive: "Whatever it took, wherever it took him, he had to find her."[5] Ethan does eventually find his niece living among the Comanche and even speaking their language: Debbie has become Scar's wife, and she declares that the Indians are now her people. During the film's climatic moment, the cavalry surrounds the Comanche village and Martin kills Chief Scar; Ethan relentlessly pursues Debbie and vows to kill her. But blood ties prove stronger than culture; Ethan suddenly abandons his revenge, lifts his frightened niece off her feet and says, "Let's go home, Debbie."

It is fitting, then, that Debbie returns to civilization and the cavalry destroys the Comanche village. The rampant slaughter of innocent lives, *The Searchers* seems to say, will cease only when one race exterminates the other. *The Searchers'* outcome is undeniably racist, but the message is disturbingly realistic: beneath the veneer of civilization lies a terrifying savagery.

The Searchers was not the first film to expose the frontier's ugly white racism. A few postwar Westerns had foreseen this gloomy trend. In 1946, *Duel in the Sun* revealed that Indians are condemned to a life of bigotry among the frontier community. The mixed-blooded heroine, Pearl Chavez, is the target of anti-Indian prejudice within the MacCanles' household. Paramount's *Arrowhead* (1953) anticipates *The Searchers* in that both its Indian and white protagonists have a fanatic hatred for the other race. Bannon (Charlton Heston) bears a long-standing grudge against the Apaches after the murder of his parents; Toriano (Jack Palance) is an educated Indian, a "murderous and treacherous chief who leads his people in a bloody rebellion against the U.S. Cavalry." A studio ad warns that although Toriano may be dressed in a jacket and tie, "under these gentlemanly garments beat a savage heart."[6] Although *Arrowhead* implies that Indians can be neither tamed nor civilized, it simultaneously suggests that peace between the two races is not possible. In one scene, Bannon sneaks upon his Indian enemy, slashes his wrist, and forces him to become a blood brother. The gesture is a mockery of postwar brotherhood, the flip side of *Broken Arrow's* interracial harmony.

Broken Lance (1954) continues the postwar skepticism by refusing to offer a pat solution to Indian/white tensions. Unlike *Broken Arrow*, the film instead states that racism is "something born and bred" in most folks and that a few heroic individuals are unlikely to change century-old attitudes. The leading character (Robert Wagner) is part Indian and he ultimately marries a white woman but without the community's cooperation. The lack of community support was common to many fifties Westerns, namely *The Gunfighter* (1950) and *High Noon* (1952); *Broken Lance* echoed the same theme of the alienated hero fighting community pressure. Without community support, individuals can do little to resist social evil. Thus, the movie's Indian/white couple rides off into the horizon and must fend for themselves within a bigoted world.

Broken Lance, *Arrowhead*, and *Duel in the Sun* appeared years before the federal government would abandon its postwar program of Indian assimilation into white society. Forced into urban centers by "Federal Termination," American Indians faced unemployment and discrimination in a program that was supposed to make them more self-sufficient. But Hollywood Westerns had already revealed that communal bigotry and social prejudice destroyed any hopes for a lasting interracial harmony. Studio blacklisting and communist witch-hunting produced a generation of filmmakers who questioned government institutions and challenged traditional American values. Recent court decisions had eroded studio monopolistic power and loosened stringent censorship regulations, thus allowing filmmakers more autonomy and freedom. War pictures began to expose the futility of combat with *The Bridges at Toko-Ri* (1954) and to question the nobility of military heroes in *Attack* (1956). Melodramas undermined the stable, all-American family in *Caught* (1948) and *All that Heaven Allows* (1955). Other films, including *No Way Out* (1950) and *Blackboard Jungle* (1955), exposed Black/white racial tensions. Similarly, the country's changing social climate gave rise to Westerns that undercut the heroic cowboy myth and destroyed the post World War II ideal of a peaceful Indian/white coexistence.

Devil's Doorway

Anthony Mann, formerly a director of low-budget thrillers and bleak *noir* films, paved the way for pessimistic, "adult" Westerns years before *The Searchers*. Mann directed eleven Westerns in the 1950s, each presenting a non-idealistic hero, a powerless community, a lonely and baroque landscape, and a cynical attitude toward frontier Indian/white relations. Mann's heroes are troubled and scarred by a painful emotional past; they are often driven by a vengeance and explode into a violent, passionate hysteria when forced to face themselves (like James Stewart in *The Man from Laramie*, 1955). A sense of moral outrage pervades Mann's Westerns, a feeling that "nice guys" always finish last. If Mann's heroes resemble Ford's protagonist in *The Searchers*, it is because both directors bridge the transition from a noble, idealistic Western cowboy to one of a vulnerable character pushed to extremes by circumstances beyond his control.[7]

In *Devil's Doorway* (1950), the tragic hero is an American Indian. Based upon a short story by Guy Trosper (titled "The Drifter"), *Devil's Doorway* is about Lance Poole (Robert Taylor) and his struggle to retain rights to his ancestral Shoshone lands in Wyoming. Lance returns home from the Civil War with a Congressional Medal of Honor, yet encounters discrimination and hostility because of his Indian status. Lance's family has been occupying Sweet Meadows for generations, but Wyoming has opened the land to ambitious homesteaders. Although Lance ate, slept, and fought with whites in the army, why should things be different back home? "Our people are doomed," his father says. And then, as if to foreshadow his people's demise, Lance's father explains, "An Indian without land loses his soul" (and, consequently, his identity).

Lance thus emerges as the movie's alienated hero, doomed because of his Indian status. He constantly encounters prejudice: the local bar will not serve alcohol to Indians, and the government will not allow noncitizens to own land. (Indians were not granted U.S. citizenship until 1924.) Lance's longtime friend, the town's marshal, likens the prevalent racism to a disturbing analogy: "Indians got no more rights than a dog." Lance's only victory is through death, an action that celebrates the uncompromising quality of Mann's characters. The Shoshone hero chooses suicide over compromise; he gathers his people to dynamite the land, salutes a soldier, and deliberately walks into cavalry gunfire (wearing his Civil War uniform). Lance's death in his cavalry uniform kills the white man in him, leaving the Indian an embattled symbol of oppression.

Devil's Doorway argues that Indians and whites are separated not by inherent differences, but by social attitudes. Lance's initial appearance disguises his Indian heritage as he enters the local bar (dressed in his sergeant's uniform) and speaks eloquent English. But an Indian-hater turns to his partner and sneers, "You notice how sour the air got? You can always smell 'em." The studio's promotional campaign places actor Taylor in military uniform among non-Indian and Indian characters, thus blurring his true identity.[8] The *New York Times* agreed: "[Lance] is the only role that is not a stereotype."[9] Lance can easily pass for white, but he will always be an unwelcome alien within his own country.

Gradually, fifties Westerns began to explore the Indians' status within society and cast a cynical eye toward whites. These movies shed some of their postwar idealism while challenging America's claim of racial tolerance. In *River of No Return* (1954), a priest observes, "I came here to administer to the Indian. I think the white man will need me more." *The Last Hunt* (1955) shows that Charlie, an Indian-hating white man, refuses to acknowledge his own savagery. "Charlie don't like himself so much so he don't like the Injun [sic] any better," explains one character. In *The Last Wagon* (1956), director and cowriter Delmer Daves reexamines *Broken Arrow*'s optimism when a white girl remarks, "I hate Indians." Later, she becomes indebted to a Comanche for saving her life and helping her "grow up."

Next to *The Searchers*, *Run of the Arrow* (1957) emerges as one of the decade's most dramatic indictments against white society. This dark Western is written, produced, and directed by Sam Fuller, and its story of a white man who lives among the Lakota Sioux predates *Dances With Wolves* by thirty-three years. *Run of the Arrow* features Rod Steiger as a disillusioned Confederate veteran who joins the Lakota as a personal rebellion against the Yankees. ("The savages have more pride in us!" he hisses.) Steiger proves himself a Lakota warrior and even marries one of their women (Sarita Montiel); he learns to live, hunt, and fight as a Lakota, but admits that his god will always be Christian.

The U.S. Cavalry clashes with the Indians and Steiger protects his Lakota friends, but his wife points out that he can never kill whites in good conscience. The Lakota capture a Yankee enemy and skin him alive, an act of savagery and brutality that horrifies Steiger and undermines any chance for an interracial peace. As Steiger and his Indian wife depart the Lakota village, the movie's closing statement leaves the matter of hostile Indian/white relations unresolved: "The ending of this story can only be written by you."

Although Steiger remains with his Lakota bride, the couples' future appears dismal. By the late 1950s, the romantic Indian/white union of *White Feather*—with the offspring's smooth transition to civilization—was destroyed by communal bigotry. The captive white woman and her mixed-blooded son in *Trooper Hook* (1957)

Rod Steiger (*second left*) marries Sioux woman Sarita Montiel in a blood brother ceremony in *Run of the Arrow*. The movie's story of a white man living among the Sioux preceded *Dances With Wolves* by thirty-three years.

Courtesy of Bison Archives.

instead face a racist and ignorant society. The movie's white heroine (Barbara Stanwyck) is torn between her Caucasian husband (who refuses to accept her half-Indian son) and her former Apache lover (who demands the boy's return). Furthermore, the townspeople condemn the woman for giving her body to an Indian instead of killing herself, and they scorn her young boy. Social tolerance is impossible: the Indian and her husband kill each other, and the woman finds comfort in the arms of a courageous white trooper.[10]

Two Rode Together

Two Rode Together, Ford's 1961 Western about Comanche captives, was one of the director's later films to expose the insidious effects of social and communal bigotry. The movie follows Marshall Guthrie McCabe (James Stewart) and Lieutenant Jim Gary (Richard Widmark) in their efforts to rescue several white captives from a nearby Comanche camp. The story raises some disturbing questions about its stable, all-white frontier community in which social proprieties are but a thin disguise for suppressed racism.

As in *The Searchers*, *Two Rode Together* confronts the perpetual tension between civilization and savagery. Who really is the more savage, however, is also at the crux of this Fordian Western. McCabe's harsh warning that a captive white boy has "turned savage" beyond recognition suggests that Indian culture has debased white civilization, forever castings its victims as social pariahs within the frontier community: "That kid has braids, stiff, stinkin' braids filled with buffalo grease ... forgot English. He just grunts Comanche now. Just grunts. And given the chance, sister, he'd rape you!"

The ugly remark becomes a symbol of community bigotry. The young boy violently protests his return to society, kicking, biting, and finally stabbing an elderly white woman who befriends him. Almost predictably, the tragedy unleashes the community's anti-Indian hysteria, and they target one of their own as a scapegoat. The boy's tragic lynching by an all-white mob becomes the film's most powerful statement against civilization's hypocrisy, as one studio memo explains. "The climax can be all the more powerful by having the screenplay capitalize on the fact that a savage who cannot be civilized is being hung by people who have turned savage."[11]

Clearly, the white community wants no part of Indian society, just as the Indian captives want no part of them. The town's hatred toward Indians again surfaces when McCabe brings Elena (Linda Cristal), an attractive Mexican woman and former captured wife of the Comanche warrior, Stone Calf (Woody Strode), to a social dance. (McCabe had previously killed her husband in self-defense.) Elena stands like a young debutante at her first ball: clothed in a white gown, she appears most uneasy among the lily-white guests. The "taint" of her Indian past haunts her: several cavalrymen refuse her invitation to dance, and one person sneers if she bore any children by her Indian husband. Not surprisingly, Elena concludes, "I do not belong with these people." Ultimately, McCabe chooses to join Elena in a stage bound for California, where both may live safely removed from the narrow-minded Anglo community.

The Unforgiven

The uneasy union between a white man and an Indian woman is also the subject of *The Unforgiven* (1960), a John Huston film based upon a story by Alan LeMay, author of *The Searchers*. *The Unforgiven* is set in the post–Civil War Texas Panhandle and reveals the same fanaticism as *The Searchers*, the same primal instincts that breed hatred between Indians and whites. Kiowa-born Rachel (Audrey Hepburn) is raised by a white family when both her Indian parents are massacred. But trouble erupts when Rachel's white fiancé is shot and scalped by Indians and her true identity is revealed. The man's grieved mother points to Rachel and screams, "Red nigger! Kiowa squaw!" and the community demands Rachel's removal. One of the family members, Ben Zachary (Burt Lancaster), fights to keep Rachel within his household and wages a relentless war against the Kiowa who want her back. Ben protects Rachel with a fierce determination, an obsession beyond human reason resembling Ethan Edwards' hunt to reclaim Debbie in *The Searchers*. Rachel, in turn, shoots and kills her own Kiowa brother. The conclusion is a reversal of *The Searchers*, with Ben planning to wed his Indian stepsister.[12]

If one glaring message emerges from *The Unforgiven*, it's that white racism was rampant on America's frontier. But the white woman's shouts of "red nigger!" troubled the Motion Picture Association of America, and the organization suggested that the movie's producers drop it. "It seems to us that it is bound to be deeply injurious to the feelings of Negroes in our audience," warned Geoffrey Shurlock, who succeeded Joseph Breen as head of the Production Code Administration in 1954.[13] The offensive phrase

James Stewart (*far right*) escorts Linda Cristal (*holding his arm*) despite disapproving glances in *Two Rode Together*.
Courtesy of Bison Archives.

Burt Lancaster comforts Indian stepsister Audrey Hepburn in *The Unforgiven.*

Courtesy of Bison Archives.

stayed in the movie: by 1960, audiences were more willing to accept controversial themes that would have caused an outcry only ten years earlier.[14]

By the early 1960s, then, the Indian/white blood brothers of the postwar era had crumbled into a discord of two incompatible cultures. At worst, Native Americans were hostile opponents to civilization; at best, they were persecuted victims of a racist society. A few films broke from this dichotomy and created Romantic Indian characters within popular animal pictures like *Tonka* (1958), *Island of the Blue Dolphins* (1964), and *Indian Paint* (1965). Other films attempted to resolve Indian/white tensions through irony. In the comedy-Western *Cat Ballou* (1965), Jackson Two-Bears (Tom Nardini) is a "civilized" Sioux Indian among a band of white misfits. Jackson's polite demeanor represents the non-stereotypical Indian: he wears contemporary clothes, refuses to drink liquor, and speaks perfect English (even correcting others' grammar). *Hatari!* (1962), an epic African adventure, brings about racial harmony through a blood transfusion: a white man has the only compatible type for an injured American Indian (Bruce Cabot).

THE ISOLATED URBAN INDIAN

As white frontier communities rejected Native Americans, more and more Indian characters found themselves struggling within modern society. Urban America offered little refuge from communal bigotry, so Indians became outcasts within the cities' neglected neighborhoods. Even television picked up the theme. From 1950 to 1960, Western movie production fell nearly 50 percent, with Columbia, MGM, and Paramount each releasing only one Western in 1960 (see Table 6.1). *Variety* speculated that the plunge was caused by large doses of Western series on television, which kept fans at home instead of luring them to movie theaters.[15] One short-lived television series, *Hawk* (ABC, September to December 1966), discarded the traditional Western format and placed its Indian hero in New York City. Hawk (Burt Reynolds) is a full-blooded American Indian detective, "a loner who appears haunted by his heritage," observed *Variety*. His sexy physique combined with a muscular prowess and lover-boy eyes were supposed to charm female audiences.[16] But Hawk was the remnant of a fading genre; he wandered among the narrow dark streets as a kind of marginal man isolated within America's urban centers.

Table 6.1   Feature Films and Westerns, 1945–1965

Year	Features Released	Westerns Released	% Westerns
1945	350	80	23
1950	383	130	34
1955	254	68	27
1960	154	28	18
1965	153	22	14

Source: Edward Buscombe, ed., *The BFI Companion to the Western* (New York: Da Capo Press, 1988), p. 427 (Appendix I).

The Exiles

The Exiles (1961), an independent and relatively unknown film by first-time director Kurt MacKenzie, captures the dreary inner-city life and alienation among America's Indian youth. (A few cynics dubbed the movie, "I Was a Teenage Indian.") The movie begins with photos of historic Indian leaders then tells of how the U.S. government forced them on reservations. *The Exiles* picks up nearly one hundred years later where *The Searchers* left off and reveals the consequences of a deeply rooted social bigotry while reinforcing urban Indian stereotypes. Three Indian men lead irresponsible and reckless lives in Los Angeles; the movie's black-and-white cinematography and lack of a real narrative points to their hopelessness. Brief scenes depict Apache teenagers drinking, fighting, and smoking in dingy cafes and cavernous alleys. Families are neglected and lives are washed away with alcohol. Night draws the Indian youth to the city's scenic lookout where cars congregate and a fight erupts; daylight brings only more drinking and isolation.

Requiem for a Heavyweight

Requiem for a Heavyweight (1962), another black-and-white movie, reveals how modern society not only alienates Native Americans but exploits their traditions as well. Anthony Quinn plays Mountain Rivera, an over-the-hill boxer of Indian ancestry who must sell his own heritage for money and showmanship. His manager (Jackie Gleason), desperate because he owes money to a few city thugs, pleads with Rivera to perform an "Indian gig" during a mock wrestling match. The final shot of Rivera in breechcloth and feathered headdress, prancing and whooping about the ring and waving a tomahawk, represents one of the most morally degrading Indian images in movie history.

Requiem for a Heavyweight was first produced in 1956 as a *Playhouse 90* for CBS, with Jack Palance as a non-Indian who boards a train for a new life rather than exploit himself (as a circus clown) in the wrestling arena. Columbia studios chose instead to try another angle: Either cast a Black American as Mountain Rivera (Sammy Davis Jr. and Sidney Poitier were likely candidates), or simply point to Quinn's Mexican ancestry. (Quinn's father was part Irish and his mother was Mexican with Indian blood.) But director Ralph Nelson decided that a Black character would add a whole new racial angle to the story, while a Mexican would give "the basic problem a different coloration by having [Rivera] not an American."[17] Thus, he reasoned, an American Indian character would safely avoid the issues of race and nationality while emphasizing Rivera's alienation within urban society.

The Outsider

The Outsider (1961), a biographical story of Ira Hamilton Hayes (1923–1955), drove home the point of Indian marginality within modern-day America. The movie's account of the Pima Indian and U.S. Marine Corporal who helped raise the American flag in Iwo Jima was shot in somber black and white and represented what *Jim Thorpe—All American* might have been a decade later. Ira represented the decade's marginal man, a rejection of both Indian and white societies and a far cry from the hero of *Jim Thorpe*. Instead, he typified the lonely, tragic hero of those from other dark Westerns like *The Left-Handed Gun* (1958) with Paul Newman as Billy the Kid, and *Flaming Star* (1960), featuring Elvis Presley as the half Kiowa Indian. But Ira's struggle with postwar traumatic stress was one of Hollywood's few attempts to depict the syndrome.

The story of Ira Hayes was initially too risky during the Cold War era. Paramount Pictures, which first purchased the movie's rights in 1955, was uneasy about the story's downbeat nature, but nonetheless refused to produce a "flag-waving bit of fiction unrelated to the facts."[18] On the other hand, the U.S. Marine Corp grumbled over what they perceived as the movie's anti-patriotic theme and privately indicated that they would not cooperate with its production.[19] But the prevailing mood of anti-communism gave Paramount the jitters. The movie's theme of "racial mistreatment and injustice," confessed one executive, "would be seized on for propaganda purposes by our enemies." Six months later, Paramount dropped the project.[20]

Universal Pictures later revived the controversial Ira Hayes story. Producer Sy Bartlett had apparently seen the earlier NBC television version on Ira Hayes titled *The American* (1960) starring Lee Marvin. But Bartlett believed that the TV movie glossed too much over Ira's troublesome past. "He was no hero. He was a simple Indian," Bartlett said. "I wanted to give him a proper funeral, to put the poor guy's bones to rest and give the Indians a sense of pride in him."[21] Bartlett believed that Hayes' life story "was one of the most tragic and dramatic episodes in modern American history," and he was determined to make a picture about him. In fact, Bartlett was "smitten" with the idea, according to screenwriter Stewart Stern, who had also written *Rebel Without a Cause* and *The Ugly American* (both movies featuring similar alienated heroes).[22]

In *The Outsider*, Ira (Tony Curtis) dies a tragic World War II hero, drunk and alone in the cold desert night. ("Even the manner of his death was too distasteful for the truth," Stern wrote.[23]) The first part of the film depicts the young Marine recruit during training where he gets a taste of white bigotry. His drill sergeant asks, "How many scalps you got in your pocket?" and refers to Ira as "chief." (The sergeant later softens.) During World War II, the twenty-two-year-old, shy Marine Corporal soars to national fame when he is one of six soldiers photographed raising the U.S. flag on Mount Suribachi in 1945. Hungry reporters label Ira "the greatest Indian hero since Jim Thorpe," and female fans swoon and tear at his clothes. But for the naive Pima from the Gila River Indian Reservation in Arizona, the media hype and fanfare are nothing but a sham. Ira's best friend dies in combat ("You're the first white man that ever was my friend," he tells him), a senseless tragedy that engulfs him with guilt and despair. Government officials exploit the historic Iwo Jima moment and send Ira on a highly publicized War Bond tour. The national attention leaves the small-town recruit bewildered, and he tells the Marines, "I ain't gonna be a hypocrite no more."

Ira Hayes thus becomes a marginal man, rejected by Indian and white societies. Stern took copious notes from conversations with Ira's family, friends, and commanding staff and visited the Pima-Maricopa Indian reservation in Arizona where Ira was raised. He discovered that Ira shifted between two worlds: He was educated in

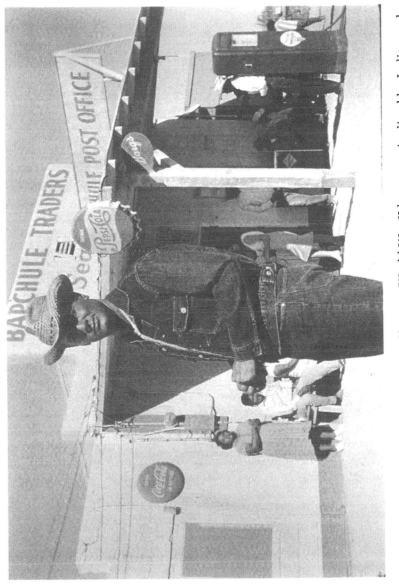

The Outsider, with Tony Curtis as Ira Hayes, a World War II hero marginalized by Indian and white societies.

Courtesy of Bison Archives.

a white school in Phoenix and later (during the Depression) moved back to the reservation. "So he never really belonged in either world," Stern noted.[24] Ira wanders from job to job and eventually retreats into a world of nightmares and alcohol. The camera often frames him in a single shot, removed from the company of other soldiers; harsh lighting splits his face into contrasting bright and dark that reinforces his marginality. Reporters discover Ira drunk and in jail, so they splatter his photo on the front page. The military is embarrassed; the Pima refer to him as a "damn disgrace." When his own tribe refuses to nominate him to its council, Ira escapes to a lonely mountain road and dies of exposure at the young age of thirty-two. He is buried at Arlington National Cemetery "with full military honors," an ironic conclusion for society's forgotten war hero. "I thought I'd better be very accurate in what I said, very careful to present Ira as he was, a real person, in a way that would be as close to the truth as I could make it," Stern said.[25]

The Outsider's theme of postwar trauma escaped many baffled reviewers. A few critics even indicated that they preferred to watch noble Indians rather than pathetic ones. Variety questioned whether an Indian would destroy himself over his best friend's death and complained, "As the hero begins to come apart at the emotional seams, so does the picture."[26] (Ira himself had once written, "I'm a vanishing American who forgot to vanish."[27]) Others grumbled over the movie's portrayal of Ira as "just another drunken Indian." "If that is all the movie-makers can make of their subject," said Time magazine, "they might better have let him rest in peace."[28]

But the Hollywood Indian could not rest in peace. As images of Indian/white coexistence collapsed, many fifties and sixties Westerns showed Native Americans fighting an embittered society and finding refuge only outside its boundaries. The communal bigotry of The Searchers and Two Rode Together had eventually alienated the movies' Native Americans in isolated reservations and neglected neighborhoods. Hollywood Indians thus emerged as the screen's persecuted victims while whites became the frontier's bloodthirsty savages. By 1970, this tension erupted into a powerful violence that would shatter the myth of Manifest Destiny and destroy the classic Hollywood Western.

7

Savagery on the Frontier

On the evening of March 23, 1973, the 45th Annual Academy Awards ceremony was coming to a close. The winner for best actor, announced Liv Ullmann and Roger Moore, was Marlon Brando for his performance as the aging Mafioso leader in *The Godfather* (1972). But Brando was nowhere. Instead, a tiny figure clad in white buckskin and wearing long black braids sashayed to the podium and brushed aside the gold Oscar statuette.

"My name is Sacheen Littlefeather," she told the astonished audience. "I'm Apache and I am president of the National Native American Affirmative Image Committee. I'm representing Marlon Brando this evening, and he has asked me to tell you in a very long speech ... that he very regretfully cannot accept this very generous award."

The audience of stars and celebrities murmured uneasily and some even whistled a few catcalls.

"And the reasons for this," continued Brando's diminutive proxy, "are the treatment of American Indians today by the film industry and on television in movie reruns and also with the recent happenings at Wounded Knee."[1]

The Academy members were aghast. In a matter of minutes, Ms. Littlefeather had summarized—in Brando's words—the crisis of contemporary American Indians. Whether Brando's motives were sincere or whether Ms. Littlefeather was really Apache (as some writers had wondered), the country's sins against its Native American people had been foisted upon Hollywood's shoulders.[2]

SETTING THE STAGE

Brando's grandstanding was perfect timing. A month before his famous Oscar rebuff, Indian activists were engaged in a bloody clash with U.S. Marshals and FBI agents at Wounded Knee, South Dakota. Members of the activist American Indian Movement (AIM) demanded swift punishment for the random murders of two Sioux men as well as an investigation into alleged Bureau of Indian Affairs misconduct. In 1972, 500 Native Americans had marched to Washington DC with their "Trail of Broken Treaties," demanding that the government disband assimilation policies and reestablish treaty relations. Angry protestors ransacked the Bureau of Indian Affairs headquarters and destroyed furniture, files, and valuable art. Activists charged that government institutions had long been bungling Indian policies; many advocated a repeal of federal assimilation and a return to the traditions and strengths of the past. Above all, they demanded political sovereignty for American Indians.

Back in Hollywood, Westerns from *The Searchers* onward had already demonstrated that Indian/white assimilation was but a fading American ideal. But by the late 1960s, Indian activism combined with Vietnam War protests and racial uprisings to set the stage for Hollywood's "anti-Westerns" and their vicious attacks against frontier white aggression. Increasingly, filmmakers revealed a hypocritical, corrupt, and violent society in response to demoralized American heroes and foundering institutions. *The Graduate* (1967), *Easy Rider* (1969), and *Zabriskie Point* (1970) showed alienated youth battling a hopelessly bigoted and materialist culture. *Catch-22* (1970) and *M*A*S*H* (1970) debunked post–World War II myths of military glory and heroism. The sacred medical institution came tumbling down with *The Hospital* (1971), and extra-marital affairs were a part of married life for *Bob and Carol and Ted and Alice* (1969). Similarly, the anti-Westerns *Little Big Man* and *Soldier Blue* shed new light on the frontier's Indian wars.

Along with the screen's increasing violence was a growing appetite for sex. A series of Supreme Court decisions eased restrictions of movie obscenity, and the MPAA's liberalized Code and Rating Administration of 1968 replaced the stringent Production Code of 1934. *Beyond the Valley of the Dolls* (1970) was the first major studio release to enter the "sexploitation" market, and *Midnight Cowboy* (1969) became Hollywood's first X-rated movie to win the Academy Award for best picture of the year. Even a few of the movies' Indian characters provided sensual material: while hard-core pornographic films like *Deep Throat* (1972) and *The Devil in Miss Jones* (1973) appeared in neighborhood movie theaters, *Indian Love Cult* (1970) had earlier highlighted the sexual adventures of Cunning Offer, Little Bird, and Princess Budding Flower. Homosexuality came out of the closet with *The Group* (1966) and *The Boys in the Band* (1970) while *Song of the Loon* (1970), billed as "the most famous gay classic of all time," featured an Indian medicine man who advocated a promiscuous lifestyle.[3]

THE FRONTIER'S WHITE SAVAGES

Hollywood's appetite for blood and gore began to shape its epic Westerns. The trend actually started in Europe: When Italian filmmaker Sergio Leone imported Clint Eastwood to star in *A Fistful of Dollars* (1964), the noisy, brutish, and action-packed "spaghetti" Western took off.[4] (Leone employed gypsies as Mexicans and Indians for his pictures.[5]) Another Italian director, Sergio Corbucci, filmed *Navajo Joe* (1966) in Spain's arid desert and cast Burt Reynolds as the tormented Indian-turned-vengeful killer. In the United States, director Sam Peckinpah added his own touches of cruelty and sadism to *The Wild Bunch* (1969).[6]

The Westerns' explosion of violence brought about a new kind of cowboy antihero. By the late 1960s, the macho, upright lawmen of *Stagecoach* and *Union Pacific* had crumbled into society's doomed outcasts. In *Butch Cassidy and the Sundance Kid* (1969), a pair of affable outlaws (Paul Newman and Robert Redford) represent the West's new breed of antiheroes whose final screen moments are frozen amidst a hail of fatal bullets. Clint Eastwood, the "Man with No Name" in Leone's trio of successful spaghetti Westerns, later returned to Hollywood as the brooding, vengeful mysterious stranger in *High Plains Drifter* (1973). As the Westerns' heir apparent to John Wayne, Eastwood wiped out the town's bad men, but when he rode off, he rode alone. The combination of antiheroism and violence also created a new breed of white savagery. Traditional glory and heroism dissipated as cowboys and frontiersmen turned into greedy, Indian-hating killers who maimed, tortured, and raped as they ventured into the frontier. These same themes previously had appeared during the 1950s (*The Last Hunt*, *The Searchers*, and *Run of the Arrow*), but the relaxed censorship regulations gave rise to even more gore and savagery a decade later.

Several years before Hollywood's era of cowboy antiheroes and violent Westerns, John Ford's *Cheyenne Autumn* exposed America's ruthless treatment of its Indians. The 1964 epic movie was Ford's last Western and by many accounts, his most problematic. Critics were sharply divided over whether his Indian portrayals were more sympathetic or merely patronizing; others praised Ford's painstaking attention to cultural and historical details only to be assailed by experts who balked at the movie's gross inaccuracies. Nevertheless, *Cheyenne Autumn* attempts to rewrite history and reveals that civilization—in the form of the military, religion, and education—destroys Indian culture and corrupts its members. The list of atrocities quickly adds up: 1,000 Northern Cheyenne are removed to Oklahoma, but only 286 remain; the Bureau of Indian Affairs fails to deliver much needed food, supplies, and medicines; one cowboy kills and scalps a hungry Cheyenne for sheer pleasure; and the army opens fire on starving Indian men, women, and children when they are detained in Fort Robinson. But at the heart of *Cheyenne Autumn* lies the real tragedy committed against the country's Native American people, the ugly blotch that brought no honor to America's history. This was the first time Ford actually admitted that Manifest Destiny was a mistake.

Tell Them Willie Boy Is Here

While *Cheyenne Autumn* was one of the first movies to show the tragedy of Manifest Destiny, later Westerns embellished white characters with an increasing appetite for blood and gore. Five years later, *Tell Them Willie Boy Is Here* (1969) would expose society's latent savagery. The movie earned a modest $2.4 million in box-office rental fees and told the story of a Paiute/Chemehuevi Indian who became the target of a vicious manhunt in 1909.[7] Robert Blake (whose alleged real-life notorieties would later match those of his on-screen characters) shoots and kills the father of his fiancée (Katharine Ross) in self-defense. As law enforcers pursue the couple across the harsh southern California desert, the incident ignites deep-rooted anti-Indian attitudes and invites bloodlust from so-called civic-minded individuals. Willie Boy's fiancée mysteriously dies (she supposedly commits suicide), and the ambivalent but sympathetic sheriff (Robert Redford) shoots and kills him. The posse gropes for Willie Boy's scalp, his boot, an ear, but the sheriff intervenes and orders the body burned. "Tell them we're all out of souvenirs," he says.[8]

Willie Boy's gray and blue tones and lifeless desert landscape create an empty, nihilistic atmosphere. The film marked Abraham Polonsky's directorial return after twenty years of blacklisting during McCarthy's anti-communism era and contains allegorical references to youth alienation and misguided Vietnam policies. Author and journalist Harry Wilson Lawton first began research on Willie Boy for a 1955 newspaper article that appeared in California's *Riverside Daily Enterprise.* Lawton's story explored the many contradictions of the Willie Boy case; his article eventually became the book, *Willie Boy: A Desert Manhunt* (1960) upon which the movie was based. (Director Polonsky was also the film's screenwriter.) Lawton chose a novelistic approach rather than a historical recreation of the actual Willie Boy manhunt. Although he said the movie differed from his book, he believed that Polonsky's version added depth to Willie Boy's story. "I like Polonsky's approach because he is psychologically faithful to the book, yet at the same time he explores the manhunt at deeper levels than the book," Lawton said in 1969.[9]

Polonsky at first had no interest in making a Western until he noticed *Willie Boy*'s theme of a generation on the run. The movie thus became a story of one man in armed revolt against an encroaching empire.[10] *Willie Boy*, he explained, spoke to young people "living in a transitional period and being driven by circumstances and values they couldn't control." Chief among those circumstances was the war in Southeast Asia. "It's fundamental to human history—this terrible thing [genocide] that we do," Polonsky said. "Not just because they're Indians, but because this is a general human situation."[11]

Little Big Man

The human situation was even more tragic in *Little Big Man* (1970). As Hollywood's quintessential anti-Western, the movie earned a whopping $15 million and spoke to American violence, youth alienation, and civilization's hypocrisy. (*Newsweek* facetiously dubbed the movie "How the West Was Lost."[12]) Arthur Penn, director of *The Left Handed Gun* (1958), *The Miracle Worker* (1962), and *Bonnie and Clyde* (1967), typically displays a strong sympathy for social outcasts and a cynicism toward human foibles. Penn labored for six years over *Little Big Man* (based upon the popular

Thomas Berger novel), which he said many studios turned down because of its attacks against white heroism. As an American Jew, Penn was deeply affected by the Holocaust and shared with Europeans a despair of the human condition. "It's almost as if all our wars and hatreds in the past have taught us nothing," he said.[13] *Little Big Man* showed another kind of genocide that Penn believed once took place in America. "You get a feeling that it's history being told another way," he said.[14]

Little Big Man's elderly Cheyenne chief, the wise Old Lodge Skins (Chief Dan George), is one of the movie's few humane characters. (The role earned Dan George an Academy Award nomination, the first time a Native North American had received the honor.[15]) Corrupt and hypocritical whites otherwise lurk around every corner. The pious Mrs. Pendrake (Faye Dunaway) devoutly recites the Bible but cheats on her husband and later becomes a prostitute; the leader of the medicine show sells bogus concoctions to gullible patrons; and the pompous, maniacal Custer suffers from an incurable delusion of grandeur. Jack Crabb (Dustin Hoffman), the movie's 121-year-old title character, is the frontier's Everyman. He's kidnapped from his Caucasian parents as a boy and raised by the Cheyenne; his near-death mishaps set up a series of allegories representing a violent and corrupt civilization.

Penn was determined to tell *Little Big Man* from the Native American point of view. He believed that Hollywood's Indian images were based upon a "pure, naked racism" and that Custer was really a "pompous, self-aggrandizing man."[16] Producer Stuart Millar put it even more bluntly: Custer was a "fanatical genocide [sic] bent on wiping the Indians out, and a sick egoist.... In our film, Custer is a dangerous paranoiac." Millar wanted *Little Big Man* to "set the record straight," which meant that Custer and his army would be the movie's villains. "We're trying to do belated justice to the Indians in this one," he explained.[17] The similarities between the movie's bloody Washita Massacre with its slaughter of Indian women and children to American killings in Vietnam are obvious. In one vivid scene, a young Cheyenne girl runs from a burning tipi, her clothes ablaze in red flames. She screams and tumbles naked to the ground. The image recalls a popular news photo from My Lai, when a terrified and nude Vietnamese girl flees a napalm explosion.[18] "It's time movies caught up with contemporary attitudes about the history of the West," observed Millar, "including attention to the significance of genocide."[19]

Sunshine (Amy Eccles) presents Jack Crabb (Dustin Hoffman) with a son in *Little Big Man*.
Courtesy of Bison Archives.

Hollywood's attention to frontier genocide brought about new allies for American Indians. The loyal Black cavalrymen (the "Buffalo Soldiers") of John Ford's *Sergeant Rutledge* (1960) fought beside their white counterparts and helped to clear the West of its Indian obstacles. But no longer would African Americans fight against Indian nations. In *The McMasters* (1970), Indians defend a Black ranch hand (Brock Peters) against local Confederate bigots. Their warrior leader offers his sister to Peters as a gesture of friendship. *Buck and the Preacher* (1971), a Western directed by and starring Sidney Poitier, shows former Black slaves in search of fertile land and freedom. "Tell him his enemies are our enemies," Poitier says to a wary Indian leader. The warriors eventually defend the Black immigrants from a murderous southern posse.

The Apotheosis of Violence: *Soldier Blue*

Critics of America's bloody Indian wars found their most sympathetic ally with *Soldier Blue* (1970). The movie's re-creation of the 1864 Sand Creek Massacre in Colorado earned a total of $4 million for its 1970/71 release and shocked audiences with its wholesale butchery and slaughter of America's Indians.[20] Director Ralph Nelson, known for his persevering and gentle heroes in *Lilies of the Field* (1963), *Father Goose* (1964), and *Charly* (1968), promised to deliver a bloodier and gorier Indian massacre than any previous Western.

Nelson was at first reluctant to direct *Soldier Blue*. He read the novel *Arrow in the Sun* (the movie's literary source) and turned it down because he thought that it was a rather routine trek story without any climax. But when screenwriter John Gay promised to include a cavalry attack on an Indian village, Nelson became interested and plunged into research on America's mistreatment of its Indians.[21]

> The more I researched, the more enraged I became. The United States negotiated over 400 treaties with Indian "Nations," as they were first called, and not one treaty was ever honored.... The [N]ative Americans helped Pilgrims, showing them how to grow corn and other crops. Their reward—extinction.[22]

So enraged was Nelson that he didn't think the script's climatic attack was big enough. He then combined the Sand Creek with the Wounded Knee Massacre, added some make-up, special effects, and stunt players, and created a detailed storyboard of the movie's gruesome finale.[23]

Soldier Blue thus became Nelson's personal antiwar statement. The filmmaker had served honorably in the Air Force during World War II, but America's recent atrocities in Southeast Asia shattered his illusions of military glory and national patriotism. "We like to think of our soldiers as epitomes of grown-up Boy Scouts incapable of evil," said Nelson. "[But] in *Soldier Blue*, I have tried to show the true face of war ... how it changes normally peaceful men into savage beasts."[24] News photos of scared and mutilated Vietnamese victims infuriated Nelson, so he channeled his anger into *Soldier Blue*'s bloody scenes. "It was about war—all war," he explained. It is war which is obscene."[25] Although Nelson denied that My Lai influenced *Soldier Blue*, he admitted that in the movie's massacre of Indian women and children, "history was repeating itself."[26]

"In 5,000 years of recorded civilization, mankind has written history in blood," begins *Soldier Blue*. The story follows the adventures of Cresta (Candice Bergen), the Caucasian former wife to a Cheyenne chief (Jorge Rivero), and Honus (Peter Strauss), a young, naïve soldier assigned to the cavalry's Indian-fighting unit. In the opening scene, Cheyenne warriors attack and kill a wagon's army escort, leaving only Cresta and Honus to fend for themselves in unfriendly Indian Territory.

But Cresta is a well-seasoned frontierswoman. Her four-letter expletives and brash behavior (she burps after meals) represent the Westerns' newly liberated feminist. She teaches Honus wilderness survival and a few tips on Cheyenne culture while affectionately calling him a son of a bitch. Their friendly interlude (which blossoms into an unlikely romance) is interrupted when soldiers ruthlessly massacre 500 innocent Cheyenne and Arapaho at Sand Creek. The cavalry rapes Indian women, cuts off their breasts, disembowels warriors, and shoots helpless children point-blank. Victorious soldiers dance with the Indians' scalps and pose in front of the human carnage for eager photographers. "We have given the Indian a lesson he will soon not forget," boasts the army colonel.

Soldier Blue's bloody theater of *Grand Guignol* offended many. "Is there some sort of chastening, ennobling gain to be realized through watching this sickening carnage?" queried the *Los Angeles Times*. Several reviewers pointed out that the movie merely reversed the bad-Indian-good-white stereotypes and rubbed the audience's noses in bloodshed. But the *New York Times* complained that the film's massacre scene did not go far enough.[27] Vine Deloria Jr., noted Standing Rock Sioux scholar and author, agreed. "Nelson is kind to his audience," he said. "Some atrocities committed by U.S. Cavalrymen against Indian women and children simply could not be shown on the screen."[28] With *Soldier Blue*, the Westerns' mythical heroes faded into the past as America's fertile frontier became a wasteland of mass Indian graves.

SURVIVAL IN THE WILDERNESS

While many anti-Westerns showed savage whites killing off innocent Indians, others explored Native American survival in a harsh environment. Life in the wilderness included its own kind of hardships and dangers in which only the fittest might survive. If violence on the frontier meant whites decimating Indians, then Native Americans had their bloody traditions of warfare and torture as well. A few Hollywood artists were simply fascinated with what they perceived as the "savage" aspects of Indian culture. For them, Indians offered curious rituals to photograph, much like the bizarre habits of people throughout the world in the Italian exploitation documentary *Mondo Cane* (1961). Although these filmmakers sensationalized Native American lifestyle, they offered a multidimensional layer to the traditional Indian stereotype.

The violence in *Ulzana's Raid* (1972), for example, suggests that in a world of hostile Indian/white relations, only moral ambiguity remains. *Ulzana's Raid* is the story of a fearsome Apache warrior (Joaquin Martinez) who escapes Arizona's San Carlos reservation and embarks upon a murdering rampage. Ulzana's pursuit becomes a game of cat-and-mouse as he cleverly eludes the posse and tortures innocent settlers along the way. The movie inverts key elements of the classic Western: When a cavalryman escorts a woman and her son through Indian Territory, Ulzana attacks, and the soldier flees the scene despite the woman's screams for help. Momentarily, he spins around and shoots her in the head, then turns the gun on himself. (In Ford's *Stagecoach*, the cavalry's bugle call instead saves the woman.) The Apaches butcher the soldier and play ball with his heart, prompting one naïve army lieutenant to denounce the Indians as un-Christian. "What bothers you, Lieutenant," says the posse leader (Burt Lancaster), "is you don't like to think of white men behaving like Indians. It kinda confuses the issue, doesn't it?" In the final scene, Ulzana chooses to die rather than succumb to white authority. "He is, in every way, a most worthy adversary," explained director Robert Aldrich.[29] Eighteen years after Massai's compromise to white civilization in *Apache*, Aldrich was finally able to allow his hero to die an Indian.

A few years later, *The White Dawn* (1974) revealed how an encounter between New England whalers and the Inuit of Canada's Northwest Territories turned to violence. The movie was based upon James Houston's 1971 novel of a true story set in the 1890s about stranded whalers on Baffin Island. The film is a far cry from Hollywood's previous Romantic versions of Inuit lifestyle in *Eskimo* and the later *Savage Innocents* (1960). In *The White Dawn*, the hunters watch in horror as the Inuit drink blood and later kill a polar bear, tear the animal apart, and eat its heart. The hunters dismiss the Inuit as savages, then help themselves to their women and introduce them to gambling and liquor. (The movie employed Inuit actors in main roles and subtitled their language.) The two cultures inevitably clash: their patience exhausted with their greedy guests, the Inuit brutally execute all three whalers. If the violence between the hunters and the Inuit appeared familiar, it's because author and screenwriter Houston had studied *A Man Called Horse* while working on *The White Dawn*. Apparently, he wanted some insight into Indian/white cultural contact.[30]

A Man Called Horse

Likewise, *A Man Called Horse* (1970) attempts to show the harsh survival within Indian culture. The movie's director, Elliot Silverstein, was well acquainted with Hollywood Westerns: for *Cat Ballou*, he successfully satirized the genre by portraying a down-and-out, heavy drinking, aging gunslinger (Lee Marvin) as the story's comedic hero. Previous Westerns, he believed, either treated Indians as enemy warriors or as partners to a cowboy hero in a dialogue of peace.[31] *A Man Called Horse* would instead look at Sioux lifestyle, which Silverstein described as "savage beauty in a primitive environment." This savagery, he reasoned, was dictated by the "Great Natural Law" and the Indians' obedience to it. Simply put, it was life feeding on life to sustain life and create life.[32]

[Native Americans] followed the same law as the animals around them; that is, survival. In order to survive, you must eat; in order to eat, you must kill. The survival of the tribe seemed more important than the survival of any individual in the tribe.... It was interesting to me because our culture tends to support the rights of individuals even when [they're] in conflict with the good of society.[33]

Unlike his contemporaries, Silverstein drew no parallels to Vietnam. Neither did he cast Indians as Noble Savages or victims of white genocide. Instead, his Indians were of a raw and brutal nature, albeit one based upon survival. When *A Man Called Horse* shows an elderly Sioux woman abandoned and left to die in the snow (a scene that infuriated Indian activist Russell Means), Silverstein believed that such an event might be possible for a people who struggled to survive in the wilderness as their food supply dwindled over time. "It's only savage if you view it from a Judeo-Christian point of view," he said. "But Indians were only obeying the law [of survival]."[34]

Silverstein never read Dorothy M. Johnson's original short story, "A Man Called Horse." First published in *Collier's* in 1950, Johnson's tale depicts the adventures of an 1840s English aristocrat who is captured by Crow Indians and eventually proves himself a warrior. Johnson's version contained no references to the Sun Dance ceremony, but Jack DeWitt's original script did.[35] Producer Sanford Howard bought the film's rights and signed DeWitt as screenwriter; he sold the story to Cinema Center Films (the short-lived theatrical arm of CBS), hired Silverstein as director, and changed the Crow to Sioux.[36] Howard employed members of the Rosebud Sioux tribe in South Dakota as extras, although the film was actually shot in Mexico. The filmmakers also added Lakota dialogue (without English subtitles), and signed on Clyde Dollar, the Sioux's resident historian, as the movie's technical consultant.

Studio perceptions of Native Americans occasionally clashed with those of the filmmakers. Apparently, an early scene of Indians chuckling at Richard Harris bathing in the nude raised a concern. Cinema Center Films believed that Indians were not supposed to laugh, so they advised Silverstein to modify the scene. Silverstein winced: his Indians might be hostile to white intruders, but they did have a range of emotions as well. "By trying to show Indians as human beings and not as savage members who prey on white people, I was threatening the vested interests," he told the *Boston Herald*.[37] Producer Howard had the movie's vested interests in mind when he politely advised Silverstein to refrain from publicly making negative comments.[38]

The filmmakers also had to contend with Richard Harris, who portrayed the movie's white captive John Morgan. The burly Irish actor had a reputation for his displays of temper and walking off the set (Silverstein actually wanted Tom Courtenay for the lead, but the production company favored Harris).[39] For *A Man Called Horse*, Harris demanded that the story revolve around his character: a clause in his contract stipulated that he approve any alterations in the script that would reduce the size and importance of his role.[40] Harris insisted that he be the first to run heroically to try to save his Indian wife (Corinna Tsopei) when she's shot rather than have the woman's elderly mother (Dame Judith Anderson) instinctively protect her daughter. Such demands served to spotlight Morgan as the movie's central hero. But occasionally, Harris had to step aside: when the script called for Morgan to eventually leave the tribe and return to England, Harris wanted to stay and become the Sioux chief.[41] Silverstein instead convinced him to leave with an escort of Sioux warriors (although Morgan does return in the sequel).[42]

Meanwhile, historian Clyde Dollar kept a watchful eye on the movie's production and often challenged the filmmakers' claims to authenticity. Such disagreements occasionally occur on a Hollywood set, but a movie about America's indigenous people at the height of Indian activism was bound to arouse controversy. Dollar was especially adamant, as he believed that the film's credibility—or lack of it—would follow him throughout his professional life.[43] Any deviation from his suggestions thus became a point of contention. He bristled when the filmmakers substituted a female pheasant for a prairie chicken (he insisted that pheasants didn't appear on the plains until the twentieth century); he objected to a berry bag in place of a basket; and he balked at Harris wearing an Apache-like headband. These blatant errors, Dollar warned, could "jeopardize any claim to fame as 'historically authentic' that *A Man Called Horse* might make."[44] But Silverstein pointed out that although historical fact was the basis of the movie, its primary goal was entertainment. "In fact," he explained, "if the scholars are offended by the berry bag then the motion picture has failed because we will have spent not enough time taking their attention to the faces of the actors."[45]

Many Indian activists were offended, especially of the movie's rather gruesome Sun Dance ceremony. In the film, Morgan is hoisted by sharp bones that pierce his pectorals and dangle his body high off the ground. (He thus attains tribal status and marries his Indian bride.) Activists criticized the depiction of the sacred ritual for

A Man Called Horse. Dame Judith Anderson (*center*) gives orders to her white captive (Richard Harris) while Corinna Tsopei (*left*) looks on.

Courtesy of Bison Archives.

portraying Indians "as a bestial race preoccupied with violence" and further denounced the movie as "humiliating and degrading."[46] Sioux activist Russell Means called the movie racist and chastised the studio for hiring Clyde Dollar, a white man, to document Rosebud Sioux history.[47] Another AIM activist, Dennis Banks, said that Greek actress and former Miss Universe Corinna Tsopei was a sellout to Native American actresses. Silverstein initially wanted Buffy Sainte-Marie for the part, but the Native Canadian singer was not interested. To him, Tsopei looked too much like a beauty contest winner among the elderly Sioux women. "She stands out like a Hollywood princess," Silverstein said. "I wanted to soften her a bit."[48]

As the controversy heightened, Dollar felt caught in the middle. He was loyal to the production company, but as the Sioux's appointed tribal historian, he tried to explain that the AIM activists did not represent the Rosebud tribe. "We consider the [AIM] protest an affront to our participation in the film," he said. Dollar's headaches grew worse when the Minnesota Department of Human Rights announced that *A Man Called Horse* "perpetuates a Caucasian superiority and neglects to consider the sensitivities of the American Indian nation." Not so, responded producer Howard, who ticked off a list of Indian experts endorsing the film's authenticity. AIM created their own list of gripes and charged that Hollywood manipulated Indians by appearing to seek authenticity and buying their services.[49]

Authenticity aside, the movie's violence and savagery captivated American audiences. *A Man Called Horse* brought a respectable $6 million during its first year and prompted two sequels, *The Return of a Man Called Horse* (1976) and *Triumphs of A Man Called Horse* (1982). Less known was *Chato's Land* (1972), a Michael Winner film starring Charles Bronson as the vengeful Apache warrior who picks off his ruthless white opponents one by one. Its story of hunters-become-hunted is identical to Winner's later *Death Wish* trilogy (also starring Charles Bronson). The movie's earning of a moderate $1.5 million pointed to the audiences' continual fascination with seventies' Westerns and their graphic violence.[50]

Jeremiah Johnson

Jeremiah Johnson (1972) is based on the true story of a nineteenth-century mountain trapper who despises war and its violence yet becomes exactly what he has despised. The rugged and scraggly looking Johnson (portrayed in the movie by the rather stately Robert Redford) actually became a kind of folk hero embodying courage and individualism. In the movie, Johnson is a deserter of military service who grows weary of bloodshed and civilization, so he seeks refuge as a trapper and learns Indian ways in the Rocky Mountains. But he runs afoul of the Crow Indians when he leads a cavalry troop through sacred tribal burial grounds. The Crow retaliate and murder Johnson's surrogate son and pregnant Indian wife. The pacifist mountain man thus turns aggressive, slaughtering the Crow and becoming a sort of legend surrounded by blood.

"The real Jeremiah Johnson," said the late Edward Anhalt (who shared screenwriting credit with John Milius), "killed 247 Crow Indians and then ate their livers, and that's not nice."[51] Indeed, the husky trapper earned the nickname of "liver-eating Johnson" because of his cannibalistic habits. Redford was not about to eat any Crow livers, so his character instead became a chivalrous Indian fighter. In fact, director Sydney Pollack (*The Scalphunters*, *Tootsie*, *Out of Africa*) had discarded an alternative ending of the film that would have shown Johnson frozen in the snow.[52] The movie's final shot instead shows the noble Johnson and the old Crow chief alone in the wilderness, giving each other a kind of peace sign. "Maybe one can read a metaphor for today's problems of useless wars and killing arising over an improper understanding between two nations or cultures," *Variety* surmised.[53] *Jeremiah Johnson* earned an impressive $22 million following its initial release and subsequent reissue in 1974 and 1975.[54]

ACTIVISM ON THE RESERVATION

While Westerns exposed violence on the frontier, other movies attempted to portray the problems of Native Americans in contemporary settings. But since the days of the early talking films, the public showed little interest in the subject. Movies that explored the bigotry and exploitation among America's Indian reservations for the most part were only of fleeting interest.

Although a film like *Flap!* (1970) ignited a controversy among Indian leaders, it failed to attract much of an audience. The contemporary story of an angry Indian war veteran (Anthony Quinn) who incites a protest was based upon Clair Huffaker's novel, *Nobody Loves a Drunken Indian*. Several Indian tribes balked at the book's offensive title, including a Navajo tribal leader. "I don't think the title is doing the Indian people justice and is in very poor taste," he said. New Mexico's Pueblo leaders appropriately pointed out that "nobody loves a drunken Indian—or a drunken anybody!"[55] Huffaker, in turn, suggested that if Indians had the patience and time to read the novel, "they'll see how shortsighted their outrage to the title is."[56] But the movie's producers were eager to quell the controversy, so they changed the title to *Nobody Loves Flapping Eagle* (the leading character's name). That disappointed a Santa Clara Indian community leader, who complained that the new title "loses a little impact." He promptly circulated a petition to restore the original one.[57]

Nevertheless, *Flap!* flopped at the box office. *When the Legends Die* (1972) also passed unnoticed, along with *House Made of Dawn* (1972), based upon N. Scott Momaday's Pulitzer Prize–winning novel, and *Journey Through Rosebud* (1972) with its story of alcoholism, poverty, and depression on South Dakota's Rosebud Indian reservation. *Variety* warned that *Rosebud*'s financial outlook was dubious and its melancholic theme unattractive.[58] As the novelty of the anti-Western and its Indian victims had begun to wear off, audiences again seemed unwilling to accept contemporary Indians as entertainment.

The Legacy of *Billy Jack*

If the modern Indian did have any appeal, America's rebellious youth found it in *Billy Jack* (1971). For several years (and several sequels), the character of Billy Jack evolved into a kind of cult hero that spoke to youth alienation and antiwar sentiment. The story of a half-Indian former war hero (Tom Laughlin) takes place on a contemporary reservation in which local townsfolk and their elected officials are really transplanted southern white bigots. Billy represents the guardian of Native American rights, and he readily employs karate (hapkido) against any white who transgresses. His Caucasian girlfriend (Delores Taylor) operates a school on the reservation, and when she's raped by a local bully, Billy kills the culprit. The police handcuff Billy and haul him away as the Indian youth rally to his defense.

Billy Jack was essentially a one-man show. The movie's actor/writer/director Tom Laughlin established an off-screen identity that seemed to merge into that of Billy Jack's. The former football player turned movie tycoon initially created the Billy Jack hero for *Born*

Losers (1967) in which he played a mild-mannered ex-Green Beret who takes on some goonish motorcyclists. Laughlin's first encounter with Indians occurred in South Dakota, where he met his actress/wife Taylor. "I had never seen anything like the reservation," he said of its depressed conditions. "The Indians lived in abandoned cars, winter and summer." When Laughlin learned that a local church had offered the Indians an open drainage pipe for a shower, he was outraged. "I was so incensed by the barbarism that I went home and wrote the *Billy Jack* thing," he said.[59] The story of a local store that refused service to an Indian family and dumped flour on them (to make them "white") found its way into a key scene in *Billy Jack*.[60]

Laughlin's rugged individualism and antiestablishment beliefs became legendary in Hollywood. Twentieth Century Fox was *Billy Jack*'s original distributor, but Laughlin accused production head Richard Zanuck of stealing the movie and butchering it. "He was the campaign chairman for Richard Nixon and didn't like the movie's anti-Nixon references," Laughlin said. Undaunted, Laughlin stole the movie's soundtrack and left Zanuck 250,000 feet of film with no dialogue or music. "We wanted to make sure the spirituality and integrity of the Indian message was not destroyed," Laughlin recalled.[61] Fox, unable to do much with a mute print, sold it back to Laughlin who then sold it to Warner Bros. But Laughlin accused Warner of trying to sabotage the movie's distribution by initially releasing it to drive-ins and porno houses. "They wanted to teach me a lesson," he said, then slapped the studio with a $51 million lawsuit. Several years later, Warner sold *Billy Jack* to NBC television, and Laughlin filed another lawsuit alleging antitrust violations. (Both suits were eventually settled.)[62] If nothing else, Laughlin's enemies had to concede that Hollywood had picked on the wrong guy.

Billy Jack attracted audiences who became increasingly sympathetic toward the American counterculture movement. Noted critic Rex Reed wrote a glowing review and drew parallels between the movie and the fight for Indian rights, the militant vs. pacifist left, and the current generation gap.[63] *Variety*, on the other hand, complained that the film's message was "rammed down the spectators' throats."[64] Nevertheless, the movie's youthful theme paid off. *Billy Jack* earned an admirable $4 million in 1971, which grew to $8.3 million for a 1973 reissue and $13 million by 1974. A sequel, *The Trial of Billy Jack* (1974), drew upon recent events of My Lai, Kent State, and even the Nixon pardon. Loyal youth fans again flocked to the box office and the movie earned $15 million that year with an additional $6.7 million in 1975.[65] But the novelty eventually wore off. The second sequel, *Billy Jack Goes to Washington* (1977), played at only limited theaters because Laughlin tried unsuccessfully to distribute the movie himself. His final installment, *The Return of Billy Jack*, was never completed.[66]

Although *Billy Jack* was a box-office winner, *One Flew Over the Cuckoo's Nest* (1975) emerged as the decade's most notable film with a modern-day Indian hero. The movie surprised many with its $57 million earnings and four major Oscar awards.[67] Critics raved about Ken Kesey's story of a cheerful immoralist (Jack Nicholson) and his fanciful escapades in a state mental hospital. Director Milos Forman, who fled the communist regime in former Czechoslovakia, had a penchant for characters who expressed themselves within a highly structured and restrictive society.[68] In *Cuckoo's Nest*, the real hero is Chief Bromden, the husky Indian who feigns muteness then ultimately smashes a window to escape the oppressive mental institution. Forman and coproducer Michael Douglas insisted upon casting a real Indian for the part and discovered the unknown six-foot six-inch Will Sampson.[69] "This was certainly a role that was positive and saw an Indian as a human being," said the Creek actor, who fought hard for Indian roles in Hollywood. "I could relate to how he felt."[70]

THE DEATH OF THE WESTERN

The immense reception to *One Flew Over the Cuckoo's Nest* ironically coincided with the Hollywood Indian's demise. The 1970s saw a sharp decline in the Westerns' popularity: the surge of 130 cowboy pictures released in 1950 plunged to a mere seven by 1977.[71] The coup de grace fell in 1980 with *Heaven's Gate*, a lavish three-hour spectacle about the bloody cattlemen wars in nineteenth-century Wyoming. *Heaven's Gate* (or, "The Movie That Killed The Western") was such an unqualified disaster that studios shied away from Westerns for the entire decade.[72] Like the aging John Wayne in *The Shootist* (1976), legendary cowboys and gunslingers thus faded into dying icons of the Old West. Outer space became the movies' new frontier as science fiction films reworked the Western genre and supplied their own colorful characters and moral conflicts. Producer Gene Roddenberry's ideas for the *Star Trek* series came from his days as head writer for television's *Have Gun Will Travel*.

Jack Nicholson (*left*) shows Will Sampson how to aim the basketball in *One Flew Over the Cuckoo's Nest.*
Courtesy of Bison Archives.

Roddenberry saw similarities between space exploration and American pioneers crossing the desert, so he created a "wagon train to the stars," or a "star trek" TV series.[73] Later, movies such as *Close Encounters of the Third Kind* (1977), *Star Wars* (1977), and *Star Trek: The Motion Picture* (1979) offered battlegrounds with modern technology and special effects that rendered the traditional cowboy useless.

The trend away from Westerns forced Hollywood Indians outside society's boundaries. *One Flew Over the Cuckoo's Nest*—in spite of Will Sampson's notable performance—had confined its Indian hero to a state mental hospital. *Harry and Tonto* (1974) placed Chief Dan George in a jail cell with Art Carney. *48 HRS.* (1982) included an Indian outlaw among a group of trigger-happy convicts. In *The Manitou* (1978) and *Nightwing* (1979), Indian characters and their mystical practices belonged to another world, far beyond civilization's comprehension.

As the Hollywood Western gradually faded, television attempted to resurrect the traditional Indian and his noble past. By the early 1970s, a series of antipollution commercials showed careless citizens littering America's lakes and forests. A sad Indian, Iron Eyes Cody, turned toward the audience with long braids, a single feather in his hair, and a tear trickling down his cheek. Hollywood's legendary Indian hero of more than one hundred motion pictures watched as contemporary America turned into a wasteland.

But the fact that the aging Cody, supposedly of Cherokee/Cree descent, was actually an Italian American was never an issue back then. Born Oscar DiCorte in Louisiana, Cody took on an identity that came to symbolize the country's quintessential Plains Indian, the last of the pure, uncorrupt Native inhabitants untouched by civilization.[74] His timing was perfect: the commercial appeared on the heels of Indian activism during which tribal resurgence and Indian autonomy meshed with the hippie back-to-nature movement. Besides, Cody's image as America's Indian hero was firmly etched in the minds of his many adoring fans and a media that preferred to cling to a comfortable stereotype. With his "Keep America Beautiful" public service television spots, he embodied the country's vision of a Noble Savage and simply looked like what America thought Indians should look like. Few were willing to part with it.

As Cody's teary-eyed noble Indian mourned the loss of America's wilderness, he simultaneously signaled the passing of the Hollywood Western and its Native American characters. A few feeble attempts like *Windwalker* (1980) briefly resurrected a Romanticized vision of Indian culture. The movie's story of the Cheyennes' struggle against their traditional Crow enemies featured British actor Trevor Howard as the Indian lead, a reminder that Hollywood was reluctant to gamble with Native American talent. Television's pro-Indian sagas—*I Will Fight No More Forever* (ABC, 1975), *Mystic Warrior* (ABC, 1984), and *Roanoak* (PBS, 1986)—struggled to fill the gap by rewriting American history. But such endeavors failed to revive the dying Western and its noble Indians. That wouldn't happen until 1990.

8

Beyond the Western

The success of Kevin Costner's *Dances With Wolves* in 1990 surprised many. Newspapers lauded the movie as "a technical marvel" and "the best Western since John Ford left us." Others praised Costner for "almost single handedly righting all the imperialistic wrongs of the entire [Western] genre."[1] Even skeptics who prematurely dubbed the project "Kevin's Gate" (a reference to the 1980 disaster, *Heaven's Gate*) were impressed. Costner, the movie's co-producer, director, and star, simply had proved the cynics wrong. His three-hour Western epic earned a hefty $184 million and captured seven Academy Awards, including best picture of the year.[2] But *Dances With Wolves*' many accolades reiterated that the Indian's movie image appeared to be firmly embedded within the American Western. Although Indian-themed non-Westerns also appeared during the decade, their weak box-office returns signaled that audiences still preferred Native Americans in epic Westerns.

Nevertheless, the American Indian was back on the screen. With the exception of a few fleeting low-budget movies like *War Party* (1988) and *Powwow Highway* (1989), the previous decade had been sparse for Hollywood's Indians.[3] Politically, *Dances With Wolves* was timely: in August of the same year, Congress declared November as American Indian Heritage Month; by October, they passed the Native American Languages Act, followed by the Native American Graves Protection and Repatriation Act (to return Indian remains and artifacts to tribes). Furthermore, the nation's quincentenary was only two years away, and if nothing else, Costner's epic reminded Americans that Indians occupied the country long before Christopher Columbus set foot on it.

American Indians quickly became hot property in Hollywood. Studios scrambled to duplicate the success of *Dances With Wolves* and created a cycle of sympathetic Indian-themed movies. Agents scouted the country for Native American actors, and producers hired Indian consultants to ward off charges of cultural or historical inaccuracy. The many claims that *Dances With Wolves* was the first movie to hire Indian actors, the first to employ authentic Native American language, and the first to cast Indians in a sympathetic light passed largely unchallenged by Indians and non-Indians alike. Instead, the film's loyal fans believed that Hollywood had finally said its long-overdue mea culpa. "For the first time ever, in [the] history of Hollywood," wrote one reviewer from the *Lakota Times*, "Native Americans are real people."[4]

RETURN OF THE WESTERN

Dances With Wolves

Dances With Wolves resurrected the Romantic image of the movies' Indians and set the tone for the decades' Westerns. Costner's vision of the Sioux before white contact echoed Jean Jacques Rousseau's Noble Savage living in a "pure state of nature," far removed from the vices and corruption of civilization. The Lakota of *Dances With Wolves* were gentle, wise, and childlike—the antithesis of their decadent white counterparts. In the movie, Costner portrays Lieutenant John J. Dunbar, a Civil War hero who longs for the Acadian wilderness and searches for a life uncontaminated by contemporary society. He finds it among the Lakota Sioux and briefly joins their idyllic community. "I've never known a people so eager to laugh, so devoted to family," he says of the Lakota. "The only word that comes to mind is harmony." Civilization, on the other hand, is vulgar and corrupt: The army tramples the Indian's sacred homeland; a deranged military officer shoots himself in the head; and white hunters deposit bloody carcasses of slaughtered buffalo across the fertile land. Dunbar and his wife (a Caucasian woman adopted by the Indians) must eventually depart into the wilderness and fend for themselves against their white enemies.

The movie's noble Indians notwithstanding, its conclusion was a source of conflict. In the 1988 paperback novel *Dances With Wolves*

Dances With Wolves. Dunbar (Kevin Costner, *left*) with Wind In His Hair (Rodney Grant) at the buffalo hunt.

Courtesy of Bison Archives.

(published by Fawcett Books), author Michael Blake made Dunbar and his wife remain with the Indians. But Costner felt differently. "Kevin was adamant that he wanted to leave [the tribe]. I don't think he ever fully embraced the feeling of 'going Native,'" Blake said. Blake initially objected to the change but realized that as the movie's screenwriter, his powers were more limited than studio producers. (Blake's adaptation of his novel won him an Academy Award for best screenplay.) But he also understood that Costner came from a different world—a white, middle-class suburban community in Orange County, California, where Blake described him as a "frat guy" with a taste for adventure. For Costner, *Dances With Wolves* was merely a James Fenimore Cooperesque vision of romance, a Boy Scout's rendition of life among the Indians. In fact, Blake remembers how Costner was "stunned speechless" over the movie's enormous reception. "He had no idea how deep this ran and what a deep effect it had on people," Blake said.[5]

Blake approached the subject differently. Years ago, the young, unknown writer earned a living in Los Angeles by working for the liberal *Los Angeles Free Press*. He read Dee Brown's *Bury My Heart at Wounded Knee* (the poignant Native American version of Western settlement) and discovered that compared to the cardboard characters of cheaply made Westerns, Indians were "real people." Brown's book stimulated him to read more about Indian culture during a period in which he felt "disenchanted with society." "[The book] was so great it coincided with how I felt life should be conducted in a more simple, fundamental way," Blake explained. "It's almost like back to the spirit, back to the soul." It was also back to nature, for Blake was an outspoken environmentalist and animal-rights activist who felt a strong kinship with the Native American community. When Costner suggested he write a novel about Plains Indians, Blake gave up his job, lived in his car, and wrote *Dances With Wolves*. "I was deeply motivated to portray Indians as people rather than as one-dimensional characters," he said.[6]

Many of the movie's white characters, however, do appear one dimensional. Indeed, the film's non-Indians—along with the evil Pawnee warriors—create a sharp contrast to the idyllic Sioux. But Blake believed that these portrayals were realistic. "The quality of people they were getting in the army out [West] was about as low as you can get," he explained of the post–Civil War military personnel. The character of Major Fambrough (who shoots himself in the head) was based upon a real army officer who actually committed suicide.

But Stands With A Fist, the white woman captive who marries Dunbar, did have a human dimension. Her life with the Sioux was based upon the story of Cynthia Ann Parker, the white girl captured by Comanches and mother of Quanah Parker (a Comanche tribal and spiritual leader and later a respected statesman).[7]

The movie's marriage of a white woman to a Caucasian man, however, carefully avoids any issue of Indian/white miscegenation. Unlike *Run of the Arrow* in 1957, in which Rod Steiger actually marries a Sioux, Dunbar instead takes a white woman as his wife. For Blake, Stands With A Fist was a literary device, a bridge for Dunbar to communicate with Native American society. "The idea of having someone that could help him access [Lakota] society made a lot of sense to me," he said.[8] In *The Holy Road* (Random House, 2002), Blake's sequel to *Dances With Wolves*, Texas Rangers attack the Indian village and recapture Dunbar's wife.

The movie's production crew struggled with problems of location and talent. In Blake's novel, Dunbar lives among the Comanche rather than the Lakota. If the movie's substitution of Sioux for Comanche appeared like another Hollywood cliché, Blake explained that the Comanche tribe in Oklahoma offered only a small talent pool. Besides, South Dakota boasted a large herd of buffalo (which the crew needed for the panoramic hunting scenes) along with many Sioux Indians who knew the Lakota language.[9] The late Native American educator Doris Leader Charge portrayed Pretty Shield, the wife of Chief Ten Bears (Floyd Red Crow Westerman) in the movie. She gave the cast a three-week cram course in the Lakota language and translated the script from English to Lakota.[10]

Costner no doubt had a huge winner on his hands. Many Native Americans were thrilled, but several critics scoffed at what they perceived as his attempt to glamorize the Sioux. Costner's movie displayed nothing of the fierceness and brutality of enemy torture and no mention of the Sun Dance that was part of Sioux life. The liberal *New Yorker* magazine pointed to the movie's childish naiveté, adding, "This is a nature-boy movie, a kid's daydream of being Indian." The *New York Times* agreed that Costner's epic was merely a nostalgic journey into Hollywood's era of bygone Westerns: "The movie teeters on the edge of *Boy's Life* literature, that is, on the brink of silliness." The weekly *Nation* was thoroughly disgusted and recommended that "the Lakota should Sioux."[11]

The critics' snide comments caused a few Native Americans to wince. *Dances With Wolves* portrayed Indian characters in a positive light, they pointed out, and showed the world that Indians were more than just screaming, scalp-hungry savages. Furthermore, Native Canadian actor Graham Greene (Oneida) earned an Oscar nomination for the movie's best supporting actor, marking the second time (after Chief Dan George) that a North American Indian received the honor. Many Indian people felt vindicated, at least by Hollywood, so cynical reviewers quickly became targets for ridicule. "Why save all their poison for *Dances With Wolves*?" wondered Tim Giago, noted Oglala Sioux columnist and publisher. Giago denounced those who criticized the movie for glorifying Sioux culture and condemning white civilization. In his words, these misguided people were simply "Indian-bashing columnists."[12]

Among other Native Americans, however, the reaction was mixed. "There's a lot of good feeling about the film in the Indian community, especially among the tribes. I think it's going to be very hard to top this one," said the soft-spoken Michael Smith (Sioux), Director of San Francisco's annual American Indian Film festival. But Blackfeet filmmaker George Burdeau was less sanguine. "I want to say 'how nice,'" Burdeau remarked. "But no matter how sensitive and wonderful this movie is, you have to ask who's telling the story. It's certainly not an Indian."[13]

Hollywood, meanwhile, continued to bask in the profits of *Dances With Wolves*. The movie's worldwide receipts of $424 million more than doubled its North American box-office earnings.[14] The Western and its Native American characters were cyclical: Two decades before *Dances With Wolves*, *Little Big Man* had set the trend for sympathetic Indian-themed movies in the 1970s, as *Broken Arrow* had established it in the 1950s. By 1990, *Dances With Wolves* had brought back the epic Western, and the decade's other popular cowboy pictures (*Unforgiven*, *Tombstone*, and *Maverick*) showed that the genre was a recurring favorite among audiences. "The fever will probably break as one or two Westerns fail, but for the moment the Western is back," the *New York Times* announced.[15] As long as Westerns were popular, Native Americans would remain on the movie screen.

The Last of the Mohicans

Two popular successors to *Dances With Wolves* were old stories told in a different light. *The Last of the Mohicans* (1992) and *Geronimo: An American Legend* (1993) reminisced of Indian life long ago and reminded audiences that the Romantic past with its "exotic" Native American inhabitants was a safe distance from the harsh realities of contemporary Indian life. Adventurous tales of Indians and whites—preferably with a handsome white male lead and his attractive love interest—were more appealing than stories of the current struggles and hardships of America's Indians. *The Last of the Mohicans* offered plenty of action and a Romantic story set against the rugged wilderness. Cooper's real villain was Magua, who clandestinely aids the French against colonial forces. But the 1992 movie version instead celebrates Magua's opposition to the British and Americans as a symbol of Indian survival and autonomy against colonial imperialism. When the Hurons defeat the British during a terrifying ambush, Magua (Cherokee actor Wes Studi) rips out the colonel's heart and proudly displays his bloody trophy. "Every Indian on the North American continent can in some way identify with this man because of the loss he has suffered," Studi said.[16]

Michael Mann, director, coproducer, and cowriter of *Mohicans*, made other changes to Cooper's original tale as well. Mann had produced TV's *Miami Vice* (NBC, 1984–1989) in which action and a kind of biracial male bonding combined to create a hit series. In 1989, he obtained the screen rights to the 1936 movie version of *The Last of the Mohicans* and added some fast-paced camera work and dramatic orchestral music. He also drew parallels between the French and Indian War (1755–1763) and contemporary U.S. foreign policy. "This was a war fought for the fur trade," he said of the battles in *Mohicans*. "In that way, it's not unlike the Gulf War [over oil] in Kuwait."[17] Mann described Cooper as "a reactionary, even reactionary for his time." "He had a horror of miscegenation," Mann said. "Our concept of the Cooper concept of the noble savage, the monosyllabic Indian, is a tremendous historical insult added to the injury of everything that happened to these people."[18]

Mann thus created his own version of early America's interracial relations. "It was very much a very ethnic polyglot community, the frontier," Mann said of colonial America. "And in that type of environment, I think there would have been intermarriage, and I don't think race would have been a big issue."[19] But like Cooper, Mann avoided the issue of intermarriage: he changed the crusty middle-aged Hawkeye into the young and sexy Daniel Day-Lewis and made Cora (Madeleine Stowe) his love interest. In the novel, Cora is attracted to Uncas; she is born of mulatto heritage but her mixed-race background completely disappears in the movie.[20] While an

Indian in Cooper's story stabs Cora as she dodges Magua's advances, Mann preserves the Hawkeye/Cora screen romance and instead sends Alice tumbling to her death. The film also shows Alice and Uncas (Inuit actor Eric Schweig) developing an unspoken passion for each other, but both die before a relationship can blossom. The real star of Mann's movie version, then, is the swashbuckling Hawkeye, who dominates many scenes and easily upstages his Indian mentor and advisor Chingachgook (an unusually subdued Russell Means).

Although *The Last of the Mohicans* was set in upstate New York, it offered the kind of action and grandeur that audiences associated with the Western. The movie brought in $72.5 million at the box office, a reminder that adventurous tales of long ago kept Hollywood's Indians frozen in America's past.[21] On the other hand, recent movies like *Dances With Wolves, Geronimo*, and *Mohicans* did provide increasing opportunities for Native Americans to play significant roles. By 1993, the number of lead and supporting Indian actors (in theatrical films and television) had jumped to 436, up from only 87 in 1985 (see Table 8.1). From 1985 to 2003, however, the number of male Indian actors has remained nearly three times that of females. In addition, 1993 saw the formation of the Native American Stunt Association, which assisted American Indian stunt performers in locating jobs and advised producers where to find them.[22]

Table 8.1   Screen Actors Guild (SAG) Employment Statistics for American Indian Performers, 1985–2003

Year[1]	Total SAG Working[2]	Male Indians	Female Indians	Total Indians	% Total Indians
1985	37,871	76	11	87	.2
1987	46,560	103	34	137	.3
1989	50,815	139	19	158	.3
1991	50,075	150	55	205	.4
1993	47,150	328	108	436	.9
1997	55,900	174	48	222	.4
1999	49,662	63	20	83	.2
2001	48,167	127	52	179	.4
2003	44,189	84	45	129	.3

[1]Statistics not available for 1995.

[2]Includes total SAG members in supporting and lead roles in all television/theatrical productions (except commercials, animation, and voice-overs).

Source: Screen Actors Guild, Affirmative Action Department, *Casting Data Total for All Productions*, 1985–2003. Data compiled based upon information supplied by producers.

The gnawing question dating back to Jim Thorpe's era of who was really Indian still lingered, however. The American Indian Registry for the Performing Arts, a Hollywood-based agency that served as a civil rights organization and clearinghouse for Native American talent, attempted to clarify this issue by screening members for tribal affiliation. The registry had assisted with auditions for *Mohicans'* 300 Indian extras, but the movie's producers did not heed the registry's request that actors bring identification cards documenting their tribal heritage. Indians and non-Indians showed up, many of whom were chagrined that the registry demanded proof of tribal membership. The registry's executive director, Bonnie Paradise (Paiute/Shoshone), was exasperated. "There are a lot of wanna-be Indians in [the audition]," she said. "It bothers me. There's no shortage of Indian talent."[23]

The registry had long wrestled with the issue of Indian identity. Since its beginnings in 1983, the organization had been trying to help American Indians find employment in the motion picture industry. The registry even created its own talent directory of Indian performers and technicians to encourage studios to hire Native Americans.[24] "They're out there, qualified American Indians," said registry board member Will Sampson. "They're all over the U.S. [Studios] just aren't looking."[25] Several years later, Sampson attracted attention when he asked eighty Caucasian actors who (he believed) had played Native Americans to morally and financially support the registry and help correct this "gross injustice," as he put it. "I realize that you were not, in any way, personally responsible for any of these casting decisions," he assured the celebrities, among them Claude Akins, Charles Bronson, Paul Newman, William Shatner, and Raquel Welch.[26] Sampson apparently tapped into their consciences, for many donated money and valuable items to the registry's auction.[27]

But financial problems continued to plague the registry. By 1993, a year that some would say was the best for Native American actors in the industry, funding sources had dried up and the registry permanently shut its doors.[28] Furthermore, the organization's advice that industry executives adhere to tribal roles when casting Indian actors troubled many in the movie business. "That starts to feel very much like Big Brother to me," said Beth Sullivan, creator and executive producer of television's *Dr. Quinn, Medicine Woman* (CBS, 1993–1998). Sullivan sympathized with Native American actors who lost opportunities to non-Indians, but she echoed the concerns of other movie executives who were reluctant to demand proof of anyone's ethnic heritage. (Such demands are not legal in the movie business.) Besides, Sullivan pointed out, a producer's responsibility is to the material and to find the best actor for the role. "I don't believe it's my job to legislate people's identity," she added.[29]

Pocahontas

Indian portrayal was a major concern for Walt Disney's thirty-third animated feature, *Pocahontas* (1995). The story of the young Native American woman who (supposedly) saved Captain John Smith's life and subsequently married John Rolfe resurrected all kinds of sensitive issues about racial and ethnic portrayals. Disney executives had already faced criticism from Arab American groups for *Aladdin*'s (1992) offensive song lyrics that depicted Mideastern culture as violent. African Americans and Hispanics later objected to *The Lion King*'s (1994) three hooligan hyenas that appeared to be thinly disguised inner-city characters. In 1992, parental concerns prompted the Disney Channel to excise the word "Injun" from its 1945 animated short, *The Legend of Coyote Rock*.[30] For *Pocahontas*, the studio thus set out to be more careful when designing Native American characters. They also hired Inuit/Cree actress Irene Bedard for the voice of Pocahontas and Sioux activist Russell Means as her father. "*Pocahontas* is a story that appealed to us because it was basically a story about people getting along together in this world," explained vice-chairman Roy Disney.[31]

Pocahontas thus avoided many of the offensive stereotypes that colored previous animated films. The movie was a vast improvement over Disney's *Peter Pan* (1953), with its buffoonish Big Chief of the Red Man and the seductive Indian princess Tiger Lily.[32] The young Pocahontas would instead be "an ethnic blend" of "softened" features: her convexly curved face was African, her dark slanted eyes Asian, and her body proportions Caucasian.[33] Her Oscar-winning hit song, "Colors of the Wind," illustrated nature's beauty and the Indians' harmonious relationship to it. "If you look at a film like *Peter Pan* where all Indians were caricatures, we are light-years from that in *Pocahontas*," said the movie's codirector Eric Goldberg. "We've gone from being accused of racism in *Aladdin* to being accused of being too politically correct in *Pocahontas*. That's progress to me."[34]

The movie's story was another matter. For Disney, *Pocahontas* was unusual: it's set in real time and a real place, unlike any of the

studio's animated features. The traditional Disney happy ending
was also missing: the loving couple (Pocahontas and John Smith) at
least appears to say good-bye forever. This differed substantially
from live-action screen versions of the young woman's life, most
of which had her marry a white man. (In *Captain John Smith and
Pocahontas* of 1953, she married twice—first to Smith and later to
Rolfe.[35]) Disney did allow the interracial romance to blossom in its
1998 direct-to-video sequel *Pocahontas II: Journey to a New World*.
In that story, the young Indian woman visits London and pairs off
with John Rolfe upon her return to America.

Particularly troublesome, however, was the movie's omission of
a few historical facts. Both *Pocahontas* and its sequel avoided her
kidnapping by the English, her conversion to Christianity, and her
untimely death (presumably from smallpox) at age twenty-one.
Many Native Americans weighed in on the issue, each voicing a
different opinion. Hanay Geiogamah (Kiowa/Delaware), an established playwright and a consultant for both *Pocahontas* and
Pocahontas II, explained that there was no harm in adapting a historical event into an animated feature as long as the studio acknowledged it. "To have put [her conversion and illness] in the film would
have taken away from the childlike simplicity of a Disney story,"
he said.[36]

Shirley "Little Dove" Custalow McGowan of Virginia's Mattaponi
tribe and a consultant for *Pocahontas* felt differently. Although
Disney had made multiple trips to Jamestown, Virginia, visited
museums, and spoken with Native American leaders and descen-
dents of Pocahontas, she was hardly impressed. "This is a great
story of respect and honor that has been lost in favor of just a
romance," she said. "I wish my name wasn't on [the film]. I wish
Pocahontas' name wasn't on it."[37] Meanwhile, Indian activist-turned-
actor Russell Means had riled a few Native Americans when he
called *Pocahontas* "the finest feature film on American Indians
Hollywood has turned out." Sioux columnist Giago responded that
the once-outspoken Means had been seduced by Hollywood profit.
"This is one case of the white man's dollar turning an activist into a
pussy cat," he said.[38]

Regardless of the Native American reaction, *Pocahontas* was
another box-office winner. The movie brought in a hefty $141.6
million, nearly twice as much as *The Last of the Mohicans*. *Spirit:
Stallion of the Cimarron* (2002), a DreamWorks Pictures' animated
feature about a wild mustang and his friendship with a Lakota

warrior, also earned a respectable $73.2 million.[39] The cycle of Indian-themed movies after *Dances With Wolves* had reestablished Native Americans as a box-office attraction in the Western (and in period adventure epics) and showed that Indian characters were popular in children's fare as well. Whether contemporary films about Indians could attract movie audiences was another matter.

HOLLYWOOD'S MODERN INDIANS

The Fate of *The Dark Wind*

The Dark Wind (1991) was one of the decade's first Indian-themed films that attempted to venture outside the Western genre. Hollywood had made similar attempts in the past, but the box-office results were disappointing. *The Dark Wind* seemed to have all the right ingredients. Based upon the acclaimed Tony Hillerman novel, the movie featured the young star Lou Diamond Phillips and had the financial backing of Robert Redford's Wildwood Enterprises. The story takes place on a contemporary Navajo reservation and shows Native Americans struggling between modern and traditional worlds. Redford had bought the rights to all Hillerman's mysteries and initially planned a series of motion pictures based upon his novels.[40]

The Dark Wind bypassed movie theaters and headed straight to video stores. The fate of the Hillerman novel would signal that modern Indian stories faced dubious prospects, at least in movie theaters. Bad luck plagued the production from the start. When Redford cast Phillips as the Navajo lead (the actor claimed part Cherokee heritage), skeptics instead referred to him as another Hollywood wannabe Indian. Meanwhile, Hopi religious leaders were unhappy with the movie's portrayal of their secret ceremonials and said that the story was too pro-Navajo.[41] New Line Cinema initially planned to release *The Dark Wind* as a joint venture with Carolco Pictures, but that collapsed when the latter headed toward bankruptcy. Regardless, movie executives were dubious that the film could ever find an audience. "The film has a lot of merit, but it's a question mark how much business it would do," said New Line president of distribution Mitch Goldman.[42] Hillerman's stories would have to wait another eleven years before Redford could successfully revive them for television's PBS *American Mystery!* series.

Thunderheart

Thunderheart (1992) was another bold attempt to resurrect contemporary Indians in movie theaters. Its original story about a young
part-Sioux FBI agent (Val Kilmer) assigned to investigate a murder
was inspired by true-life events at South Dakota's Pine Ridge
Reservation in the 1970s. *Thunderheart* was also an absorbing and
witty account of the problems that continue to plague contemporary Indian communities. The movie featured strong supporting
performances by Graham Greene and Sheila Tousey (Menominee/
Stockbridge-Munsee), who made a striking debut as a Dartmouth-
educated teacher and activist. (Tousey's character was based upon the
Native Canadian activist Anna Mae Aquash, murdered on Pine Ridge
in 1976.) British director Michael Apted (*Coal Miner's Daughter*,
Gorillas in the Mist) was obviously committed to his subject. He
also shot *Incident at Oglala* (1992), the documentary about AIM
activist Leonard Peltier and his imprisonment for the 1975 murder
of two FBI agents.

Thunderheart was the creation of John Fusco. The young screenwriter had grown up in a working-class Italian American neighborhood in Connecticut, far from the rural landscape of the Midwestern
Plains. Later in life, Fusco developed a fascination for Native
American culture. He ventured out West, wrote a few screenplays
(*Young Guns* and *Young Guns II*), and lived among the Lakota Sioux
of the Pine Ridge Reservation. "I befriended the elder and spiritual
leader, Frank Fools Crow, and studied the Lakota language. I worked
closely with the Oglala-Lakota in developing [*Thunderheart's*]
screenplay," he said.[43] Fusco then teamed up with producer Robert
De Niro who hired Apted as director. "I wanted to write a screenplay that called attention to the fact that Native American culture is
very much alive and not just a collection of quaint museum pieces,"
Fusco explained of his story set in modern times. "The Indian wars
are continuing in much more subtle ways."[44] Apted agreed; for him,
Thunderheart would bring the Hollywood Indian up to date for
American audiences. "I have this awful feeling that most people's
knowledge of Native Americans stopped with *Dances With Wolves*,"
he said.[45]

Apted's comment was uncannily accurate. Movie audiences
couldn't seem to get past the Romantic Native American image
embedded in Hollywood Westerns. *Thunderheart* earned $22.7
million, far below the enormous profits of *Dances With Wolves*.[46]

FBI agent Val Kilmer (*left*) questions tribal police officer Graham Greene in *Thunderheart*. Courtesy of Bison Archives.

Variety pointed out that although *Thunderheart* was an engross-ing mystery thriller, its attempts to reach "mytho-poetic heights" didn't quite fly. But *Screen International* seemed to touch upon a key issue: "The film has none of the misty-eyed sentimentality and white liberal guilt that permeated *Dances With Wolves*," the maga-zine noted.[47] Apparently, *Thunderheart*'s harsh contemporary set-ting was no substitute for the feel-good formula and nostalgic escape of *Dances With Wolves*.

IMAGES OF NATIVE CANADIANS

While Hollywood wallowed in its sentimental Westerns, Canadian cinema took a closer look at the harsh life of both urban and rural indigenous people. Canada's heavy influence by the documentary tradition has resulted in smaller production crews and lower bud-gets; consequently, epic Westerns (or any epics, for that matter) are the exception rather than the rule. Canadian stories of contem-porary Indians are far removed from the nostalgia of Hollywood Westerns, yet the absence of a cowboy hero taming the country's wild frontier has opened up other venues for Native Canadian men and women (also known as Aboriginal Peoples or First Nations) to assert their identities. Native Canadians have instead found a niche in movies about contemporary society, where deep tensions still divide indigenous and European cultures.

Loyalties (1986) not only exposed underlying racist attitudes but revealed the powerful strength within Native Canadian women. The contemporary story of the friendship between a stuffy upper-class wife of a British physician and her spunky Métis housekeeper cel-ebrates ethnic culture over Anglo Canadian values. (One reviewer com-mented that the movie was "another look at the dark side of WASP reserve."[48]) Cree/Métis actress, Tantoo Cardinal, plays Rosanne (the couple's outspoken housekeeper) and she "all but steals the film" as she struggles to support three kids and forms a steadfast bond with her female employer.[49] But the nasty skeleton eventually leaps out of the closet: when the woman's physician-husband attacks and rapes Rosannes' twelve-year-old daughter (Diane Debassige), his wife's loyalties are put to test. The movie's final moment demon-strates that the women's friendship transcends class and cultural barriers.

Loyalties gave Native Canadian actresses the catalyst they needed. Gradually, Canada's indigenous women discovered their own voice alongside their non-Native counterparts as they portrayed strong characters in contemporary situations. A new Native Canadian woman emerged. In *The Company of Strangers* (1990), a Mohawk woman (Alice Diabo) is joined by six other elderly ladies when their bus breaks down in a secluded wilderness. Together, the group shares common experiences and learns about survival. In *Medicine River* (1992), Sheila Tousey plays an expectant mother whose on-screen kiss with her Native Canadian boyfriend (Graham Greene) took a few non-Native viewers by surprise. "I guess people are used to watching Indians as strong, stoic individuals—and that Indians don't have sex," Tousey said.[50]

Still, few Canadian films play in American movie theaters.

Clearcut (1991), a contemporary story by Polish director Richard Bugajski, never found a distributor in the United States. (The movie's title refers to a controversial forestry practice in which every tree in a settled area is cut down.) *Clearcut* captured the intense rage that Canada's indigenous people felt toward centuries of white injustice. Graham Greene portrays a kind of avenging spirit or demon; in one particularly gruesome scene, he tortures the logging mill manager in an allegorical way (by skinning the man's leg), mimicking what loggers do to the forest. Bugajski had recently immigrated to Canada, and as a foreigner, he believed that America's Romantic ideal of nonviolent, victimized Indians was just another kind of misrepresentation.[51] If Bugajski countered Hollywood images of noble warriors with those of savagery and violence, he simultaneously reminded audiences that deep tensions still lay between the two races.

The issue of racial tensions was nothing new to Canadian cinema, however. Anti-Indian attitudes had already surfaced in *Running Brave* (1983), the biographical account of Billy Mills (Sioux) and his rise to an Olympic gold medalist, and *Justice Denied* (1989), the true story about of young Micmac sentenced to life for a murder he did not commit.[52] *Where the Spirit Lives* (1989) explored Canada's oppressive boarding schools but drew strong criticism from Native Canadian activists. Ojibwa storyteller, Lenore Keeshig-Tobias, labeled the movie "racist" and described its portrayal of Native Canadian people as passive and its absence of indigenous writers, producers, and actors as offensive. Noted Cree playwright Tomson Highway served as the film's consultant but reportedly walked out of the movie after the first twenty minutes.[53]

A later movie, *Black Robe* (1991), nearly triggered a national outcry. The film's story of a Jesuit's expedition through the remote icy regions of northern Quebec (circa 1634) offered a stark contrast to *Dances With Wolves.* The encounter between the friendly Algonquin and their enemy Iroquois was especially violent, with the latter torturing and killing a few members of a small traveling party. Unlike the Dunbar hero, *Black Robe*'s Jesuit priest was blinded by his own ideals, and he ultimately fails to cross the gap separating indigenous and white cultures. The movie's six Canadian film awards—including best picture of the year—hardly impressed Native Canadians, who condemned the film for its portrayal of "savage hostility" and pointed to the story's "sloppy inaccuracies" in tribal language and culture. *Black Robe*'s Australian director, Bruce Beresford, dismissed the controversy as "romantic, liberal notions of a sort of utopia," as he described it. "I think it boils down to the fact that a lot of Indians today don't like to see themselves portrayed as being antagonistic to one another," he said. Meanwhile, the French Canadians wondered why Beresford allowed Native Canadians to speak their own language but consigned the French to English dialogue. *Black Robe* was one of the few Canadian movies to find distribution in the United States, earning $8.2 million at the American box office.[54]

The icy Canadian north also provided the setting for *The Fast Runner* (*Atanarjuat,* 2002), the country's first commercial feature directed by an Aboriginal filmmaker. Based upon an ancient Inuit legend about a bitter rivalry between the male heirs of two strong leaders, *The Fast Runner* features an all-Inuit cast who speak their own Native language (the film is subtitled). Much of the movie's crew was also Inuit, including its director, Zacharias Kunuk. "[The film is] about identity and showing people where they came from, but it's also about survival," the filmmaker told the *New York Times.*[55] *The Fast Runner* was shot on location using wide screen digital video in the north Baffin region of the Arctic. The 172-minute epic became a cause célèbre for Canadian cinema, capturing six Genie Awards (Canada's version of the Oscars) and the Caméra d'Or at the Cannes Film Festival for best first film.

SMOKE SIGNALS AND BEYOND

While *The Fast Runner* was something of a herald for Canada's indigenous filmmakers, *Smoke Signals* (1998) focused the spotlight on an American Indian director. *Smoke Signals* was based upon a short story from Sherman Alexie's book, *The Lone Ranger and Tonto Fistfight in Heaven;* Alexie, a Coeur d'Alene Indian, also wrote the

Black Robe. Father Laforgue (*right*) shows the Algonquin how to write. Native Canadian actor August Schellenberg is center.

Courtesy of Bison Archives.

screenplay, and Chris Eyre (Southern Cheyenne/Arapaho) directed the movie. Eyre wasn't Hollywood's first Native American director (Edwin Carewe had preceded him), but he was the first to work with an all-Indian cast in a commercial film. *Smoke Signals* takes place in a contemporary setting and was financed by the Seattle-based company ShadowCatcher Entertainment for a mere $1.9 million.[56] Miramax Films bought the movie's U.S. distribution rights, a big feat for a first-time feature film director.

When Eyre first read *Smoke Signals*, he felt an immediate connection with the characters. Alexie's story offered honesty, a sense of humor, and "a projection of real Indians in terms of people I knew or people I'd like to know," Eyre said. *Smoke Signals* is about two young Native American men, the angry Victor (Adam Beach) and the nerdy Thomas Builds-the-Fire (Evan Adams) who journey from Idaho to Arizona to retrieve the body of Victor's dead father. "The material was so raw and so true to an aesthetic or convention that hadn't been portrayed before in mass media," Eyre explained. The problem in Hollywood, he said, is that supply and demand dictate that Indians are romanticized and continue to be romanticized in the Western. For Eyre, *Dances With Wolves* was popular simply because it gave liberals a platform to romanticize the oppression of Native Americans.[57]

Eyre had no desire to make a Western. "I'm not interested in making period pieces now because they do nothing for Indians of today," he said.[58] His second feature, *Skins* (2002), took place on a contemporary Indian reservation and was his "unofficial sequel" to *Dances With Wolves*. "These are the same [Oglala-Lakota] Indians that Hollywood made a movie on twelve years earlier. *Skins* is the reality of what happened [to the Sioux] 120 years later," he said. Eyre described his next film, *Edge of America* (2004), as a modern story of a girl's basketball team on the reservation. But this time he added a new angle. "It's about a black/red relationship to the exclusion of an Anglo-driven storyline," he said.[59]

Smoke Signals demonstrated that contemporary Native American stories could appeal to mainstream audiences. Mark Gill, former president of Miramax, Los Angeles, explained that *Smoke Signals* hit a human cord, which was "very specific in its telling but was universally understandable to a broad audience."[60] In addition to targeting Native American groups, Miramax was able to cross over to non-Indian filmgoers as well. The studio's marketing research showed that most audiences assumed a movie about Indians would

Director Chris Eyre (*left*) and writer Sherman Alexie on location for *Smoke Signals*. Eyre prefers to place his Native American characters in contemporary settings.

Courtesy of Bison Archives.

be solemn, so Miramax emphasized *Smoke Signals'* comedy.[61] "*Smoke Signals* allowed us to go in a different direction," Gill explained. "It also had charm, humor, a bit of optimism, and was emotionally uplifting." The movie's earnings of $6.7 million were impressive for a low-budget, independent film. Still, its box-office receipts—while strong by art film standards—were minuscule compared to contemporary Hollywood Westerns (see Table 8.2). But Gill pointed out that while audiences for Maori movies were also limited, *Whale Rider* (2003) became popular. "We've been living in a very strong culture that has tended to homogenize people, and we're just now starting to get comfortable with subsets of that culture and the human truths that come out of those experiences," he said.[62]

Perhaps audiences are becoming more comfortable with contemporary Indian experiences as well. Although moviegoers prefer nostalgic Westerns, many have discovered that television offers an alternative outlet for stories about today's Indian communities. A few TV movies and miniseries have also included behind-the-scenes Native American artists: Greg Sarris (Kashaya Pomo) served as coproducer, screenwriter, and author for HBO's *Grand Avenue*

Table 8.2 North American Box Office Earnings: Indian Westerns and Indian-Themed Films, 1990–2003

Film Title	Year Released	Earnings ($ Millions)
Dances With Wolves	1990	184.21
Pocahontas	1995	141.60
Maverick	1994	101.63
The Last of the Mohicans	1992	72.46
Legends of the Fall	1994	66.53
Windtalkers	2002	40.91
The Indian in the Cupboard	1995	35.62
The Missing	2003	26.30
Thunderheart	1992	22.66
Geronimo: An American Legend	1993	13.74
1492: Conquest of Paradise	1992	7.19
Smoke Signals	1998	6.72
Squanto	1994	3.34
Skins	2002	0.24
The Business of Fancydancing	2002	0.17

Source: *Box-Office Domestic Figures (1990–1999)*, binder 1, as cumulated from trade papers, Margaret Herrick Library, Academy of Motion Picture Arts and Sciences; *Internet Movie Database*, www.imbd.com.

(1996), and Hanay Geiogamah was executive producer and coproducer for the Turner Network Television project, *The Native Americans: Behind the Legends, Beyond the Myths* (1993–1996). ABC-TV's miniseries *DreamKeeper* (2003) employed some 2,500 Native Americans—from extras to advisors—although its programming between Christmas and New Year's (a season typically reserved for reruns) showed that the network had low expectations for viewers.[63]

A few events have helped propel television's interest in Indian-themed stories. In 2000, the major broadcast networks signed an historic agreement with the National Association for the Advancement of Colored People and a coalition of Latino, Asian American, and Native American civil rights groups. That agreement included the networks' initiatives to increase diversity in Hollywood. NBC took initiative when it sent a representative to two reservations in South Dakota and two tribal colleges to tackle "the more challenging task" of identifying Indians who might be NBC employment material.[64] The nonprofit public television station PBS attempted to bring more diversity to its programming when they approached Robert Redford to produce the film adaptation of Tony Hillerman's *Skinwalkers* (2002) as part of its *American Mystery!* series. (Hillerman's novels had been lying dormant in Hollywood ever since *The Dark Wind* failed to find a distributor.) *Skinwalkers*' high ratings prompted PBS to program two more Hillerman-based mysteries, *Coyote Waits* (2003) and *A Thief of Time* (2004), both set on contemporary Indian reservations.[65] With Hollywood Westerns in a dearth, Hillerman saw a good reason for the TV series. "It gets some Indian actors jobs," he said.[66]

Still, the few contemporary Indian stories in movie theaters indicate Hollywood's reluctance to gamble with the subject. Movies made for television, after all, are far less costly and therefore less risky than theatrical films. Moreover, history has shown that American movie audiences prefer Indian stories confined to a remote past, safely embedded in the nostalgic Western. Chris Eyre believes that as long as audiences want Indian Westerns, studios will continue to make them. "The studios are in the supply-and-demand business. If Middle America—people in Iowa and Nebraska—wanted to pay eight bucks to see a movie about [contemporary] Indians, the studios would be making those kinds of movies," he explained. "Just because [filmmakers] have a great idea, it doesn't mean the marketplace can absorb it. I don't find the problem with the studios; I find the problem is America's intolerance for any other perspective but theirs."[67]

Conclusion

For months, Hanay Geiogamah watched hopeful Native American actors parade through the casting office. Part of his job as executive producer and coproducer on the Turner Network Television series *The Native Americans: Behind the Legends, Beyond the Myths* was to advise at all casting sessions. He recalled how he began to notice patterns of actors trying to "pep up" their Indianness: The young Indian women actresses, for example, wore skimpy, tightly-wrapped tunics and minimal make-up. All had long flowing hair.

"Squash blossoms were out. Skimpiness was in," Geiogamah said of the women's attire. "Braids were considered to be too retro-stereotyped. That begins to flow into squawhood."

When the actresses moved, their long hair would brush against their face. Most would gently toss their head back and sweep their hair with their hand. Geiogamah believed that this image was unique to the casting sessions.

"That's what [the actresses] thought the directors and producers wanted," he explained.[1]

A new female Indian stereotype in Hollywood apparently has replaced the old one. Young aspiring Native American actresses read scripts and assume that filmmakers are looking for a Disney Pocahontas type with long sleek hair, a thin body, and minimal clothing. Native American male actors also strive to fit an image: They typically wear long hair and a vest or an opened ribbon shirt over their bare tanned chest. Some will add a choker necklace to enhance their credibility.

These casting sessions raise a few complex issues. Unlike Black Americans, the distinction between Indians and whites in the American mind is not so much a question of skin color as that of culture. In the motion picture business, many non-Indians can easily pass as Indians by dressing up to fit the current image of what an Indian should be. (Iron Eyes Cody convinced people for decades that he was Native American.) Producers and directors, after all, are looking for talent and a certain type that audiences will believe is real. If the actor looks the part and is convincing, audiences are willing to go along with it. Jim Thorpe addressed this issue back in the 1930s and the American Indian Registry continued to struggle with it until their closure in 1993. Not surprisingly, Native American actors still lose out to non-Indians who pose as Indians.

On the other hand, a few Native Americans believe that being Indian actually opens up opportunities in acting. The argument that only Indians should play Indians, they say, is too simplistic. "I screen tested for the Eskimo woman that Joan Chen got in [*On Deadly Ground*]. Someone asked me how I felt about that and I said, 'More power to her,'" explained Sheila Tousey. "I think that the doors should be opened to everyone because if I want to be considered for other roles, I can't say that Joan Chen shouldn't be playing an Eskimo because she isn't Eskimo. That would be hypocritical."[2] For Tousey, casting is a two-way street: just as non-Indians play Indians, Native American actors should also look for non-Indian roles. Wes Studi, most noted for his portrayal of Geronimo (in *Geronimo: An American Legend*), has successfully crossed over into non-ethnic specific roles in *Street Fighter* (1994), *Heat* (1995), and *Deep Rising* (1998). Angel Rivera, the national director of affirmative action and diversity for the Screen Actors Guild, advises others to do the same. "Some of the Native American actors are limiting their choices by being too 'Indian-centric' on casting calls when they can go for non-Indian roles as well," he said.[3]

Yet when these Indian roles do appear, many continue to go to non-Indians. Although contemporary audiences might not so easily accept a Chuck Connors as Geronimo (in the 1962 movie version) or an Elvis Presley as a Kiowa (in *Flaming Star*), few questioned Chinese/Hawaiian actor Jason Scott Lee as an Inuit in *Map of the Human Heart* (1993) or Viggo Mortensen as a Sioux pony express courier in *Hidalgo* (2004). The issue is further complicated when non-Indian actors claim Indian heritage. In Hollywood, assuming an ethnic identity is not unusual: Russian actress/dancer/costume designer Natacha Rambova (1897–1966) was really Winifred Shaunessey Hudnut from Salt Lake City, and Latin lover Ricardo Cortez (1899–1977) was Jacob Kranze from Austria. The practice continues: in 2001, a *Los Angeles Times* story on name change petitions revealed that actor Pete S. Choi had stepped into the new role of Pete Red Sky.[4]

With actors of Latin American heritage, the issue of Indian identity in Hollywood becomes even more complex. Some Latino actors claim indigenous ancestry, but the American Indian Registry took the position that only people of North American Indian descent should be included in their organization. The registry maintained that actors of Mexican or South American Indian ancestry (e.g., Pato Hoffmann) should therefore fall into the category of Latino performers. Not surprisingly, the registry's policy led to some confusion and even conflict. But beneath the controversy over who is really an Indian lies the fact that the Native American population in Hollywood is so small (compared to other minority groups) that the loss of even a few roles to non-Indians means proportionately more Indian actors out of work. Indians have no "superstars," and they don't have the numbers as Latinos or Black Americans to be able to call attention to their concerns. As Jay Silverheels once noted, "A boycott by [Hollywood] Indians would not mean the loss of money that a Negro boycott could bring."[5]

Silverheels' observation raises an important question: how much really has changed for Hollywood's Indians? After all, sympathetic portrayals of Indians in *The Silent Enemy*, *Broken Arrow*, and *Little Big Man* appeared long before *Dances With Wolves*, and a few notable Native American actors such as Will Rogers, Jay Silverheels, and Will Sampson achieved screen prominence before Wes Studi, Eric Schweig, and Adam Beach came along. Decades ago, Indians spoke their own languages in *Eskimo* and *Wagon Master* (the 1950 John Ford Western in which the Navajos finally speak Navajo), and Native American filmmaker Edwin Carewe directed major studio features (although the majority were non-Indian themed). "It seems that every twenty years or so, a powerful Native American film comes out and awakens audiences to the truth about Indian life ways," said screenwriter John Fusco. "It's a cyclical occurrence. But after awhile, audiences seem to get the message and they stop going."[6] Still, others believe that much has changed for Hollywood's Indians, especially behind the camera. Hollywood veteran journalist David

Robb has observed a growing number of Native American film-makers during the last twenty years. "What the American Indians wanted more than anything was to play themselves on screen and to write and direct their own stories, which today they are doing more than ever," he said.[7]

Appendix A: Motion Pictures Screened

Below are two lists of motion pictures screened for this book that contain portrayals of Native American characters. The first list is of short silent films (one and two reels) as well as three-reelers known as "featurettes." The second list contains feature-length movies including those made for television, mini-series, and animated films. Foreign titles represent American films distributed abroad and translated into another language.

Short Films

Across the Plains (1911)
Admiral Cigarette (1897)
Apache Father's Vengeance, An (1913)
Apache Renegade, The (1912)
Arrow of Defiance (1912)
Attack on Fort Boonesboro (1906)
Ballyhoo's Story, The (1913)
Battle at Elderbush Gulch, The (1914)
Battle of the Red Man (1912)
Blackfoot Halfbreed, The (1911)
Blazing the Trail (1912)
Broken Doll, The (1910)
Brush Between Cowboys and Indians (1904)
Buck's Romance (1912)
Call of the Wild, The (1908)
Chief's Daughter, The (1911)
Comata, the Sioux (1909)
Coming of Columbus, The (1912)

Corporal's Daughter, The (1915)
Cowboy Sheik, The (1924)
Cowboys and Indians (1907)
Curse of the Red Man, The (1911)
Custer's Last Fight (1912)
Daniel Boone (1907)
Dead Man's Claim, The (1912)
Deerslayer, The (1911)
Deerslayer's Retribution, The (1912)
Early Days in the West (1912)
Englishman and the Girl, The (1910)
Fall of Black Hawk, The (1912)
Fanget af Indianere (1915)
Flaming Arrow, The (1913)
Flight of Redwing, The (1910)
For the Papoose (1912)
For the Sake of the Tribe (1911)
Frenzy of Fire-Water (1912)
Friendly Indian, The (1909)
Girl of the Plains (1910)

Girls of Pinetree Ranch (1911)
Green Backs and Red Skins (1915)
Grey Cloud's Devotion (1911)
Ham and the Redskins (1915)
Her Primitive Man (1917)
Hiawatha (1909)
Hiawatha (1913)
Indian, The (1914)
Indian Brothers, The (1911)
Indian Chief's Generosity,
    An (1910)
Indian Maiden's Lesson, The (1911)
Indian Massacre, The (1912)
Indian Runner's Romance (1909)
Indian Vestal, The (1911)
Indienne Delaissée (1913)
Invaders, The (1912)
Iola's Promise (1912)
Kentuckian, The (1908)
Kit Carson (1903)
Kit Carson in Search of the Wagon
    Nut (1912)
Last Drop of Water, The (1911)
Last of Her Tribe, The (1912)
Last of the Line (1914)
Last of the Mohee-Cans, The (1926)
Leather Stocking (1909)
Legend of the Corn (1920)
Life of an American Cowboy (1906)
Life of Buffalo Bill, The (1912)
L'Indienne á Boireau (1913)
Little Dove's Romance (1911)
Little Indian Weaver, The (1928)
Man's Lust for Gold (1912)
Massacre, The (1912)
Mended Lute, The (1909)
Midnight Phantasy, A (1903)
Mohawk's Way, A (1910)
Old Water Jar, The (1911)
On the War Path (1911)
Pocahontas (1908)

Pueblo Legend, A (1912)
Ramona (1910)
Red Eagle, The (1911)
Red Eagle's Love Affair (1910)
Red Girl, The (1908)
Red Girl and the Child, The (1910)
Red Man, The (1909)
Red Man and the Child, The (1908)
Red Man's Honor (1912)
Red Man's View, The (1909)
Redskin's Bravery (1911)
Renegade, The (1908)
Renegade's Vengeance (1914)
Rescue of Child from Indians (1903)
Romance of the Western Hills, A
    (1910)
Rose O'Salem Town (1910)
Seminole's Sacrifice, The (1911)
Sioux Ghost Dance (1894)
Spirit of the Gorge (1911)
Squaw Man's Sweetheart, The (1912)
Squaw's Love, The (1911)
Strongheart (1914)
Struggle, The (1913)
Swiftwind's Heroism (1912)
Temporary Truce, A (1912)
Tourists, The (1912)
Two Wagons—Both Covered (1923)
Uncovered Wagon, The (1923)
Up-to-Date Squaw, An (1911)
Vanishing Race, The (1917)
Vanishing Tribe, The (1912)
Was He a Coward? (1911)
Wenona's Broken Promise (1911)
Wheels of Destiny (1911)
White Fawn's Devotion (1910)
White Man Takes a Red Wife, The
    (1910)
White Man Who Turned Indian, The
    (1924)
Yaqui Cur, The (1913)

Feature-Length Movies

These include television movies, miniseries, and animation.

Across the Plains (1939)
Across the Wide Missouri (1951)

Allegheny Uprising (1939)
America (1924)

Annie Oakley (1935)
Apache (1954)
Arizona Nights (1927)
Arizona Whirlwind (1944)
Arrowhead (1953)
Back to God's Country (Canadian;
    1919)
Badman's Territory (1946)
Battle at Apache Pass (1952)
Before the White Man Came (1920)
Behold My Wife! (1935)
Bend of the River (1952)
Big Sky, The (1952)
Big Trail, The (1930)
Billy Jack (1971)
Black Robe (Canadian; 1991)
Blazing Saddles (1974)
Blood on the Moon (1948)
Blue Blazes Rawden (1918)
Braveheart (1925)
Broken Arrow (1950)
Broken Chain, The (TV; 1993)
Broken Cord (TV; 1992)
Broken Lance (1954)
Bronco Billy (1980)
Buck and the Preacher (1971)
Buffalo Bill (1944)
Buffalo Soldiers, The (TV; 1979)
Bugles in the Afternoon (1952)
Calamity Jane (1953)
Call Her Savage (1932)
Call of the North (1914)
Canyon Passage (1946)
Captive God, The (1916)
Cat Ballou (1965)
Chato's Land (1972)
Cheyenne Autumn (1964)
Chief Crazy Horse (1955)
Cimarron (1930)
Clearcut (Canadian; 1991)
Cold Journey (Canadian; 1972)
Colorado Territory (1949)
Comanche Territory (1950)
Comancheros, The (1961)
Company of Strangers, The
    (Canadian; 1990)
Covered Wagon, The (1923)
Crazy Horse (TV; 1996)

Custer's Last Fight (1925)
Custer's Last Stand (1936)
Dakota (1945)
Dance Me Outside (Canadian; 1994)
Dances With Wolves (1990)
Daniel Boone (1936)
Dark Wind, The (1991)
Davy Crockett and the River Pirates
    (1956)
Deerslayer, The (1957)
Desert Gold (1936)
Devil Horse, The (1924)
Devil's Doorway (1950)
Diplomaniacs (1933)
Distant Drums (1951)
Dodge City (1939)
DreamKeeper (TV; 2003)
Drum Beat (1954)
Drums Along the Mohawk (1939)
Duel in the Sun (1946)
End of the Trail, The (1932)
Eskimo (1933)
Exiles, The (1961)
Fast Runner, The (Canadian; 2002)
Fighting Cowboy, The (1933)
Fighting Mad (1939)
Flaming Frontier (1926)
Flaming Star (1960)
Fort Apache (1948)
Frontier Fury (1943)
48 HRS. (1982)
49th Parallel (British; 1941)
1492: Conquest of Paradise (1992)
General Custer at Little Big Horn
    (1926)
Geronimo (1939)
Geronimo (1962)
Geronimo (TV; 1993)
Geronimo: An American Legend (1993)
Girl Crazy (1943)
Girl of the Golden West (1915)
Go West (1940)
Golden Strain, The (1925)
Golden West, The (1932)
Grand Avenue (TV; 1996)
Grey Owl (Canadian; 1999)
Half-Breed, The (1916)
Hallelujah Trail, The (1965)

Harry and Tonto (1974)
Hatari! (1962)
Heart of Wetona, The (1919)
Hiawatha (1952)
Hidalgo (2004)
Hombre (1967)
How the West Was Won (1962)
Hudson's Bay (1941)
Igloo (1932)
I Killed Geronimo (1950)
I'm from the City (1938)
In the Days of the Thundering Herd (1914)
In the Land of the War Canoes (1914)
Indian Agent (1948)
Indian in the Cupboard, The (1993)
Indian Love Call (1936)
Indian Paint (1965)
Iron Horse (1924)
I Will Fight No More Forever (TV; 1975)
Jamestown (1923)
Jeremiah Johnson (1972)
Jim Thorpe—All American (1951)
Johnny Reno (1966)
Just Squaw (1919)
Justice Denied (Canadian; 1989)
Kit Carson (1940)
Lakota Woman: Siege at Wounded Knee (TV; 1994)
Last Hunt, The (1955)
Last of His Tribe, The (TV; 1992)
Last of the Mohicans, The (1920)
Last of the Mohicans, The (1936)
Last of the Mohicans, The (1992)
Last of the Mohicans, The (TV; 1977)
Last of the Redman (1946)
Last Round-Up, The (1947)
Last Wagon, The (1956)
Laughing Boy (1934)
Lawless Plainsmen (1942)
Law Rides Again, The (1943)
Legend of the Lone Ranger, The (1981)
Legend of Walks Far Woman, The (TV; 1980)
Legends of the Fall (1994)
Light in the Forest, The (1958)
Li'l Abner (1959)
Little Big Man (1970)

Little Wild Girl (1928)
Lone Ranger and the Lost City of Gold, The (1958)
Loyalties (Canadian; 1986)
Major Dundee (1964)
Man Called Horse, A (1970)
Man from Laramie, The (1955)
Man of Two Worlds (1934)
Manitou, The (1978)
Map of the Human Heart (Canadian/European; 1993)
Mara of the Wilderness (1965)
Massacre (1934)
Maverick (1994)
McLintock (1963)
McMasters, The (1970)
Medicine River (Canadian; 1992)
Missing, The (2003)
My Little Chickadee (1939)
Mystery Ranch (1932)
Naked in the Sun (1957)
Nanook of the North (1922)
Navajo (1952)
Navajo Joe (1966)
'Neath the Arizona Skies (1934)
Nightwing (1979)
North of 36 (1924)
North West Mounted Police (1940)
Northwest Passage (1940)
One Flew Over the Cuckoo's Nest (1975)
One Little Indian (1973)
Outcasts of Poker Flat, The (1937)
Outlaw Josey Wales, The (1976)
Outsider, The (1961)
Overland Telegraph, The (1924)
Paleface, The (1921)
Paleface, The (1948)
Pawnee (1957)
Peter Pan (animated; 1953)
Plainsman, The (1937)
Pocahontas (animated; 1995)
Pocahontas II: Journey to a New World (animated; 1998)
Pony Post (1940)
Powwow Highway (British; 1988)
Primitive Lover, The (1922)
Ramona (1936)
Red Raiders (1927)

Red River (1948)
Redskin (1929)
Renegades (1989)
Renfew of the Royal Mounted (1937)
Requiem for a Heavyweight (1962)
Ride 'Em Cowboy (1942)
Ride Ranger Ride (1937)
Riel (Canadian; 1979)
Rio Grande (1950)
River of No Return (1954)
Road to Yesterday, The (1925)
Roanoak (TV; 1986)
Roll, Wagons, Roll (1940)
Rooster Cogburn (1975)
Run of the Arrow (1957)
Run, Simon, Run (TV; 1970)
Running Brave (Canadian; 1983)
Santa Fe Trail (1940)
Saskatchewan (1954)
Scalphunters, The (1968)
Scarlet West (1925)
Searchers, The (1956)
Seminole (1953)
Sergeant Rutledge (1960)
She Wore a Yellow Ribbon (1949)
Silent Enemy, The (1930)
Silent Tongue (1992)
Silly Billies (1936)
Skins (2002)
Smith! (1969)
Smoke Signals (1998)
Snowshoe Trail, The (1926)
Soldier Blue (1970)
Son of Morning Star (TV; 1991)
Spirit: Stallion of the Cimarron
        (animated; 2002)
Squanto (1994)
Squaw Man, The (1914)
Squaw Man, The (1931)
Stagecoach (1939)
Stagecoach (1966)
Stagecoach (TV; 1986)
Stand at Apache River, The (1953)
Starpacker, The (1934)
Susannah of the Mounties (1939)
Taza, Son of Cochise (1954)
Tecumseh: The Last Warrior (TV; 1995)
Tell Them Willie Boy Is Here (1969)

Ten Gentlemen from West Point (1942)
Test of Donald Norton, The (1926)
Texan, The (1920)
Texas Rangers (1936)
They Died with Their Boots On (1941)
Thunderheart (1992)
Tin Star, The (1957)
Tomahawk Territory (1952)
Tom Sawyer (1930)
Tonka (1958)
Too Many Girls (1940)
Two Flags West (1950)
Two Rode Together (1961)
Ulzana's Raid (1972)
Unconquered (1947)
Unforgiven, The (1960)
Union Pacific (1939)
Valley of the Sun (1942)
Vanishing American, The (1925)
Virginian, The (1914)
Wagon Master (1950)
Walk the Proud Land (1956)
War Party (1989)
Western Union (1941)
Westward Ho the Wagons! (1956)
When the Legends Die (1972)
Where the Rivers Flow North (1993)
Where the Spirit Lives (Canadian;
        1989)
White Buffalo, The (1977)
White Dawn, The (1974)
White Eagle (1932)
White Feather (1955)
White Oak (1921)
Whoopee! (1930)
Wild and Woolly (1917)
Wild Horse Mesa (1925)
Winchester '73 (1950)
Winds of the Wasteland (1936)
Windtalkers (2002)
Windwalker (1980)
Winterhawk (1975)
With Sitting Bull at the "Spirit Lake
        Massacre" (1927)
Wolf Call (1939)
Wolf Song (1929)
Woman God Forgot, The (1917)
Young Buffalo Bill (1940)

Appendix B: Motion Picture Archives

Below are two lists of archival collections consulted for this book: manuscripts (paper materials) as well as motion picture screening facilities.

Manuscripts and Collections

Abraham Polonsky Collection, Wisconsin Historical Society, Wisconsin Center for Film and Theater Research, Madison.

American Museum of Natural History, Department of Library Services/Special Collections, New York City.

Cecil B. DeMille Archives, L. Tom Perry Special Collections, Harold B. Lee Library, Brigham Young University, Provo, Utah.

David O. Selznick Archives, Harry Ransom Humanities Research Center, University of Texas at Austin.

Delmer Daves Papers, Department of Special Collections, Stanford University Libraries, Palo Alto, California.

Elliot Silverstein Collection, Margaret Herrick Library, Academy of Motion Picture Arts and Sciences, Beverly Hills, California.

John Ford Manuscripts, The Lilly Library, Indiana University, Bloomington.

Marty Weiser Collection, Margaret Herrick Library, Academy of Motion Picture Arts and Sciences, Beverly Hills, California.

Memoirs of Thomas H. Ince (manuscript collection), Museum of Modern Art Library, New York City.

Metro-Goldwyn-Mayer Archives, Cinema-Television Library, University of Southern California, Los Angeles.

Motion Picture Association of America, Production Code Administration Files, Margaret Herrick Library, Academy of Motion Picture Arts and Sciences, Beverly Hills, California.

National Archives & Record Administration, Office of War Information, Bureau of Motion Pictures, General Records of the Chief, Suitland, Maryland.

The Oral History Program at Columbia University: Popular Arts Project, New York City.

The Papers of D. W. Griffith: 1897–1954, Doheny Library, University of Southern California, Los Angeles.

Paramount Collection, Margaret Herrick Library, Academy of Motion Picture Arts and Sciences, Beverly Hills, California.

Ralph Nelson Papers, Department of Special Collections, Charles E. Young Research Library, University of California, Los Angeles.

RKO Radio Pictures Studio Collection, Arts Library Special Collections, Charles E. Young Research Library, University of California, Los Angeles.

Stewart Stern Collection, Cinema-Television Library, University of Southern California, Los Angeles.

Thunderbird Collection, Braun Research Library, Southwest Museum, Los Angeles.

Twentieth Century Fox Produced Scripts, Arts Library Special Collections, Charles E. Young Research Library, University of California, Los Angeles.

Warner Bros. Archives, School of Cinema-Television, University of Southern California, Los Angeles.

William Wyler Collection, Margaret Herrick Library, Academy of Motion Picture Arts and Sciences, Beverly Hills, California.

Screening Facilities: 16 mm and 35 mm Prints

The British Film Institute, National Film and Television Archive, Research Viewing Services, London.

Czech Film Archive (Národní filmový archiv), Prague, Czech Republic.

George Eastman House, International Museum of Photography and Film, Motion Picture Collection, Rochester, New York.

Library of Congress, Motion Picture, Broadcasting and Recorded Sound Division, Washington DC.

The Museum of Modern Art, Department of Film and Video, New York City.

University of California, Los Angeles, Film and Television Archive, Archive Research and Study Center, Los Angeles.

Notes

Citations from newspaper and magazine articles include page numbers when available. Page numbers were not available for articles from the clippings files of the Academy of Motion Picture Arts and Sciences' Margaret Herrick Library, the New York Public Library at Lincoln Center, and Bison Archives, Los Angeles.

Introduction

1. Even sympathetic reviewers pointed out that although the Friars' cause was just, it was nonetheless "confusing" and "unbelievably contrived." See *Choice* 10 (October 1973): 1205. Richard T. Jameson, former editor of *Film Comment*, faulted the Friars for a "hysterical superficiality and an unacknowledged racism of their own" (*Movietone News*, 25 September 1973).

2. For various reasons, I was unable to receive permission to access the studio files of the Walt Disney Company, Columbia Pictures, Tig Productions (Kevin Costner's movie company), the Clint Eastwood Collection (Wesleyan University), and the later sound era of Metro-Goldwyn-Mayer. Many of the files of Universal Pictures are limited to production logistics and publicity materials from 1945 to 1960. Although previous scholars have accessed some of these files, recent concerns of piracy and copyright in the movie business have made studios more protective of their property, including paper materials. In some cases, the studios were unable to retrieve vast production materials that had never been organized or catalogued.

3. Deterioration of silent films is a common problem due to erosion of the original nitrate-based stock, which was superseded about 1950 by the more stable and long-lasting acetate base (usually referred to as "safety film"). Film archivists estimate that only 10–15 percent of silents remain in viewable condition today, and the painstaking and expensive restoration cannot keep pace with the rate of continuing deterioration.

Chapter 1: Hollywood and the Silent American

1. *Moving Picture World* (hereafter *MPW*), 16 October 1909, p. 545. Young Deer's Vitagraph film was *Red Wing's Gratitude* (1909). *MPW* is perhaps the most comprehensive of silent film trade papers. Although *Variety* actually began publishing in 1905, its initial focus was vaudeville and legitimate theater; short one- and two-reel films were not reviewed in the early years. *MPW* was first published in 1907 and was devoted exclusively to film.

2. *MPW*, 6 May 1911, p. 999. *MPW* noted that Young Deer was a Winnebago actor from Nebraska (5 August 1911, p. 276). However, the Winnebago say that there was no tribal member by the name of Young Deer or Youngdeer. David Smith (historian, Little Priest Tribal College, Nebraska), e-mail to author, 19 June 2003.

3. According to a count of reviews from *MPW*, the number of Indian-themed films peaked around October of 1910 and again in July of 1911, when more than sixteen were released during a one-month period.

4. *MPW*, 31 December 1910, p. 1548; 17 June 1911, p. 1365; 24 June 1911, p. 1457.

5. *MPW*, 30 September 1911, p. 992; 21 October 1911, p. 207.

6. *The Sioux Ghost Dance* was actually a kinetoscope picture—a continuous strip of film which would, when cranked through a machine, be viewed through a peephole and give the illusion of motion. In the United States, films were not projected in public theaters until 1896.

7. *MPW*, 11 June 1910, p. 1015.

8. *MPW*, 3 October 1908, p. 263; 1 October 1910, p. 788; 26 February 1910, p. 300; 14 May 1910, p. 775; 28 January 1911, p. 194; 17 February 1912, p. 581.

9. "The Papers of D.W. Griffith: 1897–1954" (Copyright by Killiam Shows, Inc., 1982), p. 78, Doheny Library, University of Southern California (USC), Los Angeles.

10. Advertisement for *Comata, the Sioux* quoted in Eileen Bowser, ed., *Biograph Bulletins: 1908–1912*, New York: Farrar, Strauss and Giroux, 1973.

11. For a comparison of Griffith's Black and Indian characters, see Jack Temple Kirby, "D. W. Griffith's Racial Portraiture," *Phylon: The Atlanta University Review of Race & Culture* 34 (June 1978): 118–127. Kirby notes that "while Indians were viewed as fully capable of functional evolution (unlike blacks), and while they were a noble race (unlike blacks), they were just as unassimilable with white society" (p. 122).

12. Advertisement for *The Call of the Wild*, *MPW*, 31 October 1908, p. 344.

13. *MPW*, 31 July 1909, p. 196. Young Deer also played one of the lead Indian roles in *The Mended Lute*.

14. Advertisement for *Heredity* quoted in Bowser, *Biograph Bulletins*.

15. *MPW*, 25 July 1908, p. 72; 20 March 1909, p. 342.

16. *MPW*, 25 September 1909, p. 429; 14 January 1911, p. 97; 7 October 1911, p. 66.

17. *MPW*, 10 December 1910, p. 1360; 25 March 1911, p. 656.

18. *MPW*, 18 December 1909, p. 880; 6 May 1911, p. 1020.

19. *MPW*, 9 April 1910, p. 554.

20. *MPW*, 27 September 1910, p. 696; 21 May 1910, p. 834; 18 March 1911, p. 600.

21. *MPW*, 18 March 1911, pp. 581, 587.

22. *MPW*, 1 April 1911, p. 767. The event upon which *The Curse of the Red Man* was based had actually occurred in 1909. Bosworth was off by two years.

23. In *The Curse of the Red Man*, the tragic hero was a Maricopa Apache. *MPW*, 11 February 1911, p. 320.

24. *MPW*, 7 October 1911, p. 32.

25. *MPW*, 14 May 1910, p. 775; 7 January 1911, p. 31; Bowser, *Biograph Bulletins*. Jim Sleeper, in *Great Movies Shot in Orange County that Will Live Forever (or at least until 1934)* (Trabuco Canyon: California Classics, 1980) claims that Griffith's *Ramona* was shot on the same location that the story occurred (p. 21).

26. *MPW*, 11 March 1911, p. 523. The article states that Essanay had used the Banning Reservation Indians near Redlands. Most likely, *MPW* was referring to the Morongo Reservation, near the town of Banning, California.

27. The identity of Princess Mona Darkfeather (1882–1977) is revealed in Billy H. Doyle's "Lost Players," *Classic Images* 219 (September 1993): 54–55. Darkfeather said she was of Spanish and English descent; in an interview for *Movie Pictorial* (13 June 1914), she denied any Indian heritage. Film historian Kevin Brownlow in *The War, the West and the Wilderness* (New York: Alfred A. Knopf, 1978) had identified Darkfeather as a Seminole (pp. 256, 328), but her background had not been verified at the time of the book's publication. The same issue arises with Buffalo Child Long Lance and Iron Eyes Cody (see subsequent discussions in this book).

28. *MPW*, 3 September 1910, p. 520; 2 September 1911, p. 630.

29. On the Western's popularity, see *MPW*, 25 February 1911, p. 430; 3 June 1911, p. 1241; 1 July 1911, p. 1508. For an idea of their decline, see *MPW*, 16 September 1911, p. 773; 2 December 1911, p. 700.

30. *MPW*, 4 November 1911, p. 381.

31. *MPW*, 9 December 1911, p. 810; 27 January 1912, p. 298.

32. Steve Higgins, "Thomas H. Ince: American Filmmaker," in *The First Film Makers*, ed. Richard Dyer MacCann (Metuchen, New Jersey: The Scarecrow Press, 1989), p. 71. Prior to relocating to southern California, Ince had been a director with the Independent Motion Picture Company, which was later absorbed by Universal Pictures.

33. "Memoirs of Thomas H. Ince," manuscript for a biography published under his name and ghostwritten in *The Exhibitor's Herald*, 13 December 1924, pp. 10, 15, 23, Museum of Modern Art Library, New York City; Higgins, "Thomas H. Ince: American Filmmaker," p. 71.

34. "Memoirs of Thomas H. Ince," p. 17; *MPW*, 24 August 1912, p. 277; 1 February 1913, p. 476. *MPW* erroneously stated that the Oglala Pine Ridge Reservation was in North Dakota.

35. "Memoirs of Thomas H. Ince," pp. 17, 18. An act of Congress in 1892 prohibited the sale of alcohol to Indians on reservations and to those under the guardianship of the government.

36. "Memoirs of Thomas H. Ince," p. 19. An estimated count of Ince's Westerns was taken from "Synopses of Productions Made by Thomas Ince

during the Period April 1912 to August 1915," Charles E. Young Research Library, Department of Special Collections, University of California, Los Angeles (UCLA).

37. *MPW*, 19 February 1916, pp. 1111–1112.

38. Paul J. Eisloeffel and Andrea I. Paul trace the history of the Black Hills Feature Film Company in "Hollywood on the Plains: Nebraska's Contribution to Early American Cinema," *Journal of the West* 33 (April 1994): 13–19. In "Buffalo Bill and Wounded Knee: The Movie," Paul discusses the making of Cody's sweeping epic, *The Indian Wars*. See *Nebraska History* 71 (Fall 1990): 182–190. Brownlow also devotes a section to Buffalo Bill's film company in *The War, the West and the Wilderness*, pp. 224–235.

39. *MPW*, 23 November 1912, p. 761; 7 December 1912, p. 969. *MPW* indicated that Universal's Indians were unknowingly polluting the Los Angeles River that flowed across the studio's property. Authorities suspected that a typhoid strain originated in the Indian camp, so it was moved to another side of the ranch. See *MPW*, 23 November 1912, p. 761.

40. *MPW*, 15 February 1913, p. 667; 6 December 1913, p. 1206.

41. *The Indian Massacre* is also known by its British title, *The Heart of an Indian*. Both titles refer to the same film.

42. *MPW*, 27 April 1912, p. 322. The article, "Bison-101 Headliners," by Louis Reeves Harrison, apparently described American Indians as "inferior" to whites, noting that they were "incapable of contributing anything of value to human evolution" (p. 320). The author points out that despite the Indian's "savage" nature, Ince's films avoided extreme characterizations and did not excessively fault Indian people.

43. The original 1912 version of *Custer's Last Fight* was only three reels. Although some sources list the film's title as *Custer's Last Raid*, *MPW* identified it as *Custer's Last Fight*. See 22 June 1912, p. 1143. In 1925, a longer, five-reel version of the same film was released by the Quality Amusement Corporation. While the earlier version adopted a patriotic tone, added footage in 1925 produced a notoriously anti-Indian point of view.

44. *His Squaw, The Colonel's Adopted Daughter, The Hour of Reckoning* from "Synopses of Productions Made by Thomas Ince," UCLA.

45. *MPW*, 21 January 1911, p. 137; 11 February 1911, p. 302; 15 June 1912, p. 1014; 16 July 1912, p. 35; 24 August 1912, p. 760; 14 September 1912, p. 1067; 28 September 1912, p. 1266; 29 June 1912, pp. 1218–1219; 8 June 1912, p. 954. Accord to *MPW*, *The Yaqui Girl* was Pathé's first West Coast production. The film was reviewed on 31 December 1910, p. 1548.

46. Lillian St. Cyr (1884–1974) was born in Nebraska of Winnebago heritage. She acted in films (including Tom Mix Westerns) until she retired in the early 1920s. Later, she became active in American Indian affairs in New York City and Washington DC. See *Variety* (obituary), 20 May 1974. Vital records indicate that in 1906, St. Cyr marred J. Younger Johnson, possibly Young Deer's original surname. Both parties identified themselves as "colored." (Superior Court of the District of Columbia, Marriage License, J. Younger Johnson to Margaret L. St. Cyr, 9 April 1906.) However, in both the 1930 U.S. Census (San Francisco, CA) and a 1930 Affidavit for Marriage License (Cochise County, AZ., James Youngdeer to Helen Gilchrist, 16 July 1930), Young Deer said he was of the white race.

47. *Los Angeles Times*, 5 April 1915, p. 18. Young Deer was apparently attempting to show his friends a "new trick" with glass when he cut himself.

48. *MPW*, 26 April 1913, p. 367.

49. *Santa Ana Daily Register*, 2 May 1913, p. 8; 3 May 1913, p. 8; 19 May 1913, p. 1; 24 July 1913, p. 1; 19 September 1913, p. 1; 29 September 1913, p. 1; 30 September 1913, p. 1. Sleeper provides an in-depth account of Young Deer's activities in Orange County. See Sleeper, in *Great Movies*, pp. 29–33. Residents of Long Beach, California, will recognize one of the slave ring's coconspirators as the millionaire/philanthropist, George H. Bixby.

50. *Los Angeles Times*, 24 November 1913, p. 8, sec. 1; 30 November 1913, p. 4, sec. 2; 27 December 1913, p. 12, sec. 2; 3 April 1914, p. 12, sec. 2; 7 October 1914, p. 10, sec. 2; 3 November 1914, p. 10, sec. 2; 4 December 1914, p. 10, sec. 2. Sleeper relates a story in which an elderly woman who knew Young Deer remembered how the producer once stopped her and her friend on a street and asked if they'd like a ride to Los Angeles. She responded, "Why, if we'd gone, that would have been the last anyone would have seen of us." See Sleeper, in *Great Movies*, p. 147, 50f.

51. *New York Times*, 4 August 1912; *MPW*, 13 October 1913, p. 258.

Chapter 2: A Cultural Division

1. Jesse L. Lasky Feature Play Company, "Motion Picture Directory of *The Squaw Man*," New York, 1914, Academy of Motion Picture Arts and Sciences (hereafter AMPAS), Margaret Herrick Library, Beverly Hills, CA.

2. In 1914, Young Deer worked as a writer/director for England's Motograph Studios and the British & Colonial Kinematograph Company. His films include: *The Belle of Crystal Palace*, *The Black Cross Gang*, *Queen of the London Counterfeiters*, *The Water Rats of London*, and *The World at War* (all 1914). He later directed *Who Laughs Last* (1920) and *Lieutenant Daring R.N* (1924). Back home, *Variety* lists Young Deer as a minor player in *Man of Courage* (1922). Young Deer's date of death is yet another mystery. Although Eugene M. Vazzana's *Silent Film Necrology* (2001) says he died in New York City on April 17, 1946, a search through the city's Department of Records and Information Services Municipal Archives (all boroughs) showed no death record for a Young Deer in that year.

3. Review of *The Squaw Man* (play), *New York Times*, 29 October 1905, p. 4. According to the *Times*, William S. Hart, later to become the screen's cowboy hero of the 1920s, played the villain Cash Hawkins on the New York stage. *The Squaw Man* was first performed as a one-act play in 1904 then expanded to four acts in 1905.

4. Cecil B. DeMille, "DeMille's Epic Story of Films," *Life*, 19 October 1959, p. 166. The article is a part of DeMille's uncompleted autobiography. Later, Donald Hayne assembled the material for the book, *The Autobiography of Cecil B. DeMille* (New Jersey: Prentice-Hall, 1959).

5. "Motion Picture Directory of *The Squaw Man*," AMPAS.

6. AFI Catalog: Silent Films, *The Squaw Man's Son* (1917), American Film Institute (2002), retrieved February 7, 2004 at www.afi.com/members/catalog.

7. The California Civil Code Section 60 of 1872 prohibited marriages only between white persons and Negroes or mulattos. It was later amended to prohibit marriages between whites and Mongolians and then whites and members of the Malay race. In 1948, the Supreme Court of California ruled that these prohibitions were unconstitutional.

8. *Variety*, 2 November 1917, p. 49. Another film, *The Captive God* (1916), tells a similar story of a Spanish explorer (William S. Hart) shipwrecked off the shores of Mexico. He falls in love with and presumably marries Montezuma's daughter (Enid Markey).

9. *Variety*, 2 February 1917, p. 24; 14 July 1922.

10. *Variety*, 27 September 1918. Will Rogers (1879–1935) actually began as a cowboy, performing rope tricks and riding stunts in Wild West shows and circuses. He later rose to international fame as an author, lecturer, and screen actor. A fatal plane crash in 1935 brought Rogers' career to an abrupt end.

11. Jan-Christopher Horak offers an interesting discussion of Tourneur's off-screen space in "Maurice Tourneur's Tragic Romance," in *The Classic American Novel and the Movies*, eds. Gerald Peary and Roger Shatzkin (New York: Frederick Unger Publishing Co., 1977), pp. 10–19.

12. For a history of Cooper's tale in Hollywood, see Kenneth W. Scott, "Hawk-Eye in Hollywood: The James Fenimore Cooper Hero Still Awaits a Truly Appreciative Producer," *Films in Review* 9 (December 1958): 575–579. Scott writes that in the 1920 version, Cora slashes her wrists before she falls off the cliff. I believe that Magua instead cuts her wrist with a knife while prying loose her grasp on the rocky precipice.

13. *Variety*, 25 February 1916, p. 23; 7 April 1916, p. 21; 21 July 1916, p. 17. Only one reel of *Ramona's* original fourteen (the 1916 version) is known to survive.

14. Edwin Carewe (1883–1940) began as a stage actor before directing in Hollywood. He's credited for making Dolores Del Rio into a star, and he reached the zenith of his career in the 1920s. See *Variety* (obituary) 24 January 1940; *New York Times* (obituary) 23 January 1940. Carewe and his two brothers (Finis, a writer/director, and Wallace, a writer/producer/director) all appear on the 1907 Chickasaw rolls of the Five Civilized Tribes.

15. *Variety*, 1 July 1911, p. 1526.

16. *New York Clipper*, 4 February 1905, p. 1183.

17. *Dotted Line*, 9 November 1925, p. 7, AMPAS. The *Dotted Line* was the weekly in-house journal of the Producers Distributing Corporation (the production company behind *Braveheart*).

18. *The Half-Breed* (1916) was reedited and rereleased in 1924. (The 1922 film, *The Half-Breed*, is unrelated.) *Tongues of Flame* (1918) was a remake of the 1916 original and starred Al Whitman and Marie Walcamp. (The 1924 version of *Tongues of Flame* is unrelated.) Although trade papers referred to the lead in the 1916 *The Half-Breed* as "Lo Dorman," his name in the movie was Leaping Brook.

19. *Variety*, 4 June 1920, p. 29; 30 July 1920, p. 35.

20. *MPW*, 1 March 1913, p. 901. The 1913 version of *Hiawatha* was recently rediscovered and restored by the Motion Picture, Broadcasting and Recorded Sound Division of the Library of Congress. Although the cast included North American Indians, an actor by the name of "Soon-goot" played the title role.

21. *New York Times*, 12 June 1922, p. 18; *Los Angeles Times*, 24 July 1923, p. 119. Claude Massot's *Nanook* ("*Kabloonak*") in 1995 was a Canadian/French feature film about the making of *Nanook of the North*.

22. Shari M. Huhndorf, "Nanook and His Contemporaries: Imagining Eskimos in American Culture, 1897–1922," *Critical Inquiry* 27 (Autumn 2000): 125.

23. *Los Angeles Times*, 27 May 1923, p. 13, sec. 4. A few recent scholars have argued that far from being a classic documentary, *Nanook* is an "invented construct formed by imperialist, masculinist, and racist forces." See Sherrill Grace, "Exploration as Construction: Robert Flaherty and 'Nanook of the North,'" *Essays on Canadian Writing* 59 (Fall 1996): 123–146.

24. Bill Holm and George Irving Quimby, *Edward S. Curtis in the Land of the War Canoes: A Pioneer Cinematographer in the Pacific Northwest* (Seattle: University of Washington Press, 1980), pp. 13, 33. Anthropologists Holm and Quimby had reedited Curtis' original silent film and added a soundtrack of tribal singing with instrumental music. The new version, released in 1973, is retitled, *In the Land of the War Canoes: Kwakiutl Indian Life in the Northwest Coast*. A filmed biography, *The Shadow Catcher: Edward S. Curtis and the North American Indian* (1974; Teri C. McLuhan, dir.) documents the life and work of the noted filmmaker/photographer.

25. *Variety*, 22 March 1923, p. 28; 26 April 1923, p. 37; 24 January 1924, p. 21.

26. Lasky's comment is from Tim McCoy and Ronald McCoy, *Tim McCoy Remembers the West: An Autobiography* (Garden City, NY: Doubleday & Co., 1977), p. 162.

27. Grauman's Hollywood Egyptian Theatre Program, *The Covered Wagon*, 1923, AMPAS.

28. Diana Serra Cary, "Baby Peggy and Indian Chiefs in Hollywood," *American West* 22 (January/February 1985): 49–50. The author, former child star "Baby Peggy," recounts her visit in the article to *The Covered Wagon*'s Indian Village.

29. Daniel Simmons, or "Chief Yowlatchie" (1891–1966) took voice lessons before establishing himself as a soloist and opera singer. He performed at the Hollywood Bowl and at New York's Metropolitan Opera House. As an actor, Simmons' career spanned more than twenty-five years. Some sources identify him as a member of the Puyallup tribe. See *New York Times*, 19 November 1930; *Daily News* (Los Angeles), 18 September 1947.

30. *New York Times*, 20 September 1925; *The Vanishing American* Souvenir Program, New York Public Library at Lincoln Center, Library & Museum of the Performing Arts, New York City.

31. Carlton Jackson, *Zane Grey* (New York: Twayne, 1973), pp. 80–81. Jackson relies upon Grey's personal correspondence regarding church reactions to his missionary portrayals.

32. Grey, "The Vanishing American," *Ladies Home Journal* 39 (April 1923): 235. Grey's unpublished version is discussed in Joseph Wheeler, "Zane Grey's Impact on American Life and Letters: A Study in the Popular Novel," PhD diss. George Peabody College for Teachers, 1975, 181–183.

33. *Variety*, 30 September 1925, p. 31; Joseph Darmenberg, ed., *The Film Daily Yearbook of Motion Pictures* (New York: Film and Television Daily), p. 253.

34. *Variety*, 10 August 1927; 14 September 1927; 14 December 1927; 18 January 1928; 25 January 1928; 28 November 1928; 12 December 1928.

Chapter 3: Indian Adventures and Interracial Romances

1. *Variety*, 16 October 1929; 25 December 1929; 19 March 1930.

2. *Variety*, 22 October 1930; 29 October 1930; 5 November 1930; 19 November 1930; 18 February 1931.

3. Molly Spotted Elk, an Indian actress of Penobscot descent, played Chief Chetoga's daughter in the picture. For a fascinating account of her life and the filming of *The Silent Enemy*, see Bunny McBride, *Molly Spotted Elk: A Penobscot in Paris* (Norman: University of Oklahoma Press, 1995).

4. Long Lance's father, Joe Long, regarded himself as a descendent of the Eastern Cherokee although he was not registered on any tribal rolls. See Donald B. Smith, *Long Lance: The True Story of an Imposter* (Lincoln: University of Nebraska Press, 1982), pp. 14–15, 43–50, 100–128 passim. Smith is a Canadian historian whose biography is a meticulously researched account of Long Lance's life.

5. Douglas Burden to J. B. Shackelford (Museum cinematographer), 9 November 1927, Douglas W. Burden Papers, folder 275, Department of Library Services/Special Collections, American Museum of Natural History, New York City; Shackelford to Burden, 8 December 1927, folder 275, Special Collections, American Museum of Natural History. The film's cinematographer was Marcel Picard.

6. *Variety*, 20 May 1930.

7. "Inuit," meaning people (the singular is Inuk), has replaced the traditional term Eskimo.

8. Hunt Stromberg to W. S. Van Dyke, 17 December 1932, p. 3, Metro-Goldwyn-Mayer Archives, Cinema-Television Library, USC (hereafter MGM/USC).

9. Stromberg to Van Dyke, 7 June 1932, p. 2; 28 May 1932, p. 3, MGM/USC.

10. Stromberg to Van Dyke, 7 June 1932, p. 1; 15 July 1932; 22 July 1932; 26 July 1932, MGM/USC. Van Dyke discusses the filming of *Eskimo* in Robert C. Cannom, *Van Dyke and the Mythical City, Hollywood* (Culver City, CA: Murray & Gee, 1948), pp. 244–248.

11. Stromberg to Van Dyke, 23 August 1932, p. 1, MGM/USC. For a fascinating account of Ray Mala's life in Hollywood, see Ann Fienup-Riordan, *Freeze Frame: Alaska Eskimos in the Movies* (Seattle: University of Washington Press, 1995), pp. 64–95. According to the author, Wise "remains the most prolific film star the state has yet produced" (p. 95).

12. Stromberg to Van Dyke, 2 September 1932, pp. 1, 2; 15 July 1932, p. 2; 29 September 1932, MGM/USC. MGM executive Irving Thalberg wished to change the Inuit dialogue to English.

13. Notes by Stromberg, "Angle and Tentative Construction of *Eskimo*," 5 April 1932, p. 30, MGM/USC.

14. "Continuity and Second Revised Final Script, *Man of Two Worlds*," 22 September 1933, p. 9, box RKO-S-281, RKO Radio Pictures Studio Collection

(collection 3), Arts Library Special Collections, Charles E. Young Research Library, UCLA (hereafter RKO/UCLA).

15. *New York Times*, 15 November 1933.

16. *Variety*, 21 November 1933; *Los Angeles Times*, 28 January 1934, p. 1, sec. 2.

17. *Variety*, 15 May 1934; James Wingate (Hays Office public relations director) to W. D. Kelly, 12 April 1934, Motion Picture Association of America, Production Code Administration, AMPAS (hereafter MPAA).

18. Oliver La Farge to John Huston, 19 July 1932, William Wyler Papers, AMPAS.

19. B. D. Weeks to Will H. Hays, 19 April 1932; Lamar Trotti (Hays Office assistant) to Maurice McKenzie, 29 April 1932, MPAA.

20. Todd McCarthy and Joseph McBride, "John Lee Mahin: Teamplayer," in *Backstory: Interviews with Screenwriters of Hollywood's Golden Age*, ed. Pat McGilligan (Berkeley: University of California Press, 1986), p. 257. Mahin, alas, would regret his own advice. Years later, he admitted that the picture was awful, and that La Farge threw a drink in his face when told that Mahin had written the script (p. 257).

21. *Laughing Boy*, temporary script okayed by Stromberg, 25 October 1933, MGM/USC.

22. The Production Code of the Motion Picture Producers and Distributors of America, Inc., 1930–1934, states that "miscegenation (sex relationship between the white and black races) is forbidden" (Part II, Item 6). No mention is made of miscegenation between whites and any race other than Black Americans.

23. Joseph I. Breen to Wingate, 17 November 1933, MPAA.

24. Inter-office memorandum, local censors, *Laughing Boy*, MPAA. New York originally rejected the film in April 1934 but passed it with deletions in May. Ohio also advised numerous deletions.

25. Wingate to E. J. Mannix, 25 November 1933; Wingate to Irwin Esmond, 12 April 1934, MPAA. No indicated response from the Department of the Interior was found in the files.

26. *Variety*, 15 May 1934.

27. Robert Presnell to Hal B. Wallis, 13 July 1933, file 2064, Warner Bros. Archives, School of Cinema-Television, USC (hereafter WB/USC).

28. Wallis to Presnell, 26 October 1933, WB/USC.

29. Wingate to Jack Warner, 12 October 1933; 9 December 1933, WB/USC.

30. *Variety*, 23 January 1934. Most New York papers praised the film's theme: see *Evening Post*, 18 January 1934; *New York World-Telegram*, 18 January 1934; *Evening Telegram*, 18 January 1934; *Brooklyn Eagle*, 26 January 1934. The *New York Times* was decidedly mixed, admitting that the film was interesting but weakened by its "fiery melodramatics" (18 January 1934).

31. "William Shaeffer Collection," September 4, 1926 to August 9, 1936, WB/USC. *Massacre*'s negative cost was $399,000, and its foreign and domestic receipts totaled $528,000.

32. Chief Thunderbird, or Richard Davis (1866–1946), attended Carlisle, portrayed legendary Indian heroes in movies, and served as an advisor for DeMille's Westerns. See *The Pasadena Star News* (obituary), 6 April 1946. Oddly enough, while Thunderbird lived in Long Beach CA, he signed a

membership questionnaire to join the Knights of the Ku Klux Klan (Alabama) in 1924. On the application, he indicated that he was a Christian, a full-blooded Cheyenne, and 100 percent American. "Membership Questionnaire," Knights of the Ku Klux Klan, Thunderbird Collection, Braun Research Library, Southwest Museum, Los Angeles.

33. J. Kelly (secretary to Will Hays) to Hazel Plate, 6 November 1934, MPAA.

34. *Moving Picture Herald* noted that *Call Her Savage* reached a high of $58,000 at New York's Roxy Theater (10 December 1932, p. 53). A week later, the movie fell to $13,800 at New York's Loew's (17 December 1932, p. 42). The movie was the Box Office Champion for December 1932.

35. Maurice McKenzie to Lamar Trotti, 19 April 1932, MPAA.

36. Jason Joy to Winfield Sheehan, 24 August 1932; Wingate to Sheehan, 11 November 1932; Wingate to Gray Baker, 14 November 1932, MPAA.

37. Joy to Sheehan, 24 August 1932, MPAA.

38. *New York Herald Tribune*, 4 June 1939, p. 2, sec. 4.

39. Luther Standing Bear (1868–1939) joined Buffalo Bill's Wild West Show before finding employment as an Indian extra with producer Thomas Ince. *Los Angeles Times*, 28 January 1934, p. 1, sec. 2; *New York Herald Tribune*, 4 June 1939, p. 2, sec. 4. He continued to act until his death, but his movie career was temporarily curtailed in 1935 when he was sentenced to jail for one year for committing a statutory offense against an eight-year-old, half Paiute girl. See *Los Angeles Times*, 19 March 1935, p. 8, sec. 1; 20 March 1935, p. 8, sec. 1; 6 May 1935, p. 1, sec. 2; 23 February 1939, p. 23.

40. *New York Herald Tribune*, 4 June 1939, p. 2, sec. 4. In the article, Many Treaties identified himself as a Blackfeet Indian. It is worth noting that not all studios showed a pay discrepancy between Indian and non-Indian extras. Daily production worksheets of RKO's *Cimarron*, for example, indicate that cowboy and Indian bits each received $10/day; box RKO-P-10, RKO/UCLA.

41. *New York Times*, 16 August 1939; *New York World Telegram*, 26 September 1936.

42. On Thorpe's activities in Hollywood, see *Variety*, 14 June 1932, p. 3; 14 February 1933, p. 2; 30 October 1934, p. 1; 15 May 1935, p. 1; 30 September 1936; *New York American*, 16 January 1936; *New York Herald Tribune*, 25 September 1936; 6 April 1941.

43. *Los Angeles Times*, 24 September 1936.

44. Jack Warner, memorandum to Brian Foy (production supervisor, *Treachery Rides the Range*), 12 December 1935, WB/USC.

45. Thorpe's quote is from the *Los Angeles Times*, 24 December 1936.

46. EB [Emily Barrye], memorandum to Cecil B. DeMille, 31 October 1935, box 351, folder 7, Cecil B. DeMille Archives, L. Tom Perry Special Collections, Harold B. Lee Library, Brigham Young University, Provo, UT (hereafter CBD); DeMille to Louella O. Parsons (Hollywood columnist), 6 October 1936, box 353, folder 5, CBD.

Chapter 4: War and Its Indian Allies

1. Hollywood "racially integrated" military units in many popular war films, including *Star-Spangled Rhythm* (1942), *Bataan* (1943), *Crash Dive*

(1943), *Sahara* (1943), and *This Is the Army* (1943). In these films, Black Americans were often performing a service to their country in violation of more traditional "segregated" customs. For a further discussion of this theme, see Thomas Cripps, *Slow Fade to Black: The Negro in American Film, 1900–1942* (New York: Oxford University Press, 1977), pp. 249–389. Clayton R. Koppes and Gregory D. Black offer another point of view in *Hollywood Goes to War: How Politics, Profits, and Propaganda Shaped World War II Movies* (New York: Free Press, 1987).

2. C. J. Dunphy and staff to Zukor, Le Baron, DeMille, and Gilliam, n.d., "Advertising Approach to *The Plainsman*" (and suggested displays for the film), box 353, folder 1, CBD.

3. Bill Pine, Memo to DeMille, 18 February 1936, box 342, folder 12, CBD.

4. FC [Frank Calvin], memorandum to Joe Egli, 10 August 1936, box 351, folder 7, CBD. The Hungarian actor Victor Varconi was chosen for the role of Painted Horse.

5. *New York Times*, 3 September 1936.

6. "Blue Ribbon Award for the Month of January, 1937," box 353, folder 13, CBD; *Variety*, 20 January 1937. The film grossed $59,000 the first week, which the theater's management claimed was the highest amount under the present policy.

7. Westerns accumulated nearly $9.6 million in worldwide receipts by August 1939, and *Variety* announced that major studios were pouring $15 million into "horse operas." See *Variety*, 8 March 1939, p. 7; 23 August 1939, p. 3; 1 March 1939, p. 5.

8. Paramount press sheets from *Geronimo*, 1 August 1939 to 31 July 1940, Paramount Collection, AMPAS.

9. Breen to Luigi Luraschi (Paramount), 15 February 1939; Luraschi to Breen, 17 February 1939, MPAA.

10. A. M. Botsford to Paul Sloane, 22 February 1939; Botsford to Russell Holman, 31 July 1939; Paramount Collection, AMPAS.

11. Sloane, memorandum to Fred Leahy, 28 July 1939, pp. 2–3, Paramount Collection, AMPAS.

12. *New York Daily News*, 8 February 1940; *New York Times*, 8 February 1940.

13. *New York Herald Tribune*, 4 February 1940. The writer had mentioned that Jim Thorpe was another exception to this rule.

14. Several writers have erroneously stated that Thundercloud was not given screen credit for *Geronimo*. His name, in fact, appears as the last in a list during the title credits. Possibly, the bottom portion of the screen frame was inadvertently cut off when transferring to subsequent release prints for television and videotape (which cuts off a noticeable portion of the picture frame).

15. John de Valle, notes on *Geronimo*, 15 March 1940, Paramount Collection, AMPAS. Victor Daniels (1899–1955) worked on cattle ranches and in rodeos before receiving recognition as the screen's first Tonto. Although newspapers reported that Daniels was Cherokee and born in Oklahoma, his social security application (12 January 1937) indicated he was born south of Tucson, Arizona. Later in life, Daniels turned to coproducing and attempted to sell shares in motion pictures. In 1951, he was accused of violating the Corporate Securities Act for selling shares without a permit. See *LA Herald*

Examiner, 23 March 1951; *Daily News* (Los Angeles), 23 March 1951, 25 October 1951; *Hollywood Citizen-News,* 24 October 1951; *New York Times* (obituary), 3 December 1955.

16. Analysis Chart, *Northwest Passage,* 18 December 1939, MPAA.

17. In addition to the movie's scenes of retribution, Joe Breen told the studio to delete the scene of the Ranger gnawing on the Indian's head. Breen to Louis B. Mayer, 23 August 1939, MPAA.

18. *Variety,* 8 February 1940. Interestingly, a 1938 Gallup survey showed that the novel *Northwest Passage* was more popular among women than men.

19. *Variety,* 11 February 1940, p. 18; 13 March 1940, p. 9. Decades later, scholars attacked the movie as "the single most ferocious prewar film" ever known, citing the Indian massacre as particularly gruesome. See Raymond Durgnat and Scott Simmon, *King Vidor: American* (Berkeley: University of California Press, 1988), p. 190. As discussed, I find the Indian massacre more tempered and the Indian characters more ambiguous than what the authors assert.

20. "Line on the Golden Spike Itself," Notes for speeches and interviews on *Union Pacific,* April 1939, box 374, folder 7, CBD.

21. Hayne, *The Autobiography of Cecil B. DeMille,* p. 370.

22. DeMille, "In Chicago Tonight" (comments regarding premiere of *North West Mounted Police*), 27 October 1940, box 387, folder 6, pp. 2–3, CBD.

23. F. Calvin researched and compiled notes for *North West Mounted Police* from the following sources: *Harper's Magazine* (December 1891), *The War Trail of Big Bear* by William Cameron, *History of the Northwest Rebellion of 1885* by C. P. Mulvaney, *The Silent Force* by M. Longstreth, *Information Respecting the History, Condition, and Prospects of the Indian Tribes of the United States* by Henry Schoolcraft, and *North American Indians* by Edward S. Curtis; typed August–October 1939, box 377, folder 4, CBD.

24. *New York Times,* 5 July 1939.

25. DeMille to Archer Winsten (critic, *New York City Post*), 28 November 1940, p. 1, box 388, folder 17, CBD.

26. Ibid., p. 3, CBD.

27. Gladys Rosson to Baron Valentin Mandelstamm, 29 January 1940, box 384, folder 7, CBD. The letter indicated that DeMille personally had chosen the name Loupette.

28. "Rough Draft of New Line Suggested by Mr. Zanuck—To Work in with First Draft Continuity of 10/12/37," *Hudson's Bay,* n.d., pp. 3, 4–6, box FX-PRS-809, Twentieth Century Fox Produced Scripts (collection 10), Arts Library Special Collections, Charles E. Young Research Library, University of California, Los Angeles (hereafter TCF/UCLA); "Conference with Mr. Zanuck on New Treatment of 1/14/38," *Hudson's Bay,* pp. 1–2, box FX-PRS-809, TCF/UCLA.

29. "Rough Draft of New Line Suggested by Mr. Zanuck," *Hudson's Bay,* 12 October 1937, p. 12, box X-PRS-809, TCF/UCLA.

30. The term "Blackfoot" refers to a nation of Algonquin-speaking Indians from Canada. In the United States, the Blackfoot are referred to as Blackfeet.

31. Shirley Temple Black, *Child Star: An Autobiography* (New York: Warner Books, 1989), pp. 269–272. The author had mentioned that twelve Blackfeet

Indians were transported from Montana for *Susannah of the Mounties*, including thirteen-year-old Martin Goodrider.

32. "Conference with Zanuck on Temporary Script of 11/12/38," *Susannah of the Mounties*, 23 November 1938, pp. 4–5, box FS-PRS-122, TCF/UCLA.

33. *New York Evening Journal*, 24 June 1939; *New York Star Telegram*, 24 June 1939; *Variety*, 21 June 1939.

34. *Variety*, 29 May 1940, p. 5; 8 January 1941, p. 20; 24 June 1942, p. 8; *New York Times*, 1 November 1940.

35. In his ghostwritten autobiography, *My First Hundred Years in Hollywood* (New York: Random House, 1964), Jack L. Warner describes—albeit cautiously—his own political sentiments prior to and during World War II.

36. Raoul Walsh, *Each Man in His Time: The Life Story of a Director* (New York: Farrar, Strauss and Giroux, 1974), p. 325.

37. Aeneas MacKenzie, memorandum to Hal Wallis, 13 May 1941, file 2303, WB/USC.

38. MacKenzie, memorandum to Wallis, 13 May 1941, file 2303, WB/USC.

39. Herman Lissauer (head of Warner Bros. research department), memorandum to MacKenzie, 17 June 1941, file 1018, WB/USC.

40. Colonel E. R. Householder to William Guthrie (at Warner Bros.), n.d., MPAA; Hal Wallis, memorandum to Robert Fellows, 10 June 1941, file 2303, WB/USC.

41. *New York Times*, 19 October 1941. MacKenzie's quote is from MacKenzie, memorandum to Wallis, 13 May 1941, file 2303, WB/USC.

42. Melvin Levy, memorandum to Fellows, 30 April 1941, file 2303, WB/USC.

43. Lee Ryan, memorandum to Fellows, n.d., file 2303, WB/USC. A previous citation (file 1018) had referred to *The Battle of the Little Big Horn*, by Chief Joseph White Bull (as told to Stanley Vestal), which describes the latter's role in the battle. Lee Ryan was the captain of Warner Bros.' security department; how much influence he had on the movie's actual content is questionable. It is worth noting that the film did show Crazy Horse requesting Sitting Bull to join a war council with other Indian leaders.

44. Walsh, *Each Man in His Time*, p. 327.

45. As quoted from John Collier, *Annual Report of the Commissioner of Indian Affairs* (Washington, DC: Government Printing Office), June 1942, pp. 238, 240; June 1943, p. 237; June 1944, pp. 235–236, 252.

46. "Government Information Manual for the Motion Picture Industry," Summer 1942, record group 208, National Archives & Record Administration, Office of War Information, Bureau of Motion Pictures (Hollywood Office), General Records of the Chief, Suitland, Maryland (hereafter, OWI). While it is not within the scope of this chapter to examine the function of the OWI, it is worth noting that the agency did scrutinize Westerns for domestic and foreign release. Koppes and Black, in "Blacks, Loyalty, and Motion-Picture Propaganda in World War II," *Journal of American History* 73 (September 1986), explain that every studio (except Paramount) submitted all scripts to the OWI for review, and that by mid-1943, the agency's recommendations were almost always followed (p. 393).

47. Review of *Road to God's Country* by Lillian R. Bergquist, 13 April 1943, OWI.

48. Review of *Road to God's Country*, n.d., OWI.

49. Collier, *Annual Report*, June 1942, p. 236.

50. Review of "Untitled Bill Elliott" [working title] by Lillian Bergquist, 5 May 1943, p. 3, OWI.

51. Review of "Untitled Bill Elliott," n.d., OWI.

52. Review of *Frontier Fury* by Sandy Roth, 27 February 1943, OWI; *Variety*, 15 September 1943, p. 10.

53. Review of *The Law Rides Again* by Larry Williams, 28 May 1943, OWI.

54. "Conference with Mr. Zanuck on Final Script of 7/12/43," *Buffalo Bill*, 14 July 1943, pp. 3–4, box FX-PRS-442, TCF/UCLA.

55. "Notes on Screening of the Picture," 12 October 1943, p. 7, box FX-PRS-442, TCF/UCLA.

56. "Conference with Mr. Zanuck on Revised Final Script of 7/19/43," *Buffalo Bill*, 22 July 1943, p. 7, box FX-PRS-442, TCF/UCLA.

57. *Variety*, 26 April 1944, p. 14. Fox studios had requested 40 percent of the theater's profits along with a preferred playing time for the movie, an unusual arrangement for a Western at that time.

58. *Brooklyn Daily Eagle*, 19 April 1944.

Chapter 5: Red Becomes White

1. *Variety*, 21 March 1945, p. 11. The Writers' War Board also criticized newspapers, magazines, short stories, and ad copies for perpetuating stereotypes.

2. *Variety*, 12 March 1947, p. 2.

3. *New York Times*, 16 March 1947. *Variety* also noted the trend toward socially liberal themes: "H'wood Yens 'Significant' Pix—On Prowl for Message Films," 11 December 1946, p. 1.

4. Historian Thomas Cripps devotes several pages to the portrayal of race in *Duel in the Sun*. Cripps faults Selznick for falling back upon Hollywood's old racial stereotypes when portraying Vashti, the Black maid, and the seductive half-breed Pearl. See *Making Movies Black: The Hollywood Message Movie from World War II to the Civil Rights Era* (New York: Oxford University Press, 1993), pp. 193–196. In my opinion, Pearl's character challenged traditional stereotypes and added another dimension—albeit exaggerated—to Indian women.

5. David Thomson, *Showman: The Life of David O. Selznick* (New York: Alfred A. Knopf, 1992), p. 448.

6. David O. Selznick to Charles Koerner (coproduction head at RKO), 1 September 1944, box 596, p. 4; David O. Selznick Archives, Harry Ransom Humanities Research Center, University of Texas, Austin (hereafter, DOS). Joseph Breen to William Gordon (producer at RKO), 2 August 1944, box 596, p. 1, DOS.

7. Producer Howard Hughes had riled the Production Code Administration in 1943 when he exhibited *The Outlaw* without the Code's seal of approval; he

reissued *The Outlaw* in 1946 with a Code seal and a lurid advertising campaign that embarrassed the Hays Office. The PCA revoked the Seal of Approval and Hughes sued: the court ruled against the producer, and church and civic pressure forced many theater owners to cancel the film's engagement.

8. *The Song of Bernadette* was the story of Bernadette Soubirous of Lourdes, who witnessed a vision of the Virgin Mary in a grotto in 1858. See review in *New York Times*, 27 January 1944. Jennifer Jones was personally groomed by Selznick and later married him.

9. *Duel in the Sun*, Script notes by King Vidor, 24 June 1945, box 399, p. 1, DOS. Director King Vidor quit *Duel* following a heated argument with Selznick. William Dieterle replaced Vidor, but the Screen Directors Guild stipulated that Vidor receive sole credit. See Selznick to Daniel O'Shea, 5 September 1945, box 591; Vanguard Films, Letter to Screen Directors Guild, 11 April 1946, box 1015; Henry Herzbrun to Selznick, 8 February 1946, box 1015, DOS.

10. Selznick to Koerner, 1 September 1944, box 596, p. 6, DOS.

11. *Variety*, 22 January 1947; *New York Times*, 26 January 1947.

12. A Technicolor strike had delayed *Duel*'s prints until its Los Angeles premiere on December 30, 1946, and the last day to submit the film for the Academy Awards' qualification was December 31. Selznick had temporarily bypassed the Legion's approval, since the Academy deadline and the Technicolor strike allowed no time for a Legion prescreening.

13. Joseph Breen to Rev. Patrick Masterson (Legion of Decency), 21 February 1947, MPAA.

14. *New York Times*, 14 March 1947. *Variety* reported that *Duel* was initially cut from four to two-and-a-half hours: "Duel Gets Sliced," 30 January 1946, p. 3. Other popular films of 1946, namely Paramount's *Blue Skies* (an Irving Berlin musical) and Goldwyn's *The Best Years of Our Lives* (awarded the Oscar for Best Picture) were also given a B rating by the Legion, apparently a common classification.

15. *Variety*, 21 May 1947 (New York); 15 January 1947 (Los Angeles); *Hollywood Reporter*, 31 December 1946. *Time* reported that after one week in Los Angeles, *Duel in the Sun* did 25 percent better than *Gone with the Wind*; 27 January 1947.

16. Internet Movie Database (1990–2004), *Daughter of the West* (1949), retrieved July 30, 2004 from www.imdb.com.

17. "Use Tolerance, Americanism to Win Heavy Publicity," *Black Gold* Pressbook, New York Public Library at Lincoln Center.

18. *New York Herald Tribune*, 5 September 1947; *New York Times*, 5 September 1947.

19. Press review of *Black Gold* and posters, advertisements from the film, *Black Gold* Pressbook, New York Public Library at Lincoln Center.

20. *New York Times*, 13 September 1950. The paper responded with an editorial, criticizing the *Hiawatha* cancellation as a point of ridiculousness "reached and passed in unreasoned hysteria" (14 September 1950). The movie was finally released in 1952, and critics noted its message of peace between warring nations. See *Variety*, 10 December 1952, p. 6.

21. Hayne, *The Autobiography of Cecil B. DeMille*, pp. 385–386; Larry Ceplair and Steven Englund, *The Inquisition in Hollywood: Politics in the Film*

Community, 1930–1960 (Berkeley: University of California Press, 1983), pp. 368–369.

22. Hayne, *The Autobiography of Cecil B. DeMille*, p. 394.

23. "Suggestions for Promotion of *Unconquered*," n.d., box 430, folder 7, pp. 6, 10, CBD.

24. "Selling Ideas for *Unconquered*," Pressbook, New York Public Library at Lincoln Center.

25. Ann Del Valle, Interview with Cecil B. DeMille, 30 October 1958, box 353, folder 6, reel 1, CBD.

26. Mr. and Mrs. Robert C. Franklin, Interview with Delmer Daves, the Oral History Program at Columbia University: Popular Arts Project, ser. 3, vol. 7, no. 322, June 1959.

27. "Magnitude, Theme Lend Importance to Coming Movie," *Broken Arrow* Pressbook, New York Public Library at Lincoln Center. On Maltz' contribution, see "Mending *Broken Arrow*: Writers Guild Considers Award for Blacklisted Screenwriter of 1950 Film," *Los Angeles Times*, 29 June 1991, p. 1, sec. F.

28. "Jewelry of Apache Men," and "Games Played by Apache Children," typed 12 May 1949 from Morris Edward Opler's *An Apache Life-Way* (University of Chicago Press, 1941), pp. 21, 53–54, 395–396, Delmer Daves Papers (M192), Department of Special Collections, Stanford University Libraries, Palo Alto, CA (hereafter, Daves Papers).

29. O'Connor (*The Hollywood Indian*, p. 54) was especially critical of the fictitious wedding ceremony. Interestingly, in an oral history account, Ace Daklugie (son of Juh, Chief of Nednhi Apaches) stated that while Arnold seemed to know a good deal about Apache Indians, there was no marriage rite in Apache culture such as that described in *Blood Brother*. See Eve Ball, *Indeh, An Apache Odyssey* (Provo, UT: Brigham Young University Press, 1980), p. 31. Ball claims that the novel is valuable for historical authenticity, except for a few details.

30. Delmer Daves to Thomas Cripps, 2 March 1971.

31. *Arrow*, final script, 20 May 1949, Daves Papers.

32. A note on the revised final script (11 June 1949, Daves Papers) indicates that the previous title was *Warpaint*, which suggests a somewhat hostile tone. The title was later changed to *Arrow*, perhaps referring to Cochise's original nickname for Jeffords. The resulting title *Broken Arrow* conveys the antithesis of *Warpaint*.

33. Association of American Indian Affairs [AAIA] endorsement of *Broken Arrow*, released June 12 and distributed to newspaper syndicates; *Broken Arrow* Pressbook, New York Public Library at Lincoln Center.

34. Oliver La Farge, "AAIA Restatement of Progress and Policies in Indian Affairs," 8 February 1950; "AAIA, 1950," Papers of Philleo Nash, Truman Library, quoted in Larry J. Hasse, "Termination and Assimilation: Federal Indian Policy, 1943 to 1961," PhD diss. Washington State University, 1974.

35. *Los Angeles Times*, 25 May 1970. Additional information on Jay Silverheels (1912–1980) was obtained from *Brantford Expositor* [Canada], 19 February 1971, p. 24; 6 March 1980, p. 1; 16 December 1981; *Toronto Star*, 6 March 1980; *Los Angeles Times*, 8 August 1975 p. 17, sec. 4; 6 March 1980, p. 1, sec. 2.

36. Contrary to popular belief, George Armstrong Custer was not an army general during the Battle of Little Bighorn, but a lieutenant colonel.

37. *New York Times*, 26 November 1954. The producers of *Sitting Bull* caused an uproar among the Standing Rock Sioux community when they decided to film the picture in Mexico using Mexican extras. See F. David Blackhoop (Chair, Fort Yates Tribal Council, North Dakota), to William Langer (Twentieth Century Fox), 24 February 1954, MPAA; *Variety*, 24 February 1954, p. 18; 10 March 1954, p. 13. Producer W. R. Frank claimed that he wanted to shoot the picture in the Dakotas but was unable to swing a financial deal with the locals. *Variety*, 1 September 1954, p. 7; 8 September 1954, pp. 5, 18.

38. Edwin T. Arnold and Eugene L. Miller, *The Films and Career of Robert Aldrich* (Knoxville: The University of Tennessee Press, 1986), pp. 24, 25. Burt Lancaster, who initially preferred the studio's conclusion for *Apache*, later regretted the changes (pp. 25–27).

39. The *New York Times* (18 July 1952) had alerted readers that *The Story of Will Rogers* was "not an important film" and that it "rambles around quite a lot."

40. "Production Notes on *Jim Thorpe—All American*," n.d., p. 1, WB/USC.

41. Everett Freeman to J. R. Nichols (Commissioner of Indian Affairs, 1949–1950), 1 June 1950, WB/USC. Freeman also shared screenwriting credit on the movie.

42. Robert W. Wheeler, *Jim Thorpe: World's Greatest Athlete* (Norman: University of Oklahoma Press, 1978), pp. 110, 164. In 1973, the Amateur Athletic Union restored Thorpe's amateur standing, allowing the International Olympic Committee to follow suit. In 1982, the committee unanimously voted to return both gold medals to Thorpe's children (pp. vii–viii).

43. *Los Angeles Times*, 2 September 1940. Information on Jim Thorpe's life in Hollywood was taken from *New York Times*, 9 July 1944, p. 3, sec. 2; 6 December 1949; 29 March 1953 (obituary); *Time*, 6 April 1953; *Los Angeles Times*, 7 November 1933; 29 March 1953 (obituary).

44. Lancaster's quote is from the *New York Times*, 15 November 1982 and Wheeler, p. 256. In 1993, Indian activist Russell Means portrayed the ghost of Jim Thorpe in Disney Channel's *Wind Runner*.

45. Milton Sperling, Inter-office correspondence to Freeman, 1 December 1949, box 1761, WB/USC.

46. Thorpe had actually died of a heart attack while eating dinner at his trailer home in Lomita, California. *Los Angeles Times* (obituary), 29 March 1953.

Chapter 6: A Shattered Illusion

1. James Monaco, *How to Read a Film* (New York: Oxford University Press, 1977), p. 253 (photo caption).

2. In *John Ford: The Man and His Films* (Berkeley: University of California Press, 1986), author Tag Gallagher ranks *The Searchers* among the top twenty movies of 1956 with a domestic rental fee of $4.5 million (p. 500).

3. John Ford, interoffice memorandum, 26 January 1955, p. 1, box 6, folder 21, John Ford Manuscripts, The Lilly Library, Indiana University, Bloomington

(hereafter JFM); Patrick Ford, memorandum, 1 February 1955, p. 1, box 6, folder 21, JFM.

4. "Synopsis for *The Searchers*," n.d., p. 4, WB/USC. The description of Ethan's character is from Patrick Ford's interoffice memo, 1 February 1955, JFM.

5. Publicity materials for *The Searchers*, WB/USC.

6. Publicity materials for *Arrowhead*, Paramount Press Sheets, 1952–1953, Paramount Collection, AMPAS.

7. For an excellent discussion of Anthony Mann's style in his Westerns, see Jim Kitses, "Anthony Mann: The Overreacher," in *Horizon's West: Anthony Mann, Budd Boetticher, Sam Peckinpah; Studies of Authorship within the Western*, ed. Jim Kitses (London: Thames and Hudson, 1969), pp. 29–87.

8. Posters and advertisement for *Devil's Doorway* Pressbook, New York Public Library at Lincoln Center.

9. *New York Times*, 10 November 1950.

10. For a discussion of postwar racial attitudes in Hollywood Westerns, see John H. Lenihan, *Showdown: Confronting Modern America in the Western Film* (Urbana: University of Illinois Press, 1970), pp. 55–89.

11. Undated and unsigned memorandum from *Two Rode Together*, box 7A, folder 11, JFM.

12. The white man/Indian woman romantic union in *The Unforgiven* and other films prompted *Variety* to complain that the movies' interracial marriages were open only to white males. See 22 March 1961, p. 5. But a few exceptions were *The Vanishing American* (1955) and *Foxfire* (1955). By 1967, Sidney Poitier had wed wealthy white Katharine Houghton in *Guess Who's Coming to Dinner*.

13. Geoffrey M. Shurlock to Bernard Smith (Hecht-Hill-Lancaster Productions), 15 January 1959, MPAA.

14. Director John Huston was disappointed with *The Unforgiven* and accused the producers of turning a story of racial intolerance into a swashbuckler. "Despite some good performances," wrote Huston, "the overall tone is bombastic and over inflated." See John Huston, *An Open Book* (New York: Alfred A. Knopf, 1980), pp. 283–284.

15. *Variety*, 14 May 1958, p. 19; 24 September 1958, p. 3. Television's Western series climbed to an all-time high of 48 in 1959, up from only three in 1950. See Edward Buscombe, ed., *The BFI Companion to the Western* (New York: Da Capo Press, 1988), pp. 426, 428 (Appendix I). The *New York Times* also noted that television had "pulled the bottom from under big movie Westerns"; 28 April 1957.

16. *Variety*, 14 September 1966. *Hawk* was rereleased on NBC and reviewed on 5 May 1976.

17. Ralph Nelson, notes to Rod Serling (screenwriter), 25 July 1961, box 20, collection 875, the Ralph Nelson Papers, Department of Special Collections, Charles E. Young Research Library, UCLA (hereafter Ralph Nelson Papers).

18. Robert J. Richman, interoffice correspondence to Sidney Justin (Paramount's resident legal counsel), 5 July 1955, p. 1, "The Saga of Ira Hayes," Paramount Collection, AMPAS.

19. "The Saga of Ira Hayes," undated and unsigned document, Paramount Collection. The notation was in reference to a telegram dated 8 December 1955.

20. Richman to Justin, 5 July 1955, p. 2, "The Saga of Ira Hayes," Paramount Collection, AMPAS.

21. Kent R. Brown, private interview with Sy Bartlett, 21 August 1971 in *The Screenwriter as Collaborator: The Career of Stewart Stern* (NY: Arno Press, 1980), p. 164.

22. Brown, private interview with Stewart Stern, 12 August 1971 in *The Screenwriter as Collaborator*, p. 165.

23. Stern, notes from William Bradford Huie's *The Hero of Iwo Jima*, recorded 24 August 1959, p. 44, Stewart Stern Collection, Cinema-Television Library, USC, Los Angeles.

24. Brown, private interview with Stern, 12 August 1971 in *The Screenwriter as Collaborator*, p. 168.

25. Brown, private interview with Stern, 12 August 1971 in *The Screenwriter as Collaborator*, p. 165.

26. *Variety*, 21 February 1961.

27. Stern, notes from "Ira Hayes," recorded 27 November 1959, Stewart Stern Collection.

28. *Time*, 2 February 1962.

Chapter 7: Savagery on the Frontier

1. Anthony Holden, *Behind the Oscar: The Secret History of the Academy Awards* (New York: Simon & Schuster, 1993), pp. 289–292; Emanuel Levy, *And the Winner Is… The History and Politics of the Oscar Award* (New York: The Ungar Publishing Company, 1987), pp. 321–322. Holden believes that Sacheen Littlefeather was an actress masquerading as an Apache (p. 291).

2. Sacheen Littlefeather was born Marie Louise Cruz in Salinas, California. The former model and actress was named "Miss Vampire USA" in a promotional contest for television's *Dark Shadows* (ABC, 1966–1971) and later appeared in the movie *Winterhawk* (1975). Her acting career never really took off, however, but she attracted much attention when she posed in see-through chiffon and turquoise jewelry for *Playboy* magazine in October 1973. See *Los Angeles Times*, 30 March 1973; *Los Angeles Herald-Examiner*, 29 March 1973; 10 December 1974.

3. Advertisement for *Song of the Loon*, *Los Angeles Times*, 23 October 1974. The movie was originally released in 1970 and rereleased in 1974 and 1976.

4. See *Variety*, 31 August 1966, p. 20; *New York Times*, 27 November 1966; 12 August 1967; 9 June 1968; 13 September 1968. Germany actually produced a series of Westerns in the early 1960s that preceded the Italian spaghetti boom. German author Karl Friedrich May (1842–1912) wrote a series of novels starring Old Shatterhand and his Apache companion, Winnetou. Beginning in 1962 with *Der Schatz Im Silberee*, West Germany filmed nearly a dozen of these tales, many featuring American actor Lex Barker as Shatterhand and French actor Pierre Brice as Winnetou. For a discussion of Karl May's books and films, see Jorg Kastner, *Das Grosse Karl May Buch: Sein Leben—Seine Bucher—Die Filme* (Bergisch-Gladbagh, Germany: Bastei-Verlag Gustav H. Lubre GmbH & Co., 1992).

5. *New York Times*, 13 September 1968.

6. Although several sources claim that Sam Peckinpah was of American Indian descent, the late director was actually born into a pioneering California family. The name Peckinpah comes from the Frisian Islands off the Netherlands coast. See *New York Times*, 31 October 1971.

7. *Variety Film Rentals*, vol. 1, 1946–1979, AMPAS. Movie rentals are based upon the movie's use for a specified length of time in return for a fee paid to the distributor. Fees include U.S. and Canadian rentals. The information is assembled from *Variety* (weekly) and *Daily Variety* anniversary issues. For a comparison, note that a popular Western like *Butch Cassidy and the Sundance Kid* earned $15 million for its 1969 release.

8. James A. Sandos and Larry E. Burgess deconstruct traditional historical accounts of Willie Boy's tragic story in *The Hunt for Willie Boy: Indian Hating and Popular Culture* (Norman: University of Oklahoma Press, 1994). While I disagree with the authors' sweeping indictment that Hollywood's Indian images "have been insults to all Native Americans" (p. 55), their book offers its own flexible model of historiography.

9. Lucile Weight, "Willie Boy... A Desert Manhunt," *The Desert Trail* (Twentynine Palms, CA), 7 May 1969 (U.S. Mss 105AN), box 10, folder 2, Abraham Polonsky Collection, Wisconsin Historical Society, Wisconsin Center for Film and Theater Research, Madison.

10. Paul Buhle and Dave Wagner, *A Very Dangerous Citizen: Abraham Lincoln Polonsky and the Hollywood Left* (Berkeley: University of California Press, 2001), pp. 206–207.

11. Eric Sherman and Martin Rubin, eds., *The Directors Event: Interview with Five American Film-Makers* (New York: Atheneum, 1970), p. 25. The material in the Polonsky Collection had few memos and letters of correspondence related to *Willie Boy*. Polonsky's personal diaries, while quite lengthy, were written in his own handwriting and difficult to read.

12. *Newsweek*, 21 December 1970. See also *Variety Film Rentals*, vol. 1, 1946–1979, AMPAS.

13. Advertising for *Little Big Man*, 1971, Cinema Center Films. (Photocopy supplied by Bison Archives, Los Angeles.)

14. Seminar with Arthur Penn, 7 October 1988, Columbia University, New York City. Penn's quote is from *New York Times*, 21 December 1969. Penn was not available for interviews.

15. Dan George (1899–1981) was of the coastal Salish in British Columbia. He made his acting debut at age sixty with the Canadian television series *Cariboo Country* and appeared in many Hollywood films including *The Outlaw Josey Wales* (1976) with Clint Eastwood.

16. Gary Crowdus and Richard Porton, eds., "The Importance of a Singular, Guiding Vision: An Interview with Arthur Penn," *Cineaste* 20 (December 1993): p. 11.

17. *Hollywood Citizen News*, 17 November 1969.

18. During the seminar at Columbia University, Penn denied that My Lai influenced this scene in *Little Big Man* because, he said, "it did not happen until after the film." My Lai occurred in March 1968; the incident became public in November 1969. *Little Big Man* was released in December 1970.

19. *New York Times*, 1 October 1969.

20. *Variety Film Rentals*, vol. 1, 1946–1979, AMPAS.

21. Ralph Nelson to Ralph Moreno (reference librarian, Mill Valley Public Library, CA), 31 December 1975, p. 1, box 59, collection 875, Ralph Nelson Papers.

22. Ibid.

23. Ibid.

24. Nelson to Moreno, 31 December 1975; Speech written by Ralph Nelson for *Soldier Blue*, n.d., box 59, collection 875, Ralph Nelson Papers.

25. Ibid.; Tape of "Film Time" (London), with Ralph Nelson, 14 May 1971, box 59, collection 875, Ralph Nelson Papers.

26. Tape of "Film Time," Ralph Nelson Papers.

27. *Los Angeles Times*, 14 August 1970; *New York Times*, 20 September 1970.

28. Memorandum from Joseph Friedman (vice president of advertising and public relations, Avco Pictures), 10 April 1970, box 58, collection 875, Ralph Nelson Papers. Friedman's memo quotes an unidentified article by Vine Deloria Jr.

29. Arnold and Miller, *The Films and Career of Robert Aldrich*, p. 174.

30. "Arrested Eskimo Culture Fascinated James Houston, 'White Dawn' Author," *Boxoffice*, 19 August 1974, pp. K–2, K–8.

31. Elliot Silverstein, telephone interview by author, 6 September 2003.

32. Silverstein to Michael Nebbia (a New York commercial director), 2 August 1968, box 3, "Staff and Crew Lists," Elliot Silverstein Collection, Margaret Herrick Library, AMPAS (hereafter Elliot Silverstein Collection).

33. Silverstein, telephone interview by author, 6 September 2003.

34. Ibid.

35. Ibid.

36. Production notes from *A Man Called Horse*, n.d., Cinema Center Films, box 3, "Post Production," p. 15, Elliot Silverstein Collection.

37. John Dempsay, "Hollywood's Golden Chains," *The Boston Herald*, 3 May 1970, box 3, "Research Notes and Memoranda," Elliot Silverstein Collection.

38. Sanford Howard to Silverstein, 26 May 1970, box 3, "Research Notes and Memoranda," Elliot Silverstein Collection.

39. Silverstein, letter to author, 23 May 2004.

40. Richard A. Shepherd (Harris' agent) to Jere Henshaw (executive, Cinema Center Films), 20 January 1969, box 2, "Script Notes," Elliot Silverstein Collection.

41. Silverstein, telephone interview by author, 6 September 2003.

42. Silverstein, memorandum to Howard, 23 October 1968, box 2, "Script Notes," Elliot Silverstein Collection.

43. Clyde Dollar to Silverstein, 24 October 1968, box 3, "Historical Authenticity," Elliot Silverstein Collection.

44. Dollar to Silverstein, 12 December 1968, box 3, "Historical Authenticity," Elliot Silverstein Collection.

45. Silverstein to Dollar, 21 December 1968, box 3, "Historical Authenticity," Elliot Silverstein Collection.

46. *Los Angeles Herald-Examiner*, 17 May 1970; *Daily Variety*, 28 April 1979; 29 April 1970; 5 May 1970.

47. Russell C. Means to Frank LePointe (editor, *Rosebud Sioux Herald*, South Dakota), 13 July 1970, p. 2, box 3, "Historical Authenticity," Elliot Silverstein Collection.

48. Will Jones, "After Last Night," *Minneapolis Tribune*, 25 April 1970, box 3, "Reviews and Publicity," Elliot Silverstein Collection; Silverstein, letter to author, 23 May 2004. Silverstein's quote from telephone interview by author, 6 September 2003.

49. *Daily Variety*, 28 April 1970; 29 April 1970; 5 May 1970; *Variety*, 6 May 1970, p. 2. Producer Howard replied to AIM in a *Daily Variety* editorial, 29 April 1970.

50. *Variety Film Rentals*, vol. 1, 1946–1979, AMPAS.

51. *Time*, 8 January 1973.

52. William R. Taylor, *Sydney Pollack* (Boston: Twayne Publishers, 1981), pp. 54–55. Neither Sydney Pollack nor John Milius were available for interviews.

53. *Daily Variety*, 5 October 1972.

54. *Variety Film Rentals*, vol. 1, 1946–1979, AMPAS.

55. *Variety*, 25 March 1968; *Daily Variety*, 10 July 1969.

56. *Hollywood Reporter*, 26 March 1968.

57. *Variety*, 2 June 1969; *Hollywood Citizen News*, 20 August 1969.

58. *Variety*, 1 March 1972. *Variety Film Rentals* lists only those movies that accumulated $1 million or more in rental fees. *Flap!*, *House Made of Dawn*, and *Journey Through Rosebud* were not listed.

59. Tom Laughlin, telephone interview by author, 1 January 2004.

60. See Joe Klein's interview with Laughlin, "The Task of Billy Jack" in *Rolling Stone*, 3 July 1975, p. 40. In 1991, at the age of sixty, Laughlin announced that he was running for U.S. president on the Democratic ticket. See *People*, 11 November 1991.

61. Laughlin, telephone interview by author, 1 January 2004. The background on Laughlin's dispute with Fox is from the *Los Angeles Times*, 9 January 1972. The staff at the Richard Nixon Library was unable to find any verification that Zanuck was Nixon's campaign chairman in 1968. Meghan Lee (archivist), Richard Nixon Library and Birthplace, e-mail to author, 10 June 2004.

62. Laughlin's quote is from the *Los Angeles Times*, 9 January 1972. For a chronology of Laughlin's lawsuits, see *Hollywood Reporter*, 2 February 1972; 21 December 1972; 22 August 1978; *Variety*, 2 February 1972; 22 November 1976; 24 November 1976; 22 August 1978.

63. Ad for *Billy Jack* with quotes from Rex Reed, Avco Center Cinema in Los Angeles, folder 63, Marty Weiser Collection, AMPAS. Weiser was a publicist for Warner Bros.

64. *Variety*, 5 May 1971. Although many press announcements boasted that Laughlin was part Indian, the actor stated that he was not. See *Variety*, 28 June 1972, p. 7.

65. *Variety Film Rentals*, vol. 1, 1946–1979, AMPAS.

66. *Hollywood Reporter*, 18 April 1977; 7 November 1985. All three *Billy Jack* movies were directed by T. C. Frank, a pseudonym for actor/director Tom

Laughlin. The movie's screenwriters, Frank and Teresa Christina, were pseudonyms for Laughlin and his wife, Delores Taylor.

67. *Variety Film Rentals*, vol. 1, 1946–1979, AMPAS.

68. Thomas J. Slater, *Milos Forman: A Bio-Bibliography* (Westport, CT: Greenwood Press, 1987), pp. 1–2.

69. Milos Forman and Jan Novak, *Turnaround: A Memoir* (New York: Villard Books, 1994), p. 212.

70. Unpublished interview with Will Sampson, 5 October 1983, American Indian Registry for the Performing Arts, Los Angeles, CA, pp. 9–11. During his brief acting career, Sampson (1934–1987) played in more than two dozen feature and television movies. But kidney failure, weight loss, a heart-lung transplant, and a long bout with alcoholism brought about his premature death at age 53. See *Variety* (obituary), 10 June 1987.

71. Buscombe, *BFI Companion*, p. 426 (table 1).

72. For a few caustic reviews of *Heaven's Gate*, see *New York Times*, 19 November 1980; *Variety*, 26 November 1980.

73. John Jauna, *Cult TV: A Viewer's Guide to the Shows America Can't Live Without* (New York: St. Martin's Press, 1985), p. 57.

74. Iron Eyes Cody's Italian identity was first revealed in an article by the author in *The Times-Picayune* (New Orleans), 26 May 1996, p. 1, sec. D. The actor was born in Louisiana in 1904 and began to appear in Hollywood films in the early 1930s. A later exposé, "Make-Believe Indian" by Ron Russell, appeared shortly after Cody's death in *New Times* (Los Angeles), 8 April 1999.

Chapter 8: Beyond the Western

1. *Hollywood Reporter*, 5 November 1990; *Los Angeles Times*, 22 November 1990; *Boston Globe*, 21 November 1990.

2. *Variety*, 8 January 1992, p. 7. The movie's earnings are based upon box-office receipts for the year ending 1990.

3. Internet Movie Database (1990–2004), *War Party* (1988) and *Powwow Highway* (1989), retrieved January 6, 2004, from www.imdb.com. Both movies grossed less than $1 million.

4. *Lakota Times*, 27 November 1990. The weekly *Lakota Times* (currently, *Indian Country Today*) is the largest circulating American Indian publication in the country.

5. Michael Blake, telephone interview by author, 21 October 2003. Costner was not available at the time for interviews. Several years after *Dances With Wolves*, Costner had irked the Sioux when he and his brother Dan proposed to build a huge casino and resort on national forest land in South Dakota that tribal leaders said belonged to the Indians. See *New York Times*, 24 February 1995, p. 12, sec. A.

6. Blake, telephone interview by author, 21 October 2003.

7. Ibid.

8. Ibid. It is worth noting that in *Run of the Arrow*, Steiger and his Indian wife did remain married. In *A Man Called Horse*, however, Morgan's Sioux wife was killed in an Indian raid.

9. Ibid.

10. *New York Times*, 7 October 1990, p. 15, sec. 2.

11. *New Yorker*, 17 December 1990 (1995); *New York Times*, 9 November 1990, p. 1, sec. C; *Nation* (editorial), 15 April 1991, p. 1.

12. For Tim Giago's retort, see his editorial, "Columnists Should Dance With Facts!" *The Lakota Times*, 10 April 1991. Giago was the newspaper's president and founder.

13. *San Francisco Chronicle*, 10 November 1990, p. 3, sec. C; 11 November 1990, p. 1, sec. E.

14. Internet Movie Database (1990–2004), *Dances With Wolves* (1990), retrieved March 23, 2004, from www.imdb.com.

15. *New York Times*, 1 May 1993, p. 11, sec. C.

16. Studi's quote from Publicity from *The Last of the Mohicans* (movie press kit), Twentieth Century Fox, 1992, p. 7, AMPAS. In addition to his acting career, the multitalented Studi is an author, sculptor, and musician (he plays bass guitar). He's also a spokesperson for the Indigenous Language Institute, which supports the revitalization and preservation of Native languages threatened with extinction. See *People*, 20 October 2002, p. 10.

17. *Los Angeles Times*, 20 September 1992. Michael Mann was not available for interviews.

18. Peter Keough, "*Last of the Mohicans* Politically Corrected for Film Audiences," *Chicago Sun-Times*, 18 October 1992, p. 13.

19. Ibid.

20. In Cooper's novel (chapter 16), Cora's mother is a mixed-blooded descendent of the West Indies. Alice is Cora's half sister.

21. Internet Movie Database, (1990–2003), *The Last of the Mohicans* (1992), retrieved November 20, 2003, from www.imdb.com.

22. *Hollywood Reporter*, 29 March 1993.

23. *Los Angeles Times*, 16 March 1991. Paradise was the last of the registry's many executive directors during its ten-year existence.

24. *Hollywood Drama League*, 21–27 June 1984.

25. Unpublished interview with Will Sampson, American Indian Registry, 5 October 1983, p. 15.

26. *Variety*, 24 March 1986. The article was possibly referring to Newman's role in *Hombre* (1967), in which he played a white man raised by Apaches.

27. Hanay Geiogamah (former registry executive director), telephone interview by author, 17 December 2003.

28. *Variety*, 17 June 1986; *Hollywood Reporter*, 20 December 1993. Registry board members had discussed reviving the organization once it closed, but that never happened.

29. *Indian Cinema Entertainment*, Winter 1995, pp. 7, 9. The article includes an interview with Beth Sullivan. *Indian Cinema Entertainment* was the quarterly newsletter published by the American Indian Film Institute in San Francisco. The newsletter ceased publication in 2001.

30. *Wall Street Journal*, 29 July 1992, p. 1, sec. B. Other cable channels (namely, Nickelodeon, TBS, and TNT) also deleted scenes involving smoking, racial stereotypes, and gratuitous violence from early cartoons.

31. *Pocahontas* production information (movie press kit), The Walt Disney Co., 1995, p. 33, AMPAS.

32. In the MPAA's analysis of *Peter Pan*'s racial portrayals, the organization labeled both Indian characters as sympathetic. Analysis of Film Content, *Peter Pan*, 17 November 1952, MPAA.

33. *Allure*, June 1995. Animator Glen Keane describes his creation of the Pocahontas character in an interview with the magazine.

34. *New York Times*, 11 June 1995.

35. *Variety*, 18 November 1953.

36. Hanay Geiogamah, interview by author, 31 December 2003, Los Angeles, CA.

37. *Virginian-Pilot* (Norfolk), 20 June 1995, p. 1, sec. E.

38. *Los Angeles Times*, 11 June 1995, p. 27. Giago's quote from *Indian Country Today*, 13 July 1995.

39. Internet Movie Database (1990–2003), *Pocahontas* (1995) and *Spirit: Stallion of the Cimarron* (2002), retrieved November 20, 2003, from www.imdb.com.

40. *Los Angeles Times*, 22 July 1990.

41. *Variety*, 31 August 1990; *New York Times*, 24 September 1990.

42. *Los Angeles Times*, 6 April 1992.

43. John Fusco, e-mail to author, 3 December 2003. Fusco's first novel, *Paradise Salvage* (2002) was inspired by his boyhood memories of growing up in Connecticut. See *Boston Herald*, 25 January 2002, p. 61. Fusco's other screen credits include *Spirit: Stallion of the Cimarron* (2002), *DreamKeeper* (TV; 2003), and *Hidalgo* (2004).

44. Fusco's quote from *Thunderheart* production information (movie press kit), Tri-Star Pictures, 1992, p. 4, AMPAS. Fusco was also a producer with Robert De Niro and Jane Rosenthal on *Thunderheart*.

45. *Thunderheart* Production Information, p. 3, AMPAS. Apted was not available at the time for interviews.

46. Internet Movie Database (1990–2004), *Thunderheart* (1992). Retrieved February 12, 2004, from www.imdb.com.

47. *Variety*, 30 March 1992; *Screen International*, 10 January 1992.

48. *Canadian Forum*, December 1906.

49. *Cinema Canada*, December 1986. Tantoo Cardinal is one of Canada's most renowned indigenous film actresses, and she received a Genie Award nomination as best actress for *Loyalties*. In the United States, Cardinal appeared in *Dances With Wolves*, *Silent Tongue*, *Where the Rivers Flow North*, and *Legends of the Fall*.

50. *Indian Cinema Entertainment*, Winter 1994, p. 9.

51. Richard Bugajski, seminar at the Museum of Modern Art, 3 March 1992, New York City.

52. Although Billy Mills was a Sioux Indian from South Dakota, *Running Brave* was a Canadian production, filmed in Alberta. The movie was distributed in the United States by Buena Vista Pictures (a Walt Disney distribution company). Actor Robby Benson portrayed Mills. See *Toronto Star*, 1 September 1983.

53. *Globe and Mail* (Canada), 21 October 1989. Activist Keeshig-Tobias complained that the movie's production team was entirely non-Native. See also *Toronto Star*, 21 October 1989; *Kainai News*, 9 November 1989, p. 14; *Globe and Mail*, 26 January 1990. Others said that the film's leading actress, Michelle St. John, is not Native Canadian. St. John says that she is.

54. *Globe and Mail*, 21 December 1991, p. 3, sec. C. Director Beresford acknowledged that a French-language version of *Black Robe* was also in production. *Black Robe*'s earnings are from Internet Movie Database (1990–2004), *Black Robe* (1991), retrieved March 29, 2004, from www.imdb.com.

55. *New York Times*, 30 March 2002, p. 4, sec. A. Several publications said that *The Fast Runner* was the first Inuit language feature, although others (namely, *Eskimo* and *The White Dawn*) had preceded it.

56. *Star Tribune* (Minneapolis), 28 June 1998, p. 6, sec. F. In a telephone conversation (18 February 2004), Eyre said that *Smoke Signals*' budget was $1.9 million, although other published sources show different figures.

57. Chris Eyre, telephone interview by author, 18 February 2004. Sherman Alexie was not available for interviews.

58. Ibid. See also Eyre's interviews in *New York Times*, 29 May 1998, p. 10, sec. E; *Toronto Star*, 3 July 1998.

59. Eyre, telephone interview by author, 18 February 2004.

60. Mark Gill, telephone interview by author, 23 February 2004. Gill currently heads Warner Bros. Pictures' new specialty-film division, Warner Independent Pictures. *Smoke Signals* was one of the many films released during Gill's eight years at Miramax. *Smoke Signals*' earnings were from Internet Movie Database (1990–2004), retrieved February 24, 2004, from www.imdb.com.

61. *Variety*, 16 July 1998, p. 44.

62. As of November 2003, *Whale Rider* had earned $20.8 million in the U.S. Internet Movie Database (1990–2004), retrieved February 24, 2004, from www.imdb.com. Gill's quotes are from the telephone interview, 23 February 2004.

63. *Los Angeles Times*, 28 December 2003 to 3 January 2004 (TV Times sec.), p. 3; *Daily Variety*, 23 December 2003, p. 2. *DreamKeeper* attracted only a moderate 9.84 million viewers for its two-part series. See *Daily Variety*, 31 December 2003, p. 1. Greg Sarris was not available for interviews.

64. *Hollywood Reporter* (Special Issues: The 32nd NAACP Image Awards), February 2001, pp. 4, 6.

65. The *Boston Globe* reported that *Skinwalkers* achieved the "highest national ratings for any PBS show this year"; 26 November 2002, p. 8, sec. E. Nielsen Ratings were not available for *Skinwalkers*.

66. *Boston Globe*, 21 November 2002, p. 14, sec. B.

67. Jackie Biseley, "Native Cinema Emerges with a New Force," *Indian Country Today*, 10 May 2000. The article quotes Eyre in an interview.

Conclusion

1. Hanay Geiogamah, interview by author, 18 July 2003, Los Angeles.
2. *Indian Cinema Entertainment*, Winter 1994, p. 9.

3. Angel Rivera, interview by author, 8 January 2004, Los Angeles.

4. *Los Angeles Times*, 31 August 2001, p. 2, sec. B.

5. *The Expositor* (Branford, Ontario), 19 February 1971, p. 24.

6. *Indian Cinema Entertainment*, Summer 1995.

7. David Robb, telephone interview by author, 17 April 2004. Robb was an investigative reporter for twenty years at *Variety* and the *Hollywood Reporter*. In 2003, he received the First Americans in the Arts' Humanitarian Award for highlighting concerns of Indian artists and performers in Hollywood.

Selected Bibliography

The books and dissertations below represent broad overviews or categories of Native Americans in films. Articles are recent, beginning with the late 1980s to the present.

ARTICLES

Aleiss, Angela. "Native Americans: The Surprising Silents." *Cineaste* 21, no. 3 (1995): 34–35.

Appleford, Robert. "Coming out from behind the Rocks: Constructs of the Indian in Recent U.S. and Canadian Cinema." *American Indian Culture and Research Journal* 19, no. 1 (1995): 97–118.

Delanoe, Nelcya. "Memory Lapses." *Revue Française d'Etudes Américaines* (France) 13, no. 38 (1988): 386–393.

Griffiths, Alison. "Playing at Being Indian: Spectatorship and the Early Western." *Journal of Popular Film and Television* 29, no. 3 (2001): 100–111.

Jaimes, Annette M. "Hollywood's Native American Women." *Turtle Quarterly* (Spring/Summer, 1993): 40–45.

Jay, Gregory S. "White Man's Book No Good: D. W. Griffith and the American Indian." *Cinema Journal* 39, no. 4 (2000): 3–26.

Jojola, Ted. "Absurd Reality: Hollywood Goes to the Indians." *Film & History* 23, no. 1 1 (1993): 7–16.

Lefebvre, Martin. "The Characterization of the Indian in American Movies." *Recherches Amérindiennes au Québec* (Canada) 17, no. 3 (1987): 65–78.

Leuthold, Steven M. "Native American Responses to the Western." *American Indian Culture and Research Journal* 19, no. 1 (1995): 153–189.

Mihelich, John. "Smoke or Signals? American Popular Culture and the Challenge to Hegemonic Images of American Indians in Native American Film." *Wicazo Sa Review* 16, no. 2 (2001): 129–137.

Nottage, James A. "Authenticity and Western Film." *Gilcrease Journal* 1, no. 1 (1993): 54–66.

O'Connor, John E. "The White Man's Indian." *Film & History* 23, no. 1–4 (1993): 17–26.

Powers, Marla N. "New Perspectives on Native American Women." *Revue Française d'Etudes Américaines* (France) 13, no. 38 (1988): 350–357.

Prats, Armando José. "His Master's Voice(over): Revisionist Ethos and Narrative Dependence from 'Broken Arrow' (1950) to 'Geronimo: An American Legend' (1993)." *ANQ* 9, no. 3 (1996): 15–30.

Reed, T. V. "Old Cowboys, New Indians: Hollywood Frames the American Indian." *Wicazo Sa Review* 16, no. 2 (2001): 75–96.

Rollins, Peter C. "The Hollywood Indian: Still on a Scholarly Frontier?" *Film & History* 23, vol. 1–4 (1993): 1–6.

Seurin, Jean-Louis. "Images of Indians: Myth and Actual History." *Revue Française d'Etudes Américaines* (France) 18, no. 57 (1993): 235–244.

Shively, JoEllen. "Cowboys and Indians: Perceptions of Western Films among American Indians and Anglos." *American Sociological Review* 57, no. 6 (1992): 725–734.

Stanfield, Peter. "The Western 1909–14: A Cast of Villains." *Film History* 1 (1987): 97–112.

Telotte, J. P. "A Fate Worse Than Death: Racism, Transgression, and Westerns." *Journal of Popular Film and Television* 26, no. 3 (1998): 120–127.

BOOKS

Bataille, Gretchen M., and Charles L. P. Silet, eds. *Images of American Indians on Film: An Annotated Bibliography.* New York: Garland Press, 1986.

Bataille, Gretchen M., and Charles L. P. Silet, eds. *The Pretend Indians: Images of Native Americans in the Movies.* Ames: Iowa State University Press, 1980.

Churchill, Ward. *Fantasies of the Master Race: Literature, Cinema and the Colonization of American Indians.* 2nd ed. San Francisco, CA: City Lights Books, 1998.

Fienup-Riordan, Ann. *Freeze-Frame: Alaska Eskimos in the Movies.* Seattle: University of Washington Press, 1995.

Friar, Ralph, and Natasha Friar. *The Only Good Indian . . . the Hollywood Gospel.* New York: Drama Book Specialists, 1972.

Hilger, Michael. *The American Indian in Film.* Metuchen, NJ: The Scarecrow Press, 1986.

Hilger, Michael. *From Savage to Nobleman: Images of Native Americans in Film.* Lanham, MD: The Scarecrow Press, 1995 (paperback 2002).

Kilpatrick, Jacquelyn. *Celluloid Indians: Native Americans and Film.* Lincoln: University of Nebraska Press, 1999.

Morin, Georges-Henri. *Le Cercle Brisé: L'image de l'Indien dans le Western.* Paris: Payot, 1977.

O'Connor, John E. *The Hollywood Indian: Stereotypes of Native Americans in Film.* Trenton: New Jersey State Museum, 1980.

Prats, Armando José. *Invisible Natives: Myth and Identity in the American Western*. Ithaca, NY: Cornell University Press, 2002.
Rollins, Peter C., and John E. O'Connor, eds. *Hollywood's Indian: The Portrayal of the Native American in Film*. Lexington: University of Kentucky Press, 1998. Reprint, 1999.
Sadoux, Jean Jacques. *Racism in Western Films from D. W. Griffith to John Ford: Indians and Blacks*. New York: Revisionist Press, 1980.
Smith, Andrew Brodie. *Shooting Cowboys and Indians: Silent Western Films, American Culture, and the Birth of Hollywood*. Boulder: University of Colorado Press, 2003.

DISSERTATIONS

Aleiss, Angela. "From Adversaries to Allies: The American Indian in Hollywood Films, 1930–1950." PhD diss., Columbia University, 1991.
Black, Liza Elizabeth. "Looking at Indians: American Indians in Movies, 1941–1960." Diss., University of Washington, 1999.
Lucas, Barbara Champury. "Gendering Race: Representations of Native American and African-American Men in Nineteenth-Century Literature and Twentieth-Century Film." Diss., State University of New York, Stony Brook, 1997.
Lupis, Immaculate Josephine. "The Person of the American Indian as Portrayed in American Film and Video, 1894–1994." Diss., University of San Francisco, 1996.
Raheja, Michelle Hermann. "Screening Identity: Beads, Buckskins and Redface in Autobiography and Film." Diss., The University of Chicago, 2002.
Shively, JoEllen. "Cowboys and Indians: The Perception of Western Films among American Indians and Anglo-Americans." Diss., Stanford University, 1990.
Siminoski, Ted. "Sioux Versus Hollywood: The Image of Sioux Indians in American Films." PhD diss., University of Southern California, 1979.

Index

About the Author

ANGELA ALEISS is a contributing writer for such publications as the *Los Angeles Times*, *Variety*, and *The Washington Post*. She is a former teaching fellow at UCLA's American Indian Studies Center, and currently teaches at California State University, Long Beach.

4552066R00126

Made in the USA
San Bernardino, CA
24 September 2013